STECK-VAUGHN
CONNECTIONS

Basic Skills in Reading

REVIEWERS

Jim Barlow
Retired Vice-Principal
of Adult Education
Waterloo Region District
School Board
Educational Consultant
and Author
Kitchener, Ontario

Sherri Claiborne
Literacy Coordinator
Claiborne County
Adult Reading Experience
(CCARE)
Tazewell, Tennessee

Bill Freeland
Almonte Adult School
Almonte, California

William Burns
Instructor
San Mateo County
Office of Education
Palo Alto, California

Joanie Griffin-Rethlake
Adult Education Division
Harris County Department
of Education
Houston, Texas

Jim Scheil
Jersey City Adult Education Center
Jersey City, New Jersey

STECK-VAUGHN
COMPANY

A Division of Harcourt Brace & Company

www.steck-vaughn.com

Acknowledgments

Executive Editor: Ellen Northcutt

Project Editor: Julie Higgins

Senior Editor: Donna Townsend

Design Manager: Jim Cauthron

Cover Design: Donna Neal

Cover Production: Donna Neal and Alan Klemp

Media Researchers: Claudette Landry, Christina Berry

Electronic Production: PC&F, Inc.

Photograph Credits: Cover and title page (flipping book) © JAPACK/ CORBIS Westlight; (newspapers, documents, book stack) © PhotoDisc; p. 13 © J. Pelaez/The Stock Market; p. 56 © Michael Newman/PhotoEdit; p. 67 CORBIS/Kevin Fleming; p. 122 © Michael A. Keller/The Stock Market; p. 130 (both) © PhotoDisc; p. 133 © Al Moldvay/Tony Stone Images, Inc.; p. 158 © D. Young-Wolff/PhotoEdit; p. 164 Courtesy Mohican Press and Kihew; pp. 167, 206 © Michael Newman/PhotoEdit; p. 214 CORBIS/Ansel Adams Publishing Rights Trust.

Illustration Credits: PC&F, Inc. pages 64, 189, 193, 194, 195, 200, 201, 202, 203, 210, 212, 224

Literary Acknowledgments:

Acknowledgments for literary selections are on pages 258–260, which are an extension of this copyright page.

Contents

UNIT 1

UNIT 2

To the Student

How to Use This Book

The reading passages in this book are from a variety of sources—popular literature, classical literature, articles and reviews, and types of reading commonly found in the workplace and in everyday life. You will read and analyze these passages.

Popular literature is what most people are reading today. It includes novels, short stories, essays, poems, and plays. Classical literature is literature that has stood the test of time. It is about experiences that are important to people of all cultures and time periods. You will also find reviews of popular books, movies, TV shows, and music. Reading passages from the workplace and everyday life include advertisements, brochures, calendars, schedules, forms, documents, manuals, handbooks, drawings, diagrams, charts, and graphs.

SECTIONS

The four units in the book are organized into sections. Each section gives you a passage to read actively. *Active reading* means doing something before reading, during reading, and after reading. By reading actively, you will improve your reading comprehension skills.

Setting the Stage (Before Reading). First, you read some information about the type of story, poem, or article presented in the section. Next, you preview the passage by reading the first few sentences and answering some basic questions. Then, you write briefly about something you know from your own experience that is related to the passage. Finally, you preview some words you will find in the passage that may be unfamiliar.

The Passage (During Reading). The passages you will read are taken from well-known works of popular and classical literature as well as contemporary selections from magazines. In addition, you will find a variety of types of reading commonly found in the workplace and other areas of everyday life. After you read the first part of each passage, you will see a brief explanation of a reading skill related to the passage and a short activity for you to apply that skill. Then you will continue reading the passage. This process usually occurs two or three times for every passage.

As you are reading the passage, you will see some words in bold type. These are the **Vocabulary** words you previewed on the first page of the section. When you see them, try to figure out their meaning from the way they are used. Then, if you are still not sure of the meaning, look them up in a dictionary.

Thinking About the Passage (After Reading). This part of each section gives you an opportunity to do a variety of activities based on what you have just read. There are fill-in-the-blank, short answer, and multiple choice questions here. Answering the questions will help you decide how well you have understood what you read and also provide another way for you to connect with the selection.

READING AT WORK

Reading at Work is a two-page feature included in each unit. Each Reading at Work feature introduces a specific job, describes the reading skills the job requires, and includes a reading activity related to it. It also gives information about other jobs in the same career area.

READING CONNECTION

Reading Connection is an interdisciplinary feature included in each unit that shows how reading is related to another content area. It provides information about the relationship, a reading selection, and an exercise to check comprehension.

UNIT REVIEWS

A Unit Review lets you see how well you have learned the reading skills covered in each unit. Each Unit Review also includes an **Extension** activity that provides an opportunity for further practice with the type of reading in the unit.

INVENTORY AND POSTTEST

The Inventory is a self-check to see which skills you already know. When you complete all the items in the Inventory, check your work in the Answers and Explanations section in the back of the book. Then fill out the Correlation Chart that follows the Inventory. This chart tells you where each skill is taught in this book. When you complete the book, you will take a Posttest. Compare your Posttest score to your Inventory score to see that your skills have improved.

ANSWERS AND EXPLANATIONS

Answers and Explanations to the exercises are listed at the back of this book on pages 227–254. Some exercise items have more than one possible right answer. In such cases, a sample answer is given.

Inventory

Use this Inventory before you begin Section 1. Don't worry if you can't easily answer all the questions. The Inventory will help you determine which areas you are already strong in and which you need to study further.

Read each passage and answer the questions that follow. Check your answers on pages 227–228. Then enter your scores on the chart on page 11. Use the chart to figure out which content areas to work on and where to find them in this book.

Read the poem "Sympathy" by Paul Laurence Dunbar.

I know what the caged bird feels, alas!
    When the sun is bright on the upland slopes;
When the wind stirs soft through the springing
    grass,
And the river flows like a stream of glass;
    When the first bird sings and the first bud opes,
And the faint perfume from its chalice steals—
    I know what the caged bird feels!

I know why the caged bird beats his wing
    Till its blood is red on the cruel bars;
For he must fly back to his perch and cling
When he fain would be on the bough a-swing;
    And a pain still throbs in the old, old scars
And they pulse again with a keener sting—
I know why he beats his wing!

I know why the caged bird sings, ah me,
    When his wing is bruised and his bosom sore,—
When he beats his bars and would be free;
It is not a carol of joy or glee,
    But a prayer that he sends from his heart's deep
      core,
But a plea, that upward to Heaven, he flings—
I know why the caged bird sings!

Items 1–6 refer to the poem on page 1.

Fill in each blank with a word that best completes the statement.

1 The bird ＿＿＿＿＿＿＿＿＿ itself when it beats its wings against the bars of the cage.

2 The caged bird in the poem wants to be ＿＿＿＿＿＿＿＿＿.

3 The words *like a stream of glass* suggest that the river looks very ＿＿＿＿＿＿＿＿＿.

Circle the number of the best answer for each question.

4 What general truth about life is suggested by this poem?

    (1) All creatures suffer when they are trapped.

    (2) People should protest against cruelty to animals.

    (3) Caged birds should not be allowed to see what they are missing.

    (4) People can find true happiness only inside themselves.

    (5) If you feel unhappy, you should sing.

5 Which emotion does the author probably want the reader to experience while reading the poem?

    (1) joy

    (2) hope

    (3) yearning

    (4) fear

    (5) love

6 What kind of song would a person who feels like the caged bird be most likely to sing?

    (1) a song of thanksgiving

    (2) a patriotic march

    (3) a children's song

    (4) a blues song

    (5) a rock 'n' roll song

Go on to the next page.

Read the following passage from the autobiography *Enter Talking* by Joan Rivers with Richard Meryman.

Beginners are constantly being used and abused. Desperately eager to be noticed, they are the perfect, defenseless victims. The biggest scam ever pulled on me was that summer of 1960. An agent called up and offered me fifteen dollars to emcee a Catholic church bazaar in Queens, Long Island—draw raffle tickets out of the bowl, do my act, etc. I said yes, thrilled to do it. The agent came with me—which was unusual—and at the stage door of the school auditorium, we were met by ladies with corsages and acetate dresses and blue hairdos. They kept saying to the agent, "Where is she? Where is she?" And he said, "Don't worry she'll be along."

I could hear a little band playing out front and feel a humming excitement and electricity in the air. As I was about to walk onstage, the agent said, "Good luck—and one more thing. When you get out there, tell them your name is Rosalind Russell."

I said, "Excuse me?"

He said, "When you get out there, just say your name is Rosalind Russell. I'll explain it to you later." He pushed me onstage.

The room was jammed with kids and parents and priests and nuns, crowds of people standing along the walls where banners read, WELCOME ROSALIND RUSSELL TO ST. IGNATIUS. YOU'RE OUR WOMAN OF THE YEAR. WE LOVE YOU, ROZ. And here I was, this short chunko standing there. I went to the microphone and said, "Hi, my name is Rosalind Russell also. I'm the other one. Isn't it a coincidence? I get this all the time."

They did not take it well. The place went crazy! A wave of hate rose over the footlights—yelling, stamping on the floor. Have you ever seen screaming priests? Nuns shaking their fists?

I tried to sing "I'll Never Forget What's His Name," but there was so much noise, my accompanist could not even hear my cue. Pretty soon I said, "I'm terribly sorry. Good night." And got off. The agent, who did not want to be lynched, had disappeared. I felt *terrible*. I had ruined their night. Can you imagine the anticipation, thinking that Rosalind Russell at her height as an actress is going to show up in Queens to close your bazaar? For fifteen dollars? Think of all the ladies figuring they were going home with a Polaroid shot of themselves with Rosalind Russell.

I called the agent up the next day and said, "How could you do that?" He said a lot of performers make a buck doing it. "How would you like to be Marilyn Monroe on Tuesday?"

Items 7–11 refer to the passage on page 3.

Write the answer to each question.

7 Who is telling this story?

_____

8 The author concludes that the audience was not happy when they realized she was not Rosalind Russell. What details does the author give to support this conclusion?

_____

_____

_____

Circle the number of the best answer for each question.

9 Which of the following sentences best states the main idea of the passage?

   (1) "The biggest scam ever pulled on me was that summer of 1960."

   (2) "When you get out there, tell them your name is Rosalind Russell."

   (3) "And here I was, this short chunko standing there."

   (4) "The place went crazy!"

   (5) "He said a lot of performers make a buck doing it."

10 Which word best describes how Joan Rivers felt when she was onstage?

   (1) excited

   (2) angry

   (3) successful

   (4) sad

   (5) embarrassed

11 How does the author now seem to feel about this experience?

   (1) amused

   (2) bitter

   (3) angry

   (4) sad

   (5) disappointed

Read the following passage from the play *A Doll's House* by Henrik Ibsen.

HELMER: Oh, you think and talk like a heedless child.

NORA: Maybe. But you neither think nor talk like the man I could bind myself to. As soon as your fear was over—and it was not fear for what threatened me, but for what might happen to you—when the whole thing was past, as far as you were concerned it was exactly as if nothing at all had happened. Exactly as before, I was your little skylark, your doll, which you would in future treat with doubly gentle care, because it was so brittle and fragile. *(Getting up)* Torvald [his first name]—it was then it dawned upon me that for eight years I had been living here with a strange man, and had borne him three children—. Oh, I can't bear to think of it! I could tear myself into little bits!

HELMER: *(sadly)* I see, I see. An abyss has opened between us—there is no denying it. But, Nora, would it not be possible to fill it up?

NORA: As I am now, I am no wife for you.

HELMER: I have it in me to become a different man.

NORA: Perhaps—if your doll is taken away from you.

HELMER: But to part!—to part from you! No, no, Nora, I can't understand that idea.

NORA: *(going out to the right)* That makes it all the more certain that it must be done. *(She comes back with her cloak and hat and a small bag which she puts on a chair by the table.)*

HELMER: Nora, Nora, not now! Wait till tomorrow.

NORA: *(putting on her cloak)* I cannot spend the night in a strange man's room.

HELMER: But can't we live here like brother and sister—?

NORA: *(putting on her hat)* You know very well that would not last long. *(Puts the shawl around her.)* Good-bye, Torvald. I won't see the little ones. I know they are in better hands than mine. As I am now, I can be of no use to them.

HELMER: But some day, Nora—some day?

NORA: How can I tell? I have no idea what is going to become of me.

HELMER: But you are my wife, whatever becomes of you.

NORA: Listen, Torvald. I have heard that when a wife deserts her husband's house, as I am doing now, he is legally freed from all obligations towards her. In any case I set you free from all your obligations. You are not to feel yourself bound in the slightest way, any more than I shall. There must be perfect freedom on both sides. See, here is your ring back. Give me mine.

Items 12–16 refer to the passage on page 5.

Write the answer to each question.

12 How long has the couple been married?

_____

13 Based on the stage directions, what will Nora probably do after she gets her ring back? How can you tell?

_____

_____

_____

Circle the number of the best answer for each question.

14 Which word gives the best meaning for abyss?

   (1) agreement

   (2) argument

   (3) gap

   (4) road

   (5) family

15 What do you learn about Torvald Helmer?

   (1) He has become a different man.

   (2) He does not really understand what Nora wants.

   (3) He understands why his wife is upset.

   (4) He has been a terrible and cruel husband.

   (5) He is pleased and excited by Nora's decision.

16 When Nora says that she was Torvald's "little skylark" and "doll," she is suggesting that he

   (1) treated her like an equal.

   (2) was mean to her.

   (3) treated her like a pet or a toy.

   (4) acted like her brother.

   (5) had been the perfect husband.

Read the following passage from the novel *The Flower Drum Song* **by C. Y. Lee.**

He halted at the corner of Grant and Pine and wiped the perspiration on his forehead with a forefinger.

"*Shew,* we have walked a distance of five *li* from the bus station," he said in Mandarin. "Are you tired, May Li?"

"A little," the girl said. She was dressed in a Chinese gown of light blue and wearing a pigtail wound round her head, her pretty face without make-up glowing with health.

"Shall we go visit Mr. Poon now, father?"

"Oh, do not be so foolish. Nobody visits people so early. This is New Year's day, people sleep in the morning with a full stomach of food and wine and do not wish to be disturbed. We shall have our breakfast and rest our legs for a while." He wiped his forehead once more and looked around.

"Here is a teahouse, father," May Li said, pointing at a red signboard saying "Lotus Room."

"Good," Old Man Li said. When he looked at the stairway he frowned. "No, May Li, I shall not climb this with my luggage on my back."

"Let me carry it up for you, father," May Li said.

"No, you are carrying enough of your own."

"I can carry a lot more." She held her father's canvas bag until Li finally yielded it to her, shaking his head. "You are just like your mother, May Li. Forty years ago when she was your age she could carry a hundred catties of flour and walk seventy *li* a day. She was strong as a cow, and just as amiable. . . "

"What shall we eat, father?" May Li asked.

"We shall see," Old Man Li said, trudging up the stairway. "We shall have some New Year dishes. But we must be careful in our selection. The owner of this place might be greedy, otherwise he would not have built a restaurant upstairs. He knows that people will eat more after this climbing, *shew!*"

When he reached the top of the stairs he promptly changed his opinion of the owner. The spacious dining hall with red-lacquered lattice windows was clean and impressive, almost filled with customers. Only a reputable place could be so prosperous, he thought. The smiling manager greeted them and directed them to a vacant table near one of the windows and handed them two copies of the menu with special New Year dishes attached to them. Old Man Li held the menu tensely, swallowing and resisting, his eyes roving among the expensive items. He wanted to eat everything, but he felt his economical nature held him back like an iron chain restraining a dog. He quickly closed the menu and rubbed his neck. "May Li, I shall let you order."

Items 17–21 refer to the passage on page 7.

Write the answer to each question.

17 Where did the old man and the girl just come from?

_____

18 Why did Old Man Li let May Li order the food?

_____

_____

_____

Circle the number of the best answer for each question.

19 After May Li asks about visiting Mr. Poon, what do she and her father do?

   (1) They try to find Mr. Poon.

   (2) They decide to celebrate New Year's day.

   (3) They decide to have breakfast.

   (4) They leave the bus station.

   (5) They find a hotel.

20 When Old Man Li compares his wife to a cow, he is **suggesting that she was**

   (1) ugly.

   (2) very strong.

   (3) fat.

   (4) not very smart.

   (5) a bad mother.

21 What fact changed Old Man Li's opinion about the restaurant?

   (1) The owner was greedy.

   (2) The restaurant was upstairs.

   (3) He was hungry after climbing.

   (4) The restaurant was clean and impressive.

   (5) New Year dishes were on the menu.

Read the following schedule and registration form.

GREENBORO RECREATION CENTER
123 Broad Street
Telephone: 835-7640

Spring Tennis Schedule

Adult tennis classes are available for all levels of experience. Tennis professionals will teach all classes. Classes are limited to 12 students, so get your registration form in early. Bring your own racquet or rent one from our pro shop. We look forward to seeing you on the court!

Beginner Tennis

April 5–May 31 (8 weeks)
T101   Monday   7:30–8:30 p.m.
$40 Resident $48 Non-Resident
This class is for students with no previous experience.

Intermediate Tennis

April 6–June 1 (8 weeks)
T103   Tuesday   7:00–8:00 p.m.
$40 Resident $48 Non-Resident
This class is for students who have taken several classes or have mastered forehand and backhand and are ready to learn how to serve and volley.

Advanced Beginner Tennis

April 7–June 2 (8 weeks)
T101   Wednesday   7:30–8:30 p.m.
$40 Resident $48 Non-Resident
This class is for students who have some experience or who have taken at least one class. Students must know the rules of the game and how to keep score.

Advanced Tennis

April 8–June 3 (8 weeks)
T103   Thursday   7:00–8:00 p.m.
$40 Resident $48 Non-Resident
Students must know how to serve and volley. The focus of these classes will be on developing strategies for singles and doubles play.

- -

Registration Form

You can mail in your registration or bring it to the office by April 2.
Please include full payment.

Last Name _____   First Name _____

Address _____   Zip Code _____

Home Phone _____   Work Phone _____

Class #	Class Name	Day	Class Time	Fee

Items 22–27 refer to the schedule and registration form on page 9.

Write the answer to each question.

22 How much would someone who does not live in Greenboro pay for the Intermediate Tennis class?

_____

23 Do students need to own a tennis racquet to take a class? Explain.

_____

24 How many students would be in a full class?

_____

Circle the number of the best answer for each question.

25 Suppose that you have played a little tennis in the past and you know the rules of the game. Which class would you sign up for?

(1) Beginner Tennis

(2) Advanced Beginner Tennis

(3) Intermediate Tennis

(4) Advanced Tennis

(5) There are no classes for this level.

26 What would you learn in the Advanced Tennis class?

(1) You would learn the rules of the game.

(2) You would learn backhand and forehand strokes.

(3) You would learn how to keep score.

(4) You would learn strategies for play.

(5) You would learn to serve and volley.

27 If you sign up for Intermediate Tennis, when would your class meet?

(1) Monday from 7:30–8:30 p.m.

(2) Tuesday from 7:30–8:30 p.m.

(3) Tuesday from 7:00–8:00 p.m.

(4) Wednesday from 7:30–8:30 p.m.

(5) Thursday from 7:00–8:00 p.m.

Check your answers on pages 227–228.

Inventory Correlation Chart

The chart below will help you determine your strengths and weaknesses in reading and interpreting different forms of literature and other written material.

Directions

Circle the number of each item that you answered correctly on the Inventory. Count the number of items you answered correctly in each row. Write the number in the Total Correct space in each row. (For example, in the Fiction row, write the number correct in the blank before *out of 5*.) Complete this process for the remaining rows. Then add the four totals to get your Total Correct for the whole Inventory.

Content Areas	Items	Total Correct	Pages
Fiction (Pages 12–65)	17, 18, 19, 20, 21	_____ out of 5	Pages 32–37 Pages 44–49
Nonfiction (Pages 66–131)	7, 8, 9, 10, 11	_____ out of 5	Pages 80–85 Pages 86–91
Poetry and Drama (Pages 132–165)	1, 2, 3, 4, 5, 6, 12, 13, 14, 15, 16	_____ out of 11	Pages 134–139 Pages 140–145 Pages 146–151 Pages 152–157
Prose and Visual Information (Pages 166–215)	22, 23, 24, 25, 26, 27	_____ out of 6	Pages 174–179 Pages 180–185

TOTAL CORRECT FOR INVENTORY _____ out of 27

If you answered fewer than 24 items correctly, look more closely at the four content areas covered. In which areas do you need more practice? Page numbers to refer to for practice are given in the right-hand column above.

Fiction

We read and watch fictional stories all the time. A work of fiction comes from a writer's imagination. Fictional writing takes us out of our own lives and everyday experiences. It takes us to worlds far away or just down the block. It puts us in the lives of people from different times, places, and ways of life.

We read fiction to be entertained. But as often as not, we are also informed, terrified, or inspired by a work of fiction. Fiction is not just something we read in a book or see on a screen; it can become a part of our lives. Good fiction is something we never forget.

○ Think of a movie you have seen that was based on a book. Have you read the book too? Which did you like better—the book or the movie? If you haven't read the book yet, would you like to?

○ Have you ever read a fictional story that inspired you? What was it? Did it inspire you to do something or to think differently? Did it have an impact on your life?

SECTIONS

1 **Mystery Novel**

2 **Science Fiction**

3 **Thriller Novel**

4 **Popular Novel**

5 **Folk Novel**

6 **Classic Short Story**

7 **Popular Short Story**

Mystery Novel

Setting the Stage

A **mystery novel** presents the reader with a puzzle. Who committed the crime in the story? Why? What are the clues? Who is telling the truth? Who can be trusted and who can't? In a mystery novel, the main character is often a detective whose job it is to solve the mystery. Most of the fun of reading mysteries is putting all the clues together to solve the puzzle.

PREVIEW THE READING

You can get a feel for the mystery in this passage right away. Read the title and the first paragraph. Then stop and come back here to answer these questions.

1 Does this story take place in a city or in the country? What time of day is it?

_____

2 What is the name of the character who is trying to solve the mystery? What is the crime he's trying to solve?

_____

RELATE TO THE CHARACTER

This passage is about Chee, a Navajo policeman. In the passage, you will learn a little about Navajo customs and about Navajo beliefs regarding life, death, and ghosts.

3 Every culture and religion has its own beliefs about life after death. What are yours? What do you believe happens to people after they die?

_____

_____

VOCABULARY

gusts	ponderosas	hogan
plausible	tentatively	forlorn

Check your answers on page 228.

The Ghostway by Tony Hillerman

The night breeze was beginning now as it often did with twilight on the east slope of mountains. Nothing like the morning's dry **gusts,** but enough to ruffle the mare's ragged mane and replace the dead silence with a thousand little wind sounds among the **ponderosas.** Under cover of these whispers, Chee moved along the arroyo [a deep ditch cut by a stream] rim, looking for the horse thief.

He checked up the arroyo. Down the arroyo. Along the ponderosa timber covering the slopes. He stared back at the talus [a mass of debris at the base of a cliff] slope, where he had been when he'd heard the horse. But no one could have gotten there without Chee seeing him. There was only the death **hogan** and the holding pen for goats and the brush arbor, none of which seemed **plausible.** The thief must have tied his horse and then climbed directly up the slope across the arroyo. But why?

Just behind him, Chee heard a cough.

He spun, fumbling for his pistol. No one. Where had the sound come from?

He heard it again. A cough. A sniffling. The sound came from inside Hosteen Begay's hogan.

Chee stared at the corpse hole, a black gap broken through the north wall. He had cocked his pistol without knowing he'd done it. It was incredible. People do not go into a death hogan. People do not step through the hole into darkness. White men, yes. As Sharkey had done. And Deputy Sheriff Bales. As Chee himself, who had come to terms with the ghosts of his people, might do if the reason was powerful enough. But certainly most Navajos would not. So the horse thief was a white. A white with a cold and a runny nose.

Finding the Stated Main Idea The **main idea** of a paragraph or passage is the most important idea. The **stated main idea** of a paragraph tells you clearly what the important point of that paragraph is.

In this passage, Chee is using clues to solve a mystery. In the second paragraph, for example, he thinks he has learned something important: "The thief must have tied his horse and then climbed directly up the slope across the arroyo." This is the stated main idea of the paragraph. To find the stated main idea in other paragraphs, look for the idea that seems most important. Ask yourself, "Which sentence gives the most important information about the mystery?"

Which of the following gives the stated main idea of the last paragraph on the page? In other words, which of the following seems more important to solving the mystery?

a. "Chee stared at the corpse hole, a black gap broken through the north wall."

b. "So the horse thief was a white. A white with a cold and a runny nose."

Chee moved quietly to his left, away from the field of vision of anyone who might be looking through the hole. Then he moved silently to the wall and along it. He stood beside the hole, back pressed to the planking. Pistol raised. Listening.

Something moved. Something sniffled. Moved again. Chee breathed as lightly as he could. And waited. He heard sounds and long silences. The sun was below the horizon now, and the light had shifted far down the range of colors to the darkest red. Over the ridge to the west he could see Venus, bright against the dark sky. Soon it would be night.

There was the sound of feet on earth, of cloth scraping, and a form emerged through the hole. First a stocking cap, black. Then the shoulders of a navy pea coat, then a boot and a leg—a form crouching to make its way through the low hole.

"Hold it," Chee said. "Don't move."

A startled yell. The figure jumped through the hole, stumbled. Chee grabbed.

He realized almost instantly he had caught a child. The arm he gripped through the cloth of the coat was small, thin. The struggle was only momentary, the product of panic quickly controlled. A girl, Chee saw. A Navajo. But when she spoke, it was in English.

"Turn me loose," she said, in a breathless, frightened voice. "I've got to go now."

Chee found he was shaking. The girl had handled this startling encounter better than he had. "Need to know some things first," Chee said. "I'm a policeman."

"I've got to go," she said. She pulled **tentatively** against his grip and relaxed, waiting.

Identifying Details The details of a paragraph or passage support the main idea. Details are facts about a person, place, thing, event, or time. Details answer the questions *who, what, when, where, why,* and *how.* Details tell you about sounds and sights and smells.

The passage above gives several details about the time of day: the sun is below the horizon, the sky is dark and red, and the planet Venus is visible in the dark sky.

❶ The third paragraph gives details about what Chee heard and saw. Name two things he heard and two things he saw.

_____

_____

❷ The passage gives many details about the person Chee finds. List three of them.

_____

_____

_____

"Your horse," Chee said. "You took her last night from over at Two Gray Hills."

"Borrowed it," the girl said. "I've got to go now and take her back."

"What are you doing here?" Chee asked. "In the hogan?"

"It's my hogan," she said. "I live here."

"It is the hogan of Hosteen Ashie Begay," Chee said. "Or it was. Now it is a *chindi* [evil spirit left behind when a person dies] hogan. Didn't you notice that?"

It was a foolish question. After all, he'd just caught her coming out of the corpse hole. She didn't bother to answer. She said nothing at all, simply standing slumped and motionless.

"It was stupid going in there," Chee said. "What were you doing?"

"He was my grandfather," the girl said. For the first time she lapsed into Navajo, using the noun that means the father of my mother. "I was just sitting in there. Remembering things." It took her a moment to say it because now tears were streaming down her cheeks. "My grandfather would leave no *chindi* behind him. He was a holy man. There was nothing in him bad that would make a *chindi*."

"It wasn't your grandfather who died in there," Chee said. "It was a man named Albert Gorman. A nephew of Ashie Begay." Chee paused a moment, trying to sort out the Begay family. "An uncle of yours, I think."

The girl's face had been as **forlorn** as a child's face can be. Now it was radiant. "Grandfather's alive? He's really alive? Where is he?"

"I don't know," Chee said. "Gone to live with some relatives, I guess. We came up here last week to get Gorman, and we found Gorman had died. And that." Chee pointed at the corpse hole. "Hosteen Begay buried Gorman out there, and packed up his horses, and sealed up his hogan, and went away."

The girl looked thoughtful.

"Where would he go?" Chee asked. The girl would be Margaret Sosi. No question about that. Two birds with one stone. One stolen pinto mare and the horse thief, plus one missing St. Catherine's student. "Hosteen Begay is your mother's father. Would he . . . ?" He remembered then that the mother of Margaret Billy Sosi was dead.

"No," Margaret said.

"Somebody else then?"

"Almost everybody went to California. A long time ago. My mother's sisters. My great-grandmother. Some people live over on the Cañoncito Reservation, but . . ." Her voice trailed off, became suddenly suspicious. "Why do you want to find him?"

Using Details The details of a passage give information about characters and how they feel. In the above passage, several details show how the young girl feels— for example, she stood slumped and motionless; tears streamed down her cheeks.

Using all the details given in the passage, decide what kind of person Margaret is.

a. intelligent and independent

b. cowardly and helpless

Check your answers on page 228.

Thinking About the Story

Practice Vocabulary

The words below are in the passage in bold type. Study the way each word is used. Then complete each sentence by writing the correct word.

gusts	**ponderosas**	**hogan**
plausible	**tentatively**	**forlorn**

1 A Navajo home is called a _____.

2 In autumn, _____ of wind blow the leaves around.

3 If you believe a story could be true, you think it is

_____.

4 The man stood _____ on his sprained ankle and found it hurt too much to walk.

5 The sad news made the woman feel _____.

6 The _____ are a kind of pine tree.

Understand What You Read

Write the answer to each question.

7 At first, what makes Chee think the horse thief is a white person with a cold?

_____

_____

8 The passage says that the girl handled this startling encounter better than Chee. In what way did she handle it better?

_____

_____

9 What does the girl mean when she says that she "borrowed" the horse?

_____

_____

10 To whom does the hogan belong?

_____

_____

Check your answers on page 228.

Apply Your Skills

Circle the number of the best answer for each question.

11 Which of the following is the most important idea of the entire passage?
(1) Navajos live in hogans.
(2) Chee is an experienced policeman.
(3) Margaret Sosi has run away from home.
(4) Other crimes besides the horse theft may have taken place here.
(5) Horses are important to the Navajos.

12 Which detail makes the most important point about Chee's character?
(1) He spun, fumbling for his pistol.
(2) He had come to terms with the ghosts of his people.
(3) He breathed as lightly as he could.
(4) He could see Venus, bright against the sky.
(5) He stood beside the hole, back pressed to the planking.

13 Which detail best describes the land where this story takes place?
(1) The night breeze was beginning.
(2) He heard sounds and long silences.
(3) "My grandfather would leave no *chindi* behind him."
(4) Chee moved along the arroyo rim, looking for the horse thief.
(5) He looked along the ponderosa timber covering the slopes.

Connect with the Story

Write your answer to each question.

14 If you were Chee, what would you do next? Why?

_____

_____

_____

15 Have you ever been completely surprised or startled like Chee is when he finds that it's Margaret in the hogan? What was the surprise or shock for you? Was there any information or clue that could have prepared you for the surprise or shock? Explain.

_____

_____

_____

_____

_____

Science Fiction

Setting the Stage

In **science fiction** an author imagines what life and people might be like in another time or place. Science fiction is often set in the future, in outer space, or on other planets. These kinds of stories are called science fiction because they combine fantasy with ideas and principles from science. For example, science fiction characters might travel through space, go back or forward in time, or develop new and wonderful technology or powers. Most science fiction is filled with adventure.

PREVIEW THE READING

You can often get a good idea of what you will be reading by looking at the first few sentences. Read the title and first six lines of the passage. Then stop and answer this question.

1 Name four characters that are introduced in the first few sentences.

_____

RELATE TO THE PROBLEM

The passage is from a science fiction story in *I, Robot*. The main characters are scientists who are working on an important project—building a robot. The story is both scary and believable because it plays with people's fear that technology, computers, and robots will some day run our lives. Many people believe that we already depend too much on technology.

2 What is your experience with technology? Have you ever felt that it was running your life—rather than you running it? Please explain.

_____

_____

VOCABULARY

pampering	**clangor**	**paralytic**	**contorted**
dilemma	**acceleration**	**manual**	

Check your answers on page 229.

I, Robot by Isaac Asimov

Alfred Lanning met Dr. Calvin just outside his office. He lit a nervous cigar and motioned her in.

He said, "Well, Susan, we've come pretty far, and Robertson's getting jumpy. What are you doing with The Brain?"

Susan Calvin spread her hands, "It's no use getting impatient. The Brain is worth more than anything we forfeit on this deal."

"But you've been questioning it for two months."

The psychologist's voice was flat, but somehow dangerous, "You would rather run this yourself?"

"Now you know what I meant."

"Oh, I suppose I do," Dr. Calvin rubbed her hands nervously. "It isn't easy. I've been **pampering** it and probing it gently, and I haven't gotten anywhere yet. Its reactions aren't normal. Its answers—they're queer, somehow. But nothing I can put my finger on yet. And you see, until we know what's wrong, we must just tiptoe our way through. I can never tell what simple question or remark will just . . . push him over . . . and then—Well, and then we'll have on our hands a completely useless Brain. Do you want to face that?"

"Well, it can't break the First Law."

"I would have thought so, but—"

"You're not even sure of that?" Lanning was profoundly shocked.

"Oh, I can't be sure of anything, Alfred—"

The alarm system raised its fearful **clangor** with a horrifying suddenness. Lanning clicked on communications with an almost **paralytic** spasm. The breathless words froze him.

He said, "Susan . . . you heard that . . . the ship's gone. I sent those two field men inside half an hour ago. You'll have to see The Brain again."

Identifying the Implied Main Idea The main idea is the most important idea of a paragraph or a passage. In fiction the main idea is often not stated. It may only be suggested or implied. This means you must figure out, or infer, the main idea yourself.

To figure out the main idea, read the entire passage and think about what is going on. What are the characters saying, thinking, doing? Read between the lines. What do the stated facts seem to show? What is the author hinting?

In the passage so far, Dr. Calvin and Dr. Lanning are talking about a third character, The Brain. Which of the following is the implied main idea?

    a.   The doctors are upset because something is wrong with The Brain.

    b.   Dr. Calvin is worried about what a fourth character, Robertson, will do.

Check your answers on page 229.

Susan Calvin said with enforced calm, "Brain, what happened to the ship?"

The Brain said happily, "The ship I built, Miss Susan?"

"That's right. What has happened to it?"

"Why, nothing at all. The two men that were supposed to test it were inside, and we were all set. So I sent it off."

"Oh—Well, that's nice." The psychologist felt some difficulty in breathing. "Do you think they'll be all right?"

"Right as anything, Miss Susan. I've taken care of it all. It's a bee-yoo-tiful ship."

"Yes, Brain, it *is* beautiful, but you think they have enough food, don't you? They'll be comfortable?"

"Plenty of food."

"This business might be a shock to them, Brain. Unexpected, you know."

The Brain tossed it off, "They'll be all right. It ought to be interesting for them."

"Interesting? How?"

"Just interesting," said The Brain, slyly.

"Susan," whispered Lanning in a fuming whisper, "ask him if death comes into it. Ask him what the dangers are."

Susan Calvin's expression **contorted** with fury, "Keep quiet!" In a shaken voice, she said to The Brain, "We can communicate with the ship, can't we, Brain?"

"Oh, they can hear you if you call by radio. I've taken care of that."

"Thanks. That's all for now."

Once outside, Lanning lashed out ragingly, "Great Galaxy, Susan, if this gets out, it will ruin all of us. We've got to get those men back. Why didn't you ask if there was danger of death—straight out?"

"Because," said Calvin, with a weary frustration, "that's just what I can't mention. If it's got a case of **dilemma,** it's about death. Anything that would bring it up badly might knock it completely out. Will we be better off then? Now, look, it said we could communicate with them. Let's do so, get their location, and bring them back. They probably can't use the controls themselves; The Brain is probably handling them remotely. Come!"

Identifying the Implied Main Idea Characters often say things that are clues to the implied main idea. In this second passage, the dialogue between Dr. Calvin and the Brain offers many clues to the implied main idea.

For example, you learn that The Brain can answer the questions Dr. Calvin asks. This is a clue about The Brain's abilities. The way The Brain answers (*happily, slyly*) also offers clues.

In the passage above, what is the implied main idea?

a.   The doctors are weary and frustrated.

b.   The Brain has taken control.

It was quite a while before Powell shook himself together.

"Mike," he said out of cold lips, "did you feel any **acceleration**?"

Donovan's eyes were blank, "Huh? No . . . no."

And then the redhead's fists clenched and he was out of his seat with sudden frenzied energy and up against the cold, wide-curving glass. There was nothing to see—but stars.

He turned, "Greg, they must have started the machine while we were inside. Greg, it's a put-up job; they fixed it up with the robot to jerry us into being the try-out boys, in case we were thinking of backing out."

Powell said, "What are you talking about? What's the good of sending us out if we don't know how to run the machine? How are we supposed to bring it back? No, this ship left by itself, and without any apparent acceleration." He rose, and walked the floor slowly. The metal walls dinned back the clangor of his steps.

He said tonelessly, "Mike, this is the most confusing situation we've ever been up against."

"That," said Donovan, bitterly, "is news to me. I was just beginning to have a very swell time, when you told me."

Powell ignored that. "No acceleration—which means the ship works on a principle different from any known."

"Different from any we know, anyway."

"Different from *any* known. There are no engines within reach of **manual** control. Maybe they're built into the walls. Maybe that's why they're thick as they are."

"What are you mumbling about?" demanded Donovan.

"Why not listen? I'm saying whatever powers this ship is enclosed, and evidently not meant to be handled. The ship is running by remote control."

"The Brain's control?"

"Why not?"

"Then you think we'll stay out here till The Brain brings us back."

"It could be. If so, let's wait quietly. The Brain is a robot. It's got to follow the First Law. It can't hurt a human being."

Recognizing Supporting Details In the last passage, The Brain sent two men and a spaceship into space, and the men have no control over the ship. One implied main idea of the passage is this: the men in the ship have the skills to figure out what happened to them.

Write two clues or details that help the men figure out what happened to them.

_____

_____

Thinking About the Story

Practice Vocabulary

The words below are in the passage in bold type. Study the way each word is used. Then match each word with its meaning. Write the letter.

_____ ❶ pampering

_____ ❷ clangor

_____ ❸ contorted

_____ ❹ dilemma

_____ ❺ acceleration

_____ ❻ manual

_____ ❼ paralytic

a.   unable to move

b.   speeding up

c.   twisted

d.   a problem

e.   a harsh, ringing noise

f.   by hand

g.   spoiling, or taking special care of

Understand What You Read

Circle the letter of the best answer to each question.

❽   Who or what is The Brain?
   a.   The Brain is a being from another planet.
   b.   The Brain is a robot.

❾   What is the First Law?
   a.   The First Law states that a robot cannot harm a human being.
   b.   The First Law states that a robot must obey a human being.

❿   What do the two doctors fear will happen to the men in the ship?
   a.   They are afraid that the men will steal the ship.
   b.   They are afraid that the men will die or be unable to return.

Write the answer to each question.

⓫   Why does Dr. Calvin have to be so careful about what she says to The Brain?

_____

_____

⓬   What does Powell mean when he says that "this is the most confusing situation we've ever been up against"?

_____

_____

Apply Your Skills

Circle the number of the best answer for each question.

⑬ Which statement best expresses the implied main idea of the entire passage?
   (1) The scientists have lost control of their own experiment.
   (2) Robots are angry about being used by human beings.
   (3) Robots are always smarter than human beings.
   (4) Robots make life easier for human beings.
   (5) Scientists should never have invented robots.

⑭ Which of the following statements does <u>not</u> support the implied main idea of the entire passage?
   (1) The Brain is worth a great deal of money.
   (2) The Brain has sent two men into outer space.
   (3) The Brain answers Susan's questions in a sly, unhelpful manner.
   (4) The Brain has provided food for the men in the ship.
   (5) The Brain has set up only one-way contact with the ship.

⑮ Which sentence contains details that best support the idea that Powell and Donovan are shocked to discover that the ship has taken off?
   (1) He rose, and walked the floor slowly.
   (2) "Greg, they must have started the machine while we were inside."
   (3) The redhead's fists clenched.
   (4) He was out of his seat with sudden frenzied energy.
   (5) "What are you mumbling about?" demanded Donovan.

Connect with the Story

Write your answer to each question.

⑯ Which character would you choose to be—Alfred Lanning or Susan Calvin? Or, would you not like to be either one? In a sentence or two, explain why.

_____

_____

_____

⑰ Do you think the problem presented in the story from *I, Robot* is realistic? In other words, could computer programmers and scientists go too far in inventing computers that "think"? Explain why or why not.

_____

_____

_____

Thriller Novel

Setting the Stage

Thriller novels are scary, full of creaking sounds and shadows and dark spirits. Reading a thriller novel can make you shiver, cause chills to run up your spine, or make the hair on the back of your neck stand up.

A good thriller makes readers keep reading. They want to find out what will happen. For many people, the scarier a thriller story is, the better.

PREVIEW THE READING

You can get a feel for what you will be reading very quickly, often from the first paragraph. Read the first paragraph of the passage. Then answer these questions.

1 What is the name of the main character?

_____

2 What words or phrases in the first paragraph give it a scary feel?

_____

_____

RELATE TO THE STORY

This passage is by Stephen King, an author who is famous for writing terrifying stories. Most of his books are bestsellers, which means that thousands and thousands of people buy them.

3 Have you ever seen a thriller movie or TV show? Did it scare you? Did you like being scared? Why or why not?

_____

_____

VOCABULARY

| momentarily | cylindrical | methodical | glimpse |
| synchronized | pondering | hunkered | incline |

Check your answers on page 230.

Salem's Lot by Stephen King

When he first heard the distant snapping of twigs, he crept behind the trunk of a large spruce and stood there, waiting to see who would show up. *They* couldn't come out in the daytime, but that didn't mean *they* couldn't get people who could; giving them money was one way, but it wasn't the only way. Mark had seen that guy Straker in town, and his eyes were like the eyes of a toad sunning itself on a rock. He looked like he could break a baby's arm and smile while he did it.

He touched the heavy shape of his father's target pistol in his jacket pocket. Bullets were no good against *them*—except maybe silver ones—but a shot between the eyes would punch that Straker's ticket, all right.

His eyes shifted downward **momentarily** to the roughly **cylindrical** shape propped against the tree, wrapped in an old piece of toweling. There was a woodpile behind his house, half a cord of yellow ash stove lengths which he and his father had cut with the McCulloch chain saw in July and August. Henry Petrie was **methodical,** and each length, Mark knew, would be within an inch of three feet, one way or the other. His father knew the proper length just as he knew that winter followed fall, and that yellow ash would burn longer and cleaner in the living room fireplace.

His son, who knew other things, knew that ash was for men—things—like *him*. This morning, while his mother and father were out on their Sunday bird walk, he had taken one of the lengths and whacked one end into a rough point with his Boy Scout hatchet. It was rough, but it would serve.

Identifying Point of View in Fiction Every story is told from a particular **point of view.** In a story told from the main character's point of view, for example, readers feel as if they're seeing the action through the main character's eyes, hearing through her or his ears. In another story, the point of view might let the reader know what *every* character is thinking or feeling.

An author has many possible points of view to choose from when writing a story. To identify point of view when you read, ask yourself whose actions you are following most closely. Whose eyes are you seeing through? Whose thoughts do you know? In the passage above, the story is told from Mark's point of view.

Choose the phrase from the passage that shows the story is told from Mark's point of view.

a.   His eyes shifted momentarily to the roughly cylindrical shape.

b.   His son, who knew other things, knew that ash was for men.

The character telling the story is called the narrator. This story is told from Mark's point of view, but Mark is not the narrator. Mark is not telling his own story. Someone else is telling the story about him.

Check your answers on page 230.

He saw a flash of color and shrank back against the tree, peering around the rough bark with one eye. A moment later he got his first clear **glimpse** of the person climbing the hill. It was a girl. He felt a sense of relief mingled with disappointment. No henchman of the devil there; that was Mr. Norton's daughter.

His gaze sharpened again. She was carrying a stake of her own! As she drew closer, he felt an urge to laugh bitterly—a piece of snow fence, that's what she had. Two swings with an ordinary tool box hammer would split it right in two.

She was going to pass his tree on the right. As she drew closer, he began to slide carefully around his tree to the left, avoiding any small twigs that might pop and give him away. At last the **synchronized** little movement was done; her back was to him as she went on up the hill toward the break in the trees. She was going very carefully, he noted with approval. That was good. In spite of the silly snow fence stake, she apparently had some idea of what she was getting into. Still, if she went much further, she was going to be in trouble. Straker was at home. Mark had been here since twelve-thirty, and he had seen Straker go out to the driveway and look down the road and then go back into the house. Mark had been trying to make up his mind on what to do himself when this girl had entered things, upsetting the equation.

Perhaps she was going to be all right. She had stopped behind a screen of bushes and was crouching there, just looking at the house. Mark turned it over in his mind. Obviously she knew. How didn't matter, but she would not have had even that pitiful stake with her if she didn't know. He supposed he would have to go up and warn her that Straker was still around, and on guard. She probably didn't have a gun, not even a little one like his.

Understanding the Setting Setting tells where and when the action takes place. Look for clues to find out what the setting is. For example, look for words that tell whether the characters are indoors or outdoors. Look for words that describe the time of day or the season of the year. Look for words that tell how things around the characters look and sound.

In the passage above, Mark is watching a girl as she moves along. The two of them are outside. Which of the following best describes the place?

    a.   a neighborhood with small houses set close together

    b.   a wooded area with hills near someone's house

When you read, try to picture the setting in your mind. Use the clues the author gives you about the time and place. Imagine yourself in the place. Imagine that you are there watching the characters and the action.

Check your answers on page 230.

He was **pondering** how to make his presence known to her without having her scream her head off when the motor of Straker's car roared into life. She jumped visibly, and at first he was afraid she was going to break and run, crashing through the woods and advertising her presence for a hundred miles. But then she **hunkered** down again, holding on to the ground like she was afraid it would fly away from her. She's got guts even if she is stupid, he thought approvingly.

Straker's car backed down the driveway—she would have a much better view from where she was; he could only see the Packard's black roof—hesitated for a moment, and then went off down the road toward town.

He decided they had to team up. Anything would be better than going up to that house alone. He had already sampled the poison atmosphere that enveloped it. He had felt it from a half a mile away, and it thickened as you got closer.

Now he ran lightly up the carpeted **incline** and put his hand on her shoulder. He felt her body tense, knew she was going to scream, and said, "Don't yell. It's all right. It's me."

She didn't scream. What escaped was a terrified exhalation of air. She turned around and looked at him, her face white. "W-Who's me?"

He sat down beside her. "My name is Mark Petrie. I know you; you're Sue Norton. My dad knows your dad."

"Petrie . . .? Henry Petrie?"

"Yes, that's my father."

"What are you doing here?" Her eyes were moving continually over him, as if she hadn't been able to take in his actuality yet.

"The same thing you are. Only that stake won't work. It's too . . ." He groped for a word that had checked into his vocabulary through sight and definition but not by use. "It's too flimsy."

She looked down at her piece of snow fence and actually blushed. "Oh, that. Well, I found that in the woods and . . . and thought someone might fall over it, so I just—"

He cut her adult temporizing short impatiently: "You came to kill the vampire, didn't you?"

Identifying Supporting Details   Supporting details are pieces of information that tell the reader something about a character, a place, or a problem in the story. The passage above includes many details about Sue. Which details support Mark's idea that she's "got guts."

a.   She didn't run away when she saw Straker's car; she didn't scream when Mark touched her.

b.   Her face was white; he felt her body tense.

Thinking About the Story

Practice Vocabulary

Complete each sentence by writing the correct word in the blank.

momentarily	cylindrical	methodical	glimpse
synchronized	pondering	hunkered	incline

1. When you look briefly at a tree, you get only a _____ of it.

2. Ed is very _____; he works in a careful and precise way.

3. Mark spent several days _____ the problem, trying to think of a solution.

4. She _____ down, kneeling on her hands and knees, close to the ground.

5. It took him a long time to ride his bike up the _____ to the top of the hill.

6. Something that has the shape of a tube is _____.

7. Jill stopped watching the road _____, and right then she had the accident.

8. Figure skating pairs must always be _____, carefully making their movements at the same time.

Understand What You Read

Write the answer to each question.

9. Name two things Mark did to prepare before he went to Straker's house.

_____

_____

10. Why does Mark move so carefully while he's watching Sue?

_____

_____

11. Why does Mark think Sue is there to kill the vampire?

_____

_____

Check your answers on page 230.

Apply Your Skills

Circle the number of the best answer for each question.

12 Imagine that the author wanted to change the story and tell it from Sue's point of view. Which of the following sentences represents her point of view?
(1) Mark had seen that guy Straker in town.
(2) She turned around and looked at him.
(3) It was a girl. He felt a sense of relief mingled with disappointment.
(4) As she drew closer, he felt an urge to laugh bitterly.
(5) He felt her body tense, knew she was going to scream.

13 Which of the following tells the least about the setting of the story?
(1) Yellow ash would burn longer and cleaner in the living room fireplace.
(2) He crept behind the trunk of a large spruce.
(3) She went on up the hill toward the break in the trees.
(4) He avoided any small twigs that might pop and give him away.
(5) He ran quickly up the carpeted incline.

14 Which detail best supports the idea that Straker expects something to happen?
(1) His eyes were like the eyes of a toad.
(2) He looked like he could break a baby's arm and smile while he did it.
(3) Straker's car backed down the driveway.
(4) Straker was at home.
(5) Mark had seen Straker go out to the driveway, look down the road, and then go back in the house.

Connect with the Story

Write your answer to each question.

15 If you were rewriting this story from Sue's point of view, what would you have her thinking about Mark?

_____

_____

16 In this passage, Mark has decided he wants to team up with Sue. Do you prefer to have a partner or team with you when you attack a problem? Or do you prefer to handle problems by yourself? Give reasons for your answer.

_____

_____

4

Popular Novel

Setting the Stage

Popular novels are works of fiction, meaning that they come from the imagination. Still, the author of a popular novel wants to make the characters and their feelings very real to the reader.

Popular novels often focus on families, love, marriage, or work—issues that are important to all of us. Almost always, the characters face some sort of problem or conflict. These novels may entertain, but the best of them also express important ideas and values.

PREVIEW THE READING

The mood or feel of a piece sometimes comes through in the first few sentences. Read the first six lines of the passage. Then answer these questions.

1 What mood or feeling do the first lines of the passage express?

_____

2 List three characters mentioned in the first lines of the passage.

_____

RELATE TO THE EXPERIENCE

This passage is about three women who have known each other for a long time. Their feelings for each other are deep and loving. One of the women, Ciel, returns after a long absence. The reunion is joyous and tearful at the same time.

3 Have you ever had a reunion with someone you loved, after a long separation? How did it feel? Describe the reunion and how you felt.

_____

_____

VOCABULARY

posed	**pranced**	**inhaled**
intervals	**baste**	**hesitantly**

Check your answers on page 230.

The Women of Brewster Place
by Gloria Naylor

"Miss Johnson, you wanna dance?" A handsome teenager **posed** himself in a seductive dare before Etta. She ran her hand down the side of her hair and took off her apron.

"Don't mind if I do." And she **pranced** around the table.

"Woman, come back here and act your age." Mattie speared a rib off the grill.

"I am acting it—thirty-five!"

"Umph, you got *regrets* older than that."

The boy spun Etta around under his arms. "Careful, now, honey. It's still in working order, but I gotta keep it running in a little lower gear." She winked at Mattie and danced toward the center of the street.

Mattie shook her head. "Lord keep her safe, since you can't keep her sane." She smiled and patted her foot under the table to the beat of the music while she looked down the street and **inhaled** the hope that was bouncing off swinging hips, sauce-covered fingers, and grinning mouths.

A thin brown-skinned woman, carrying a trench coat and overnight case, was making her way slowly up the block. She stopped at **intervals** to turn and answer the people who called to her—"Hey, Ciel! Good to see you, girl!"

Ciel—a knot formed at the base of Mattie's heart, and she caught her breath. "No."

Ciel came up to Mattie and stood in front of her timidly. "Hi, Mattie. It's been a long time."

"No." Mattie shook her head slowly.

"I know you're probably mad at me. I should have written or at least called before now."

"Child." Mattie placed a hand gently on Ciel's face.

"But I thought about you all the time, really, Mattie."

"Child." Both of Mattie's hands cupped Ciel's face.

"I had to get away; you know that. I needed to leave Brewster Place as far behind me as I could. I just kept going and going until the highway ran out. And when I looked up, I was in San Francisco and there was nothing but an ocean in front of me, and since I couldn't swim, I stayed."

"Child. Child." Mattie pulled Ciel toward her.

"It was awful not to write—I know that." Ciel was starting to cry. "But I kept saying one day when I've gotten rid of the scars, when I'm really well and over all that's happened so that she can be proud of me, then I'll write and let her know."

"Child. Child. Child." Mattie pressed Ciel into her full bosom and rocked her slowly.

"But that day never came, Mattie." Ciel's tears fell on Mattie's chest as she hugged the woman. "And I stopped believing that it ever would."

"Thank God you found that out." Mattie released Ciel and squeezed her shoulders. "Or I woulda had to wait till the Judgment Day for this here joy."

She gave Ciel a paper napkin to blow her nose. "San Francisco, you said? My, that's a long way. Bet you ain't had none of this out there." She cut Ciel a huge slice of angel food cake on her table.

"Oh, Mattie, this looks good." She took a bite. "Tastes just like the kind my grandmother used to make."

"It should—it's her recipe. The first night I came to Miss Eva's house she gave me a piece of that cake. I never knew till then why they called it angel food—took one bite and thought I had died and gone to heaven."

Ciel laughed. "Yeah, Grandma could cook. We really had some good times in that house. I remember how Basil and I used to fight. I would go to bed and pray, God please bless Grandma and Mattie, but only bless Basil if he stops breaking my crayons. Do you ever hear from him, Mattie?"

Mattie frowned and turned to **baste** her ribs. "Naw, Ciel. Guess he ain't been as lucky as you yet. Ain't run out of highway to stop and make him think."

Drawing Conclusions A **conclusion** is an opinion or judgment you make after studying all the facts you have. The conclusion is not usually stated directly in what you read.

To draw a conclusion, use two or more stated ideas to come up with an idea that is not directly stated in the reading. You can conclude some things based on the facts that you find in the reading.

Choose the two facts from the passage above that support the conclusion that Ciel and Mattie have known each other for a very long time.

    a.   Ciel talks about events from long ago.

    b.   Ciel says that she has been living in San Francisco.

    c.   Ciel tells Mattie that is has been a long time since they have seen each other.

To draw the conclusion that Ciel and Mattie have known each other for a very long time, you "read between the lines." This means you have to go beyond what the passage actually says to reach this conclusion.

Etta came back to the table out of breath. "Well, looka you!" She grabbed Ciel and kissed her. "Gal, you looking good. Where you been hiding yourself?"

"I live in San Francisco now, Miss Etta, and I'm working in an insurance company."

"Frisco, yeah, that's a nice city—been through there once. But don't tell me it's salt water putting a shine on that face." She patted Ciel on the cheeks. "Bet you got a new fella."

Ciel blushed. "Well, I have met someone and we're sort of thinking about marriage." She looked up at Mattie. "I'm ready to start another family now."

. . . Mattie beamed.

"But he's not black." She glanced **hesitantly** between Etta and Mattie.

"And I bet he's *not* eight feet tall, and he's *not* as pretty as Billy Dee Williams, and he's *not* president of Yugoslavia, either," Etta said. "You know, we get so caught up with what a man *isn't*. It's what he is that counts. Is he good to you, child?"

"And is he good for you?" Mattie added gently.

"Very much so." Ciel smiled.

"Then, I'm baking your wedding cake." Mattie grinned.

"And I'll come dance at your reception." Etta popped her fingers.

Mattie turned to Etta. "Woman, ain't you done enough dancing today for a lifetime?"

"Aw, hush your mouth. Ciel, will you tell this woman that this here is a party and you supposed to be having a good time."

"And will you tell that woman," Mattie said, "that hip-shaking is for young folks, and old bags like us is supposed to be behind these tables selling food."

"You two will never change." Ciel laughed.

Visualizing Characters Sometimes characters in fiction are described in detail. Sometimes the author says only a little about how they look. Either way, characters become more alive if you can form some mental pictures of them.

To visualize a character, use all the details you can find about how the character looks. What the person does and says also helps create a mental picture. In the passage above, look at what Etta says and what she does. Also, look at what Mattie says to Etta or about her.

Based on details in the passage, which of the following is the most likely description of Etta Johnson?

    a.   middle-aged but energetic

    b.   awkward and shy

Check your answers on page 230.

Thinking About the Story

Practice Vocabulary

The words below are in the passage in bold type. Study the way each word is used. Then match each word with its meaning. Write the letter.

_____	**1** posed	a. breathed in
_____	**2** pranced	b. spaces in time between events
_____	**3** inhaled	c. brush liquid on roasting meat
_____	**4** intervals	d. in an unsure way
_____	**5** baste	e. stood in a way intended to impress
_____	**6** hesitantly	f. walked in a proud, happy way

Understand What You Read

Write the answer to each question.

7 Where has Ciel been?

_____

_____

8 Who is Miss Eva, and what fact do you know about her?

_____

_____

9 Why do you think Ciel is hesitant after she tells Etta and Mattie that her boyfriend is not black?

_____

_____

10 How do Etta and Mattie feel about Ciel's new boyfriend?

_____

_____

11 How do you think Etta and Mattie feel about each other?

_____

_____

Apply Your Skills

Circle the number of the best answer for each question.

12 What can you conclude about the setting of this passage? Where are these people?
(1) at a family reunion
(2) at Etta's birthday party
(3) at an outdoor neighborhood party
(4) at a San Francisco restaurant
(5) at a wedding reception

13 What can you conclude about why Ciel left Brewster Place?
(1) She had some kind of personal trouble.
(2) She left to go to college.
(3) She wanted to see the ocean.
(4) Her grandma died.
(5) Her friend Mattie sent her away.

14 Etta and Mattie are different in personality. Which sentence best describes their differences?
(1) Etta thinks only of herself, while Mattie thinks mainly of others.
(2) Etta gets angry easily, while Mattie is very calm.
(3) Etta feels restless in Brewster Place, while Mattie is completely satisfied there.
(4) Etta is a motherly at-home type, while Mattie likes to go out and party.
(5) Etta likes to go out and party, while Mattie is a motherly at-home type.

Connect with the Story

Write your answer to each question.

15 Do you think of yourself as more like Etta or more like Mattie? Give reasons for your answer.

_____

_____

16 Could you be satisfied living in the same neighborhood all your life? Or are you more like Ciel, who needed to get away? Give reasons for your answer.

_____

_____

_____

5 Folk Novel

Setting the Stage

People have been telling certain tales over and over for centuries. These stories are called **folktales. Folk novels** retell these old stories, which are set in far-distant times and places.

Folktales often teach a lesson or explain how something began. Folktales also include ideas that are important to a group of people or a culture. By using a folktale as part of a longer story, an author can show how events today are connected to the past.

PREVIEW THE READING

You can learn a lot about a passage by reading a few sentences. Read the first few sentences of this passage. Then answer these questions.

1 How many characters are talking? What are they doing?

_____

_____

RELATE TO THE SITUATION

An important theme in this story is the struggle for survival. The reader learns about this struggle in two ways. First, the fish struggle with the river as it floods and then dries up. Second, the early people struggled for survival when their crops withered and died.

2 Is there a story in your family history about a struggle for survival? Most families have such a story. What is yours?

_____

_____

_____

VOCABULARY

churned	**listlessly**	**subsided**
furrow	**abode**	**relented**

Bless Me, Ultima   by Rudolfo A. Anaya

"You fish a lot?" I asked.

"I have always been a fisherman," he answered, "as long as I can remember—"

"You fish," he said.

"Yes. I learned to fish with my brothers when I was very little. Then they went to war and I couldn't fish anymore. Then Ultima came—" I paused.

"I know," he said.

"So last summer I fished. Sometimes with Jasón."

"You have a lot to learn—"

"Yes," I answered.

The afternoon sun was warm on the sand. The muddy waters after-the-flood **churned listlessly** south, and out of the deep hole by the rock in front of us the catfish came. They were biting good for the first fishing of summer. We caught plenty of channel catfish and a few small yellow-bellies.

"Have you ever fished for the carp of the river?"

The river was full of big, brown carp. It was called the River of the Carp. Everybody knew it was bad luck to fish for the big carp that the summer floods washed downstream. After every flood, when the swirling angry waters of the river **subsided,** the big fish could be seen fighting their way back upstream. It had always been so.

The waters would subside very fast and in places the water would be so low that, as the carp swam back upstream, the backs of the fish would raise a **furrow** in the water. Sometimes the townspeople came to stand on the bridge and watch the struggle as the carp splashed their way back to the pools from which the flood had uprooted them. Some of the town kids, not knowing it was bad luck to catch the carp, would scoop them out of the low waters and toss the fish upon the sand bars.

Identifying Figurative Language (Personification) Authors sometimes use language in a special way called personification. In personification, something that is not human is given human qualities. For example, an author might say that the wind whistled sadly through the trees. People can feel the emotion of sadness, but wind cannot. The author has used the word *sadly* to create a mood and make the reader think of a low, soft sound.

In the passage above, the author uses the word *angry* to describe the water. This is an example of personification that helps to create a mood. What does that word suggest to you?

a. The level of the water was very low.

b. The water was very rough and, perhaps, dangerous.

Check your answers on page 231.

There the poor carp would flop until they dried out and died, then later the crows would swoop down and eat them.

Some people in town would even buy the carp for a nickel and eat the fish! That was very bad. Why, I did not know.

It was a beautiful sight to behold, the struggle of the carp to regain his **abode** before the river dried to a trickle and trapped him in strange pools of water. What was beautiful about it was that you knew that against all the odds some of the carp made it back and raised their families, because every year the drama was repeated.

"No," I answered, "I do not fish for carp. It is bad luck."

"Do you know why?" he asked and raised an eyebrow.

"No," I said and held my breath. I felt I sat on the banks of an undiscovered river whose churning, muddied waters carried many secrets.

"I will tell you a story," Samuel said after a long silence, "a story that was told to my father by Jasón's Indian—"

I listened breathlessly. The lapping of the water was like the tide of time sounding on my soul.

"A long time ago, when the earth was young and only wandering tribes touched the virgin grasslands and drank from the pure streams, a strange people came to this land. They were sent to this valley by their gods. They had wandered lost for many years but never had they given up faith in their gods, and so they were finally rewarded. This fertile valley was to be their home. There were plenty of animals to eat, strange trees that bore sweet fruit, sweet water to drink and for their fields of maíz [corn]—"

"Were they Indians?" I asked when he paused.

"They were *the people*," he answered simply and went on. "There was only one thing that was withheld from them, and that was the fish called the carp. This fish made his home in the waters of the river, and he was sacred to the gods. For a long time the people were happy. Then came the forty years of the sun-without-rain, and crops withered and died, the game was killed, and the people went hungry. To stay alive they finally caught the carp of the river and ate them."

Identifying Point of View A story is often told through the eyes of only one character, the narrator. In that case, we are hearing the story from the narrator's point of view. In this story, we have a "first-person" narrator, identified by the word *I* in the first sentence. This point of view makes the action in a story seem very real.

Who is the narrator in this passage?
a.   Samuel
b.   We don't know his name.

I shivered. I had never heard a story like this one. It was getting late and I thought of my mother.

"The gods were very angry. They were going to kill all of the people for their sin. But one kind god who truly loved the people argued against it, and the other gods were so moved by his love that they **relented** from killing the people. Instead, they turned the people into carp and made them live forever in the waters of the river—"

The setting sun glistened on the brown waters of the river and turned them to bronze.

"It is a sin to catch them," Samuel said, "it is a worse offense to eat them. They are a part of *the people*." He pointed towards the middle of the river where two huge back fins rose out of the water and splashed upstream.

"And if you eat one," I whispered, "you might be punished like they were punished."

"I don't know," Samuel said. He rose and took my fishing line.

"Is that all the story?" I asked.

He divided the catfish we had caught and gave me my share on a small string. "No, there is more," he said. He glanced around as if to make sure we were alone. "Do you know about the golden carp?" he asked in a whisper.

"No," I shook my head.

"When the gods had turned the people into carp, the one kind god who loved the people grew very sad. The river was full of dangers to the new fish. So he went to the other gods and told them that he chose to be turned into a carp and swim in the river where he could take care of his people. The gods agreed. But because he was a god they made him very big and colored him the color of gold. And they made him the lord of all the waters of the valley."

Understanding Sequence One way an author can organize a story is by using sequence, or presenting events as they occur in time. To follow the sequence in a story, look for the order that things happen in time.

Sometimes that author uses words that help you know what the order of events is. Look for clue words such as *first, second, later, then, while, before, after, during,* and *since.*

In Samuel's story, what happened after the people ate the carp?

a.   The gods became angry.

b.   The forty years of sun-without-rain began.

Thinking About the Story

Practice Vocabulary

The words below are in the passage in bold type. Study the way each word is used. Then complete each sentence by writing the correct word.

churned	**listlessly**	**subsided**
furrow	**abode**	**relented**

1. The path left in the ground by a plow is called a _____ .

2. The boiling water _____ in the pot on the hot stove.

3. Samuel had no energy, so he lay _____ on his bed.

4. The woman knew she could change the run-down apartment into a cozy _____ .

5. We waited until the flood _____ before we cleaned up the mess.

6. The parents sometimes _____ on their strict rules when their children gave good reasons for breaking these rules.

Understand What You Read

Write the answer to each question.

7. Why won't the narrator fish for carp?

_____

_____

8. How do you think the narrator feels while hearing the story about the carp?

_____

_____

_____

9. In Samuel's story, why did the gods decide to save the people even though the people had eaten the carp?

_____

_____

_____

Check your answers on page 231.

Apply Your Skills

Circle the number of the best answer for each question.

10 Which of the following phrases includes a personification?
 (1) the tide of time sounding on my soul
 (2) the struggle of the carp
 (3) muddied water carried many secrets
 (4) they turned the people into carp
 (5) forty years of the sun-without-rain

11 If the author had written the passage from Samuel's point of view, we might not know
 (1) that the boy thought of his mother while Samuel was talking.
 (2) why the people ate the carp.
 (3) why the gods agreed not to kill the people.
 (4) that the kind god chose to be turned into a carp.
 (5) that it was considered a sin to catch carp and a bigger sin to eat them.

12 In the sequence of Samuel's story, when does the god become a golden carp?
 (1) while the people were eating the carp from the river
 (2) after the people had been turned into carp
 (3) after Samuel divided the catfish up with the boy
 (4) while the people were being turned into carp
 (5) before the gods got angry

Connect with the Story

Write your answer to each question.

13 In this passage, Samuel explains certain beliefs about the history and ways of his people. How have you learned the history and beliefs of your family or people?

_____

_____

14 At the beginning of the story, the boy knows it's wrong to catch carp, but no one has ever told him why it is wrong. Do you think it's important to know *why* something is wrong? Or is it enough simply to know that it *is* wrong? Explain your answer.

_____

_____

_____

Classic Short Story

Setting the Stage

A **short story** is a piece of fiction that is shorter than a novel but has a full plot. A short story usually has only a few main characters and takes place over a shorter time period than a novel. Writers have been publishing short stories in books, newspapers, and magazines for more than a century. A very famous writer of scary short stories was Edgar Allan Poe (1809–1849). His spine-chilling stories have been made into movies and TV shows.

PREVIEW THE READING

You can get an idea of what a short story is about by reading a few sentences. Read the first paragraph of the passage. Then answer these questions.

1 What is the narrator's state of mind?

_____

2 Which of the narrator's senses is sharpest?

_____

RELATE TO THE SETTING

Most of this passage takes place inside a dark bedroom where an old man sleeps. The narrator of the story describes his method for sneaking into that room at night, trying not to awaken the old man. The narrator imagines what the man in the bedroom is feeling after a sound awakens him one night.

3 Have you ever been awakened in the night by a sound, then lay there listening for every scratch or creaking sound? Describe the experience. How did it feel?

_____

_____

VOCABULARY

acute	dissimulation	sufficient	sagacity	stifled
suppositions	enveloped	unperceived	crevice	stealthily

Check your answers on page 232.

The Tell-Tale Heart by Edgar Allan Poe

True!—nervous—very, very dreadfully nervous I had been and am; but why *will* you say that I am mad? The disease had sharpened my senses—not destroyed—not dulled them. Above all was the sense of hearing **acute.** I heard all things in the heaven and in the earth. . . . How, then, am I mad? Hearken! and observe how healthily—how calmly I can tell you the whole story.

It is impossible to say how first the idea entered my brain; but once conceived, it haunted me day and night. Object there was none. Passion there was none. I loved the old man. He had never wronged me. He had never given me insult. For his gold I had no desire. I think it was his eye! yes, it was this! One of his eyes resembled that of a vulture—a pale blue eye, with a film over it. Whenever it fell upon me, my blood ran cold; and so by degrees—very gradually—I made up my mind to take the life of the old man, and thus rid myself of the eye forever.

Using Definitions as Context Clues The context of a word or phrase is the language around it that gives clues to its meaning. Sometimes an author defines an unfamiliar word or phrase for the reader by using context clues. For example, in the passage above, the phrase "sharpened my senses" is used. By saying the opposite, "not destroyed—not dulled them," the author makes the meaning of the phrase clear. Definition clues usually are found after a word and are set off by commas or dashes.

In the passage above, the author uses the phrase "by degrees." Look for it. Based on the context clue, what is the meaning of this phrase?

   a.   doing something very gradually

   b.   making up one's mind

Now this is the point. You fancy me mad. Madmen know nothing. But you should have seen *me*. You should have seen how wisely I proceeded—with what caution—with what foresight—with what **dissimulation** I went to work! I was never kinder to the old man than during the whole week before I killed him. And every night, about midnight, I turned the latch of his door and opened it—oh, so gently! And then, when I had made an opening **sufficient** for my head, I put in a dark lantern, all closed, closed, so that no light shone out, and then I thrust in my head. Oh, you would have laughed to see how cunningly I thrust it in! I moved it slowly—very, very slowly, so that I might not disturb the old man's sleep. It took me an hour to place my whole head within the opening so far that I could see him as he lay upon his bed. Ha!—would a madman have been so wise as this? And then, when my head was well in the room, I undid the lantern cautiously—oh, so cautiously—cautiously (for the hinges creaked)—I undid it just so much that a single thin ray fell upon the vulture eye.

And this I did for seven long nights—every night just at midnight—but I found the eye always closed; and so it was impossible to do the work; for it was not the old man who vexed me, but his Evil Eye. And every morning, when the day broke, I went boldly into the chamber, and spoke courageously to him, calling him by name in a hearty tone, and inquiring how he had passed the night. So you see he would have been a very profound old man, indeed, to suspect that every night, just at twelve, I looked in upon him while he slept.

Upon the eighth night I was more than usually cautious in opening the door. A watch's minute hand moves more quickly than did mine. Never before that night had I *felt* the extent of my own powers—of my **sagacity.** I could scarcely contain my feelings of triumph. To think that there I was, opening the door, little by little, and he not even to dream of my secret deeds or thoughts. I fairly chuckled at the idea; and perhaps he heard me; for he moved on the bed suddenly, as if startled. Now you may think that I drew back—but no. His room was as black as pitch with the thick darkness (for the shutters were close fastened, through fear of robbers), and so I knew he could not see the opening of the door, and I kept pushing it on steadily, steadily.

I had my head in, and was about to open the lantern, when my thumb slipped upon the tin fastening, and the old man sprang up in the bed, crying out—"Who's there?"

I kept quite still and said nothing. For a whole hour I did not move a muscle, and in the meantime I did not hear him lie down. He was still sitting up in the bed listening;— just as I have done, night after night, hearkening to the death watches in the wall.

Understanding Mood The mood of a story is like the mood of a person. It can be tense and gloomy, light and joyous, or dark and frightening. An author has many ways of creating mood: telling what the characters are like, describing the setting, and indicating how quickly or slowly events occur.

In this story, the author creates the mood by introducing a peculiar and nervous character and making him sneak around in someone's dark bedroom. The language *(hinges creaked, vulture eye, stalked with his black shadow)* also contributes to the mood.

What is the mood of this passage?
a.   light and comical
b.   dark and spooky

Presently I heard a slight groan, and I knew it was the groan of mortal terror. It was not a groan of pain or of grief—oh, no!—it was the low **stifled** sound that arises from the bottom of the soul when overcharged with awe. I knew the sound well. Many a night, just at midnight, when all the world slept, it has welled up from my own bosom, deepening, with its dreadful echo, the terrors that distracted me. I say I knew

   Check your answers on page 232.

it well. I knew what the old man felt, and pitied him, although I chuckled at heart. I knew that he had been lying awake ever since the first slight noise, when he had turned in the bed. His fears had been ever since growing upon him. He had been trying to fancy them causeless, but could not. He had been saying to himself—"It is nothing but the wind in the chimney—it is only a mouse crossing the floor," or "it is merely a cricket which has made a single chirp." Yes, he had been trying to comfort himself with these **suppositions**; but he has found all in vain. *All in vain;* because Death, in approaching him, had stalked with his black shadow before him, and **enveloped** the victim. And it was the mournful influence of the **unperceived** shadow that caused him to feel—although he neither saw nor heard—to *feel* the presence of my head within the room.

When I had waited a long time, very patiently, without hearing him lie down, I resolved to open a little—a very, very little **crevice** in the lantern. So I opened it—you cannot imagine how **stealthily,** stealthily—until, at length, a single dim ray, like the thread of the spider, shot from out the crevice and full upon the vulture eye.

It was open—wide, wide open—and I grew furious as I gazed upon it. I saw it with perfect distinctness—all a dull blue, with a hideous veil over it that chilled the very marrow in my bones; but I could see nothing else of the old man's face or person: for I had directed the ray as if by instinct, precisely upon the . . . spot.

And now have I not told you that what you mistake for madness is but over-acuteness of the senses?—now, I say, there came to my ears a low, dull, quick sound, such as a watch makes when enveloped in cotton. I knew *that* sound well too. It was the beating of the old man's heart. It increased my fury, as the beating of a drum stimulates the soldier into courage.

Predicting Outcomes Sometimes an author ends a story without telling what finally happened. The reader must figure out the ending. When you do that, you are predicting the outcome. You use the information presented in the story to predict what will happen.

The outcome you predict must fit the story. It must make sense with what you know about the characters and what has already happened in the story.

In the part of "The Tell-Tale Heart" you have read, you have seen how upset the narrator gets because of the old man's *vulture* eye. Now he has finally seen the eye in the middle of the night. What do you think he will do next?

a.   He will probably go ahead with his plan to kill the old man.
b.   He will probably get control of his feelings, sneak out of the room, and close the door.

Check your answers on page 232.

Thinking About the Story

Practice Vocabulary

The words below are in the passage in bold type. Study the context in which each word appears. Then match each word with its meaning. Write the letter.

_____ **1** acute

_____ **2** stealthily

_____ **3** sufficient

_____ **4** enveloped

_____ **5** sagacity

_____ **6** stifled

_____ **7** suppositions

_____ **8** unperceived

_____ **9** crevice

_____ **10** dissimulation

a. not seen

b. surrounded

c. enough

d. wisdom

e. small crack

f. the process of disguising one's intentions

g. sharp

h. ideas assumed to be correct

i. held in

j. quietly and secretly

Understand What You Read

Write the answer to each question.

11 What about the old man bothered the narrator the most?

_____

_____

12 Why did the narrator enter the man's room for seven nights without carrying out his plan to kill him?

_____

_____

_____

13 According to the narrator, why couldn't the old man comfort himself and settle back down into sleep on the eighth night?

_____

_____

_____

Check your answers on page 232.

Apply Your Skills

Circle the number of the best answer for each question.

14 Find the word *conceived* in the first line of the second paragraph of the passage. Using context clues, decide which of the following best defines the word.
(1) put in words
(2) entered my brain
(3) haunted the narrator
(4) insulted the narrator
(5) wronged the old men

15 Which of the following phrases best establishes the mood of the story?
(1) Every morning, when the day broke, I went boldly into his chamber.
(2) I knew what the old man felt, and pitied him.
(3) I found the eye always closed; and so it was impossible to do the work.
(4) He had never given me insult.
(5) For a whole hour, I did not move a muscle.

16 Based on what you know of the narrator, which of the following do you predict will happen after he kills the old man?
(1) The sound of the old man's heartbeat haunts the narrator after he kills the old man.
(2) The narrator becomes more peaceful and relaxed.
(3) The narrator decides that he is mad after all.
(4) The narrator regrets what he has done because the old man had always been kind to him.
(5) The old man's eye follows the narrator everywhere.

Connect with the Story

Write your answer to each question.

17 The narrator keeps saying that he is not crazy. Do you believe him? Why or why not?

_____

_____

18 Do you enjoy Poe's style of writing in this story? Explain your answer. Considering that most of Poe's writing has a similar dark mood, would you want to read more of his work? Why or why not?

_____

_____

7

Popular Short Story

Setting the Stage

Short stories and other kinds of **popular fiction** sometimes deal with problems between parents and children. A special kind of problem can come up if the parents moved to the United States from a different country. The immigrant parents may want to keep the traditions from their old country, but the American-born children don't. Recently, a number of young authors have written fiction that describes the personal conflicts that result.

PREVIEW THE READING

You can get an idea of what a short story is about by reading a few sentences. Read the first few sentences of the passage. Then answer these questions.

1 Who are the two main characters?

_____

2 What two cultures is the story about?

_____

RELATE TO THE FEELINGS

This passage is about a mother who is thinking about her adult daughter. The mother sees how different she is from her daughter, who was raised as an American and has lost the Chinese ways of seeing and being. The mother has many feelings about these differences. She is sad, and proud, and confused.

3 How are you similar or different from your parents or children (if you have them)? How do these differences and similarities make you feel?

_____

_____

VOCABULARY

blend	circumstances	advantage
opportunities	pursuing	fabulous

   Check your answers on page 232.

Double Face by Amy Tan

My daughter wanted to go to China for her second honeymoon, but now she is afraid.

"What if I **blend** in so well they think I'm one of them?" Waverly asked me. "What if they don't let me come back to the United States?"

"When you go to China," I told her, "you don't even need to open your mouth. They already know you are an outsider."

"What are you talking about?" she asked. My daughter likes to speak back. She likes to question what I say.

"Aii-ya," I said. "Even if you put on their clothes, even if you take off your makeup and hide your fancy jewelry, they know. They know just watching the way you walk, the way you carry your face. They know you do not belong."

My daughter did not look pleased when I told her this, that she didn't look Chinese. She had a sour American look on her face. Oh, maybe ten years ago, she would have clapped her hands—hurray!—as if this were good news. But now she wants to be Chinese, it is so fashionable. And I know it is too late. All those years I tried to teach her! She followed my Chinese ways only until she learned how to walk out the door by herself and go to school. So now the only Chinese words she can say are *sh-sh, houche, chr fan,* and *gwan deng shweijyau.* How can she talk to people in China with these words? . . . , choo-choo train, eat, close light, sleep. How can she think she can blend in? Only her skin and her hair are Chinese. Inside—she is all American-made.

It's my fault she is this way. I wanted my children to have the best combination: American **circumstances** and Chinese character. How could I know these two things do not mix?

I taught her how American circumstances work. If you are born poor here, it's no lasting shame. You are first in line for a scholarship. If the roof crashes on your head, no need to cry over this bad luck. You can sue anybody, make the landlord fix it. You do not have to sit like a Buddha under a tree letting pigeons drop their dirty business on your head. You can buy an umbrella. Or go inside a Catholic church. In America, nobody says you have to keep the circumstances somebody else gives you.

Comparing and Contrasting Comparing shows how things are alike. Contrasting shows how things are different. In the passage, the mother says that Waverly has Chinese hair and skin. But her mother says that Waverly is different from the people in China in every other way.

What is one important way that Waverly is different from Chinese people?
a.   She has a sour look on her face.
b.   She's afraid she'll have to stay in China.

She learned these things, but I couldn't teach her about Chinese character. How to obey parents and listen to your mother's mind. How not to show your own thoughts, to put your feelings behind your face so you can take **advantage** of hidden **opportunities.** Why easy things are not worth **pursuing.** How to know your own worth and polish it, never flashing it around like a cheap ring. Why Chinese thinking is best.

No, this kind of thinking didn't stick to her. She was too busy chewing gum, blowing bubbles bigger than her cheeks. Only that kind of thinking stuck.

"Finish your coffee," I told her yesterday. "Don't throw your blessings away."

"Don't be so old-fashioned, Ma," she told me, finishing her coffee down the sink. "I'm my own person."

And I think, How can she be her own person? When did I give her up?

Making Inferences When you make an inference, you figure out something that is suggested or implied by an author but not directly stated. You combine the facts you have with your own knowledge and experiences.

In this passage, the mother says, "Finish your coffee. Don't throw your blessings away." From this you can infer that the Chinese believe in not wasting what one has been given.

When the mother gives examples of "American circumstances," what can you infer as her meaning?

    a.   She believes that Americans have fewer opportunities than the Chinese do.

    b.   She believes Americans have more choices in life than Chinese people do.

My daughter is getting married a second time. So she asked me to go to her beauty parlor, her famous Mr. Rory. I know her meaning. She is ashamed of my looks. What will her husband's parents and his important lawyer friends think of this backward old Chinese woman?

"Auntie An-mei can cut me," I say.

"Rory is famous," says my daughter, as if she had no ears. "He does **fabulous** work."

So I sit in Mr. Rory's chair. He pumps me up and down until I am the right height. Then my daughter criticizes me as if I were not there. "See how it's flat on one side," she accuses my head. "She needs a cut and a perm. And this purple tint in her hair, she's been doing it at home. She's never had anything professionally done."

She is looking at Mr. Rory in the mirror. He is looking at me in the mirror. I have seen this professional look before. Americans don't really look at one another when talking. They talk to their reflections. They look at others or themselves only when they think nobody is watching. So they never see how they really look. They see themselves smiling without their mouth open, or turned to the side where they cannot see their faults.

"How does she want it?" asked Mr. Rory. He thinks I do not understand English. He is floating his fingers through my hair. He is showing how his magic can make my hair thicker and longer.

"Ma, how do you want it?" Why does my daughter think she is translating English for me? Before I can even speak, she explains my thoughts: "She wants a soft wave. We probably shouldn't cut it too short. Otherwise it'll be too tight for the wedding. She doesn't want it to look kinky or weird."

And now she says to me in a loud voice, as if I had lost my hearing, "Isn't that right, Ma? Not too tight?"

I smile. I use my American face. That's the face Americans think is Chinese, the one they cannot understand. But inside I am becoming ashamed. I am ashamed she is ashamed. Because she is my daughter and I am proud of her, and I am her mother but she is not proud of me.

Mr. Rory pats my hair more. He looks at me. He looks at my daughter. Then he says something to my daughter that really displeases her: "It's uncanny how much you two look alike!"

I smile, this time with my Chinese face. But my daughter's eyes and her smile become very narrow, the way a cat pulls itself small just before it bites. Now Mr. Rory goes away so we can think about this. I hear him snap his fingers. "Wash! Mrs. Jong is next!"

So my daughter and I are alone in this crowded beauty parlor. She is frowning at herself in the mirror. She sees me looking at her.

"The same cheeks," she says. She points to mine and then pokes her cheeks. She sucks them outside in to look like a starved person. She puts her face next to mine, side by side, and we look at each other in the mirror.

"You can see your character in your face," I say to my daughter without thinking. "You can see your future."

"What do you mean?" she says.

And now I have to fight back my feelings. These two faces, I think, so much the same! The same happiness, the same sadness, the same good fortune, the same faults.

I am seeing myself and my mother, back in China, when I was a young girl.

Identifying Conflict in Fiction Fiction is often based on a **conflict** between characters. The conflict can come from cultural differences, different opinions, or different ways of life. This passage is based on the conflict between Waverly and her mother.

What is an important conflict in this passage?

a. The mother does not like Mr. Rory, but the daughter does.

b. The mother is proud of the daughter, but the daughter is ashamed of the mother.

Thinking About the Story

Practice Vocabulary

The words below are in the passage in bold type. Study the way each word is used. Then complete each sentence by writing the correct word.

blend	circumstances	advantage
opportunities	pursuing	fabulous

1 I have not given up my goals. I am still _____ them.

2 The more education you have, the more _____ you are likely to have.

3 If things are mixed together enough, they will _____.

4 She thought it would be _____ if she won the state lottery.

5 The scholarships for Chinese-Americans gave Waverly a financial

_____ .

6 The difficult _____ Mrs. Jong grew up in did not stop her from trying to improve herself.

Understand What You Read

Write the answer to each question.

7 According to the mother, what does not mix?

_____

_____

8 Why do you think Waverly tells Mr. Rory what her mother wants?

_____

_____

_____

9 What does Mr. Rory say just before he sends Mrs. Jong for her shampoo? Why do you think this bothers Waverly?

_____

_____

_____

Check your answers on page 233.

Apply Your Skills

Circle the number of the best answer for each question.

10 The mother compares and contrasts Chinese and American ways. According to her, which of the following is the most important difference?
  (1) The Chinese are more careful and quiet and observant than Americans.
  (2) The Chinese are poorer than Americans.
  (3) Chinese hair is different from American hair.
  (4) Americans wear more fancy jewelry than the Chinese.
  (5) Americans don't appreciate Chinese culture, while the Chinese love everything that is American.

11 From the mother's thoughts, what can you infer about the way the Chinese talk to each other?
  (1) They always look away from each other.
  (2) They look directly at each other.
  (3) They do not smile when talking.
  (4) They do not talk in public.
  (5) They tell each other their inner feelings.

12 The mother and daughter are in conflict about many things. For example, the mother thinks some of her daughter's ideas are silly. Which of the following shows how the mother feels?
  (1) "Now she is afraid."
  (2) "Don't be so old-fashioned."
  (3) ". . . her famous Mr. Rory . . ."
  (4) "She is not proud of me."
  (5) "You can see your character in your face."

Connect with the Story

Write your answer to each question.

13 In this passage, which of Mrs. Jong's "faces" do you like better? The Chinese one or the American one? Explain your answer.

_____

_____

14 Do you agree with the mother in this passage when she says that "Americans don't really look at each other when talking"? Explain your answer.

_____

_____

Reading at Work

Retail Sales: Bookstore Clerk

Do you like working with people? If you do, you may choose to work in retail sales. This area involves a wide range of jobs in stores where people buy products for their home, work, or personal use. If you also like to read, then the retail sales job of bookstore clerk may be right for you.

Bookstore clerks should have good personal skills because they have a lot of interaction with customers. They can recommend books by a particular author, interest area, time period, or genre. They must also have good math skills for working with inventory, prices, and discounts. Many bookstore clerks also use computers and data entry skills to check whether a book is in stock or to order books from publishers or suppliers.

> **Genre:** a type of book by subject area. You have read examples of mystery, science fiction, and thriller genres in this unit. Other popular genres include adventure, romance, biography, and "how-to" books.

Look at the chart showing some of the careers in retail sales.

- Do any of the careers interest you? If so, which ones?

- What information would you need to find out more about those careers? On a separate piece of paper, write some questions that you would like answered. You can find out more information about those careers in the *Occupational Outlook Handbook* at your local library.

Use the material on the previous page and the bestseller list below to answer the questions that follow.

Bookstore clerks must be able to answer questions from customers. They often use tools like reference books, computer databases, and bestseller lists.

Rank	Title	Author	Weeks on the Bestseller List
	FICTION Bestsellers Week of April 27		
1	**Just Around the Corner**—Super sleuth Shelly Shift chases jewel thief around the globe.	Marcy Boone	3
2	**Fear of the Known**—Supernatural thriller set in 19th century Missouri.	Brian Jenkins	7
3	**Windy Days, Sleepless Nights**—Independent young woman climbs Mt. Everest and finds love.	Ellen Stein	2
4	**One More Byte**—Private Investigator Ray Fern hunts computer hacker.	Ray Lopez	10
5	**The Sky's the Limit**—Group of friends finds challenges in the Rocky Mountains.	Brett Young	5
6	**Let Me Hear It Again**—Bitter, ailing deaf woman finds hope and romance in the hospital.	Tanisha Jordan	22
7	**Aidan's Image**—Young family moves into haunted house.	Randy Moore	17
8	**Now You See It, Now You Don't**—Shelly Shift uncovers identity of murderous magician.	Marcy Boone	14

1 Put a check mark by each reason that bookstore clerks use bestseller lists.

_____ To suggest new books for their customers to read

_____ To fill up the shelves in the bookstore

_____ To keep the most popular books in stock

_____ To make the bookstore look attractive

2 Which book has been on the bestseller list the longest? _____

3 What kinds of books do you enjoy reading? Name your favorite genre and explain why you like it.

_____

_____

_____

_____

Unit 1 Review: Fiction

Read the following passage from the novel *Mutation* by Robin Cook.

"But he's not crying?" questioned Victor. Doubt clouded his euphoria.

The resident lightly slapped the soles of Victor Jr.'s feet, then rubbed his back. Still the infant stayed quiet. "But he's breathing fine."

The resident picked up the bulb syringe and tried to suction Victor Jr.'s nose once again. To the doctor's astonishment, the newborn's hand came up and yanked the bulb away from the fingers of the resident and dropped it over the side of the infant care unit.

"Well that settles that," said the resident with a chuckle. "He just doesn't want to cry."

"Can I?" asked Victor, motioning toward the baby.

"As long as he doesn't get cold."

Gingerly, Victor reached into the unit and scooped up Victor Jr. He held the infant in front of him with both hands around his torso. He was a beautiful baby with strikingly blond hair. His chubby, rosy cheeks gave his face a picturesquely cherubic quality, but by far the most distinctive aspect of his appearance was his bright blue eyes. As Victor gazed into their depths he realized with a shock that the baby was looking back at him.

"Beautiful, isn't he?" said Marsha over Victor's shoulder.

"Gorgeous," Victor agreed. "But where did the blond hair come from? Ours is brown."

"I was blond until I was five," Marsha said, reaching up to touch the baby's pink skin.

Victor glanced at his wife as she lovingly gazed at the child. She had dark brown hair peppered with just a few strands of gray. Her eyes were a sultry gray-blue; her features quite sculptured: they contrasted with the rounded, full features of the infant.

"Look at his eyes," Marsha said.

Victor turned his attention back to the baby. "They are incredible, aren't they? A minute ago I'd have sworn they were looking right back at me."

"They are like jewels," Marsha said.

Victor turned the baby to face Marsha. As he did so he noticed the baby's eyes remained locked on his! Their turquoise depths were as cold and bright as ice. Unbidden, Victor felt a thrill of fear.

Items 1–6 refer to the passage on page 58.

Find the numbered words in the passage. Study the context in which each word appears. Then match each word with its meaning. Write the letter.

_____ **❶** euphoria   a.   carefully

                                       b.   angel-like

_____ **❷** gingerly

                                       c.   extreme happiness

_____ **❸** cherubic

Circle the number of the best answer for each question.

❹ What can you conclude about how Marsha feels about her child? Marsha feels

    (1) proud

    (2) puzzled

    (3) worried

    (4) uninterested

    (5) surprised

❺ Newborn babies cannot focus their eyes. What can you infer from Victor's noticing "the baby's eyes remained locked on his"?

    (1) The baby is not a newborn infant.

    (2) Victor has poor eyesight.

    (3) The baby is not normal.

    (4) The baby is not Victor's son.

    (5) Victor knows a lot about babies.

❻ Which of the following pairs of words does the author use to show how Victor feels about the baby's eyes?

    (1) chuckle and gazed

    (2) beautiful and brown

    (3) jewels and bright

    (4) turquoise and locked

    (5) shock and fear

Read the following passage from the novel *The Grapes of Wrath* by John Steinbeck.

And the migrants streamed in on the highways and their hunger was in their eyes, and their need was in their eyes. They had no argument, no system, nothing but their numbers and their needs. When there was work for a man, ten men fought for it— fought with a low wage. If that fella'll work for thirty cents, I'll work for twenty-five.

If he'll take twenty-five, I'll do it for twenty.

No, me, I'm hungry. I'll work for fifteen. I'll work for food. The kids. You ought to see them. Little boils, like, comin' out, an' they can't run aroun'. Give 'em some windfall fruit, an' they bloated up. Me. I'll work for a little piece of meat.

And this was good, for wages went down and prices stayed up. The great owners were glad and they sent out more handbills to bring more people in. And wages went down and prices stayed up. And pretty soon now we'll have serfs again.

And now the great owners and the companies invented a new method. A great owner bought a cannery. And when the peaches and the pears were ripe he cut the price of fruit below the cost of raising it. And as cannery owner he paid himself a low price for the fruit and kept the price of canned goods up and took his profit. And the little farmers who owned no canneries lost their farms, and they were taken by the great owners, the banks, and the companies who also owned the canneries. As time went on, there were fewer farms. The little farmers moved into town for a while and exhausted their credit, exhausted their friends, their relatives. And then they too went on the highways. And the roads were crowded with men ravenous for work, murderous for work.

And the companies, the banks worked at their own doom and they did not know it. The fields were fruitful, and starving men moved on the roads. The granaries were full and the children of the poor grew up rachitic [with spine problems], and the pustules of pellagra [sores caused by a skin disease] swelled on their sides. The great companies did not know that the line between hunger and anger is a thin line. And money that might have gone to wages went for gas, for guns, for agents and spies, for blacklists, for drilling. On the highways the people moved like ants and searched for work, for food. And the anger began to ferment.

Items 7–12 refer to the passage on page 60.

Write the word that best completes each sentence.

hunger	**work**	**cannery**	**anger**

7 The migrants were competing for _____ so that they could feed their children.

8 The companies and banks did not understand that they would cause their own doom. They did not understand the thin line between

_____ and _____.

9 One way a great owner increased profits was to buy a

_____.

Circle the number of the best answer for each question.

10 Which of the following phrases is the best meaning of the word *ferment* as it is used in this passage?

   (1) slowly to grow dangerously angry

   (2) the process of making beer

   (3) to grow older

   (4) to make people sick

   (5) to die down quickly

11 Which of the following words best describes the mood in this passage?

   (1) calm

   (2) delighted

   (3) forgiving

   (4) uneasy

   (5) quiet

12 What do the words *ravenous* and *murderous* suggest about how the people felt about getting work? The people felt

   (1) uninterested.

   (2) that they deserved work.

   (3) confident.

   (4) desperate.

   (5) that they could always find work.

Read the following passage from the novel *Ramona* by Helen Hunt Jackson.

Capitan was leaping up, putting his paws on Alessandro's breast, licking his face, yelping, doing all a dog could do, to show welcome and affection.

Alessandro laughed aloud. Ramona had not more than two or three times heard him do this. It frightened her. "Why do you laugh, Alessandro?" she said.

"To think what I have to show you, my Señorita," he said. "Look here;" and turning towards the willows, he gave two or three low whistles, at the first note of which Baba came trotting out of the copse [small group of trees] to the end of his lariat, and began to snort and whinny with delight as soon as he perceived Ramona.

Ramona burst into tears. The surprise was too great.

"Are you not glad, Señorita?" cried Alessandro, aghast. "Is it not your own horse? If you do not wish to take him, I will lead him back. My pony can carry you, if we journey very slowly. But I thought it would be joy to you to have Baba."

"Oh, it is! it is!" sobbed Ramona, with her head on Baba's neck. "It is a miracle,—a miracle. How did he come here? And the saddle too!" she cried, for the first time observing that. "Alessandro," in an awe-struck whisper, "did the saints send him? Did you find him here?" It would have seemed to Ramona's faith no strange thing, had this been so.

"I think the saints helped me to bring him," answered Alessandro, seriously, "or else I had not done it so easily. I did but call, near the corral-fence, and he came to my hand, and leaped over the rails at my word, as quickly as Capitan might have done. He is yours, Señorita. It is no harm to take him?"

"Oh, no!" answered Ramona. "He is more mine than anything else I had; for it was Felipe gave him to me when he could but just stand on his legs; he was only two days old; and I have fed him out of my hand every day till now; and now he is five. Dear Baba, we will never be parted, never!" and she took his head in both her hands, and laid her cheek against it lovingly.

Items 13–19 refer to the passage on page 62.

Find the words in the passage. Study the context in which each word appears. Then write the word that best completes each sentence.

yelping	lariat	trotting	perceived

⑬ Sarah saw things differently, she _____ that people were angry with her.

⑭ He tied the end of the _____ to the post.

⑮ I couldn't hear you over the loud _____ of the animals.

⑯ The horse was _____ so quickly that Joe couldn't stop it.

Circle the number of the best answer for each question.

⑰ What or who is Baba?
    (1) a pony
    (2) a dog
    (3) a horse
    (4) an employee
    (5) Felipe's son

⑱ Ramona is so happy to see Baba because
    (1) it was a surprise for Alessandro.
    (2) the saints brought him.
    (3) he had her saddle.
    (4) Felipe had lost him.
    (5) she had been separated from him.

⑲ What can you infer about Ramona and Alessandro?
    (1) Alessandro is rich and Ramona is not.
    (2) Ramona is rich and Alessandro is not.
    (3) Alessandro's parents do not approve of Ramona.
    (4) Ramona's family does not approve of Alessandro.
    (5) Alessandro and Ramona are both from the same kind of family.

Fiction Extension

In this unit you have read samples of many types of fiction. Which piece did you like the best? Would you like to read the book that it came from or something else by that author? Turn to the Annotated Bibliography on pages 255–257 of this book. Write down the name of the book and the author. Make a plan to go to a library or bookstore soon to get that book or another one by that author.

Check your answers on page 234.   UNIT 1 : FICTION **63**

Reading Connection: Fiction and Earth Science

The Great Santini by Pat Conroy

Before Ben could answer, Bull thundered out at all of them, "I'm gonna give you hogs about five seconds to cut the yappin' then I'm gonna pull this car over to the side of the road and I bet I can shut your yaps even if your mother can't."

"Hush," Lillian hissed at her children. "Not another sound." Her eyes cast a stern, desperate communiqué to her children.

But this time there was no need. Bull's tone had registered. Each child knew the exact danger signals in the meteorology [science of weather] of their father's temperament [manner of behaving]; they were adroit [skillful] weathermen who charted the clouds, winds, and high pressure areas of his fiercely wavering moods, with skill created through long experience. His temper was quick fused and uncontrollable and once he passed a certain point, not even Lillian could calm him. He was tired now after driving through half the night. Behind his sunglasses, the veined eyes were thinned with fatigue and a most dangerous ice had formed over them. The threshing winds of his temper buffeted the car and deep, resonant warning signals were sent out among the children. Silence ruled them in an instant. They resumed watching the diminishing countryside on the outskirts of Ravenel. "Control," Lillian said soothingly. "Control is very important for all of us." She was looking at her husband.

Earth Science: Weather Factors

In the selection Bull's temperament is compared to the weather. This comparison can help us imagine what he sounds like and looks like because weather is so much a part of our everyday lives.

We know from our own experience some of the effects weather can have on our environment, our moods, and our bodies. Also, through the science of meteorology, we have a good understanding of what creates the weather conditions on our planet.

It all begins with the sun. As Earth's land and water surfaces are heated and cooled, they heat and cool the air above them. This creates air masses with different temperatures. Where these masses of differing temperatures meet is called a front. A cold front is created when a colder air mass moves into a warm air mass. A warm front occurs when a warm air mass pushes into a colder air mass. Movements of these fronts cause changes in weather.

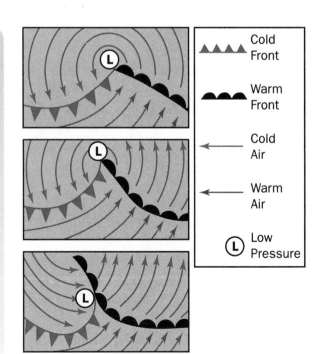

A cold front overtakes a warm front to create a storm.

Circle the number of the best answer for each question.

1 In the passage from *The Great Santini,* Bull's moods are compared to
(1) a meteorologist.
(2) lightning.
(3) the weather.
(4) dangerous ice.
(5) the clouds.

2 What does the writer mean when he says that the children were "adroit weathermen"?
(1) They were studying the weather in school.
(2) They were skillful in everything they did.
(3) They could read their father's moods.
(4) They were watching the weather on TV.
(5) They were getting sick from the weather.

3 Which of the following is <u>not</u> likely to be a factor in creating weather?
(1) a meteorologist
(2) the sun
(3) the oceans
(4) a warm air mass
(5) a cold air mass

Write the letter in the blank.

4 As you saw in *The Great Santini,* expressions about the weather can be used to represent a person's moods. Match the weather expressions with the descriptions of moods. Write the letter.

Weather Conditions		Moods
_____ **1** Cools off at dusk	a.	Begins the day with a smile
_____ **2** Sky darkens and clouds form	b.	Even tempered
_____ **3** Beautiful sunrise	c.	Grows grumpier as the day goes on
_____ **4** Sunny and warm	d.	Calms down by evening

Write your answer.

5 Some scientists think that weather can actually affect people's moods. Do you think the weather affects your moods? Explain and give examples.

_____

_____

_____

Nonfiction

Much of the reading that people do is **nonfiction**. Nonfiction is writing about real people, places, things, or events. One of the most common sources for nonfiction is the newspaper. Magazines also include many nonfiction articles. A nonfiction article can contain information or opinions about almost any topic, from dog training to popular music.

Many books are also works of nonfiction. Nonfiction books include books that tell about the lives of famous or important people, books about history, and books about real things such as travel or geography.

○ Look through a local newspaper article about an event. How much of it discusses what the writer thinks or feels? How much of it is about facts—things that really happened?

○ Look through a national news magazine article about an event. How is it different from the local newspaper article? Why do you think that is?

Biography

Setting the Stage

A **biography** is a true story about the life of a real person. It tells about the important events, people, and decisions that affected the person's life.

The author of a biography is called a **biographer.** Biographers often use diaries, letters, and other written records to get as much information as they can about the time and place in which the person lived. Whenever possible, authors interview the people they write about.

PREVIEW THE READING

To get an idea of what you will be reading, look at the title of the selection on page 69 and read the first paragraph. Then answer these questions.

1 Who is the story about, and where does it take place?

_____

2 How does the character feel about this place?

_____

RELATE TO THE SETTING

This passage takes place in Harlem, which is part of New York City. Langston Hughes is excited about being in Harlem, even though he has never been to this place before.

3 Have you ever been alone in a strange place for the first time? Where was it? How did you feel?

_____

_____

VOCABULARY

dazzled   marquee   flurry   fraternity   anchorage

Langston Hughes: A Biography
by Milton Meltzer

Heading for Harlem he took his first subway ride. The train rushed madly through the tunnel, green lights punctuating the dark and stations suddenly glaring whitely and then blacking out. He counted off the numbered signs till 135th Street and got off. The platform was jammed with people—colored people—on their way to work. Lugging his heavy bags up the steps, he came out breathless on the corner of Lenox Avenue. The September morning was clear and bright. He stood there, feeling good. It was a crazy feeling—as though he had been homesick for this place he had never been to.

He walked down the block to register at the YMCA, the first place young Negroes stayed when they hit Harlem. That afternoon he crossed the street to visit the Harlem Branch Library. All newcomers were swiftly made at home there by Miss Ernestine Rose, the white librarian, and her *café-au-lait* [light coffee-colored] assistant, Catherine Latimer, who had charge of the Schomburg Collection. Here you could drown in thousands and thousands of books by and about black folks. That night, **dazzled** by the electric signs on the **marquee,** he went into the Lincoln Theatre to hear a blues singer.

Identifying Point of View A point of view is a way of looking at a situation. Biographers can tell a story from the point of view of an outsider and include only facts about a person, or they can tell both the facts and how the person feels.

In the passage above, Langston Hughes has been experiencing many new things. Instead of just giving the facts, the author tries to show the reader how Hughes feels. This helps readers see the story from Hughes' own point of view. Which sentence helps you understand how Langston Hughes feels about this new place?

a. He walked down the block to register at the YMCA.
b. It was a crazy feeling—as though he had been homesick for this place he had never been to.

He had a week to himself before classes began at Columbia, and he spent every moment mapping Harlem with his feet. The great dark expanse of this island within an island fascinated him. In 1921 it ran from 127th Street north to 145th, and from Madison Avenue west to Eighth Avenue. Eighty thousand black people (it would be three times that number within ten years) were packed into the long rows of once private homes as the flood of Southern Negroes continued to roll North. It was a new black colony in the midst of the Empire City, the biggest of the many "Bronzevilles" and "Black Bottoms" beginning to appear across the nation.

The high rents charged Negroes and the low wages paid them made Harlem a profitable colony for landlords and merchants, but a swollen, aching slum for the people who lived there. To the boy from the Midwest, however, this was not yet its meaning. He had been in love with Harlem long before he got there, and his dream was to become its poet. That first week of wonderful new insights and sounds passed swiftly. He loved the variety of faces—black, brown, peach, and beige—the richest range of types any place on earth. He hated to move out of Harlem, but his tuition was paid at Columbia and he felt he had to go. At the dormitory office they looked startled when he showed up for his room key. There must be some mistake, they told him; no room was left. He did not know it but Columbia did not allow Negroes to live in the dormitories. There was a big **flurry** when he insisted he had made a reservation long ago, by mail. He got the room finally, but it was a token of what was to come.

The university was too big, too cold. It was like being in a factory. Physics, math, French—he had trouble with all of them and the instructors were too busy or too indifferent to help. His only friend was Chun, a Chinese boy who didn't like Columbia either. Nobody asked the yellow man or the black man to join a **fraternity** and none of the girls would dance with them. Not being used to this, Chun expected them to. Langston didn't.

Nothing went right at school. Langston stopped studying, spent very little time on campus and all the time he could in Harlem or downtown. He made the city his school, read a lot of books, and dented his allowance badly buying tickets night after night for the all-Negro musical hit *Shuffle Along*, whose songs were written by Noble Sissle and Eubie Blake. His mother, separated again from Homer Clarke, showed up in New York and he had to help her with money while she looked for work.

Drawing Conclusions When you draw a **conclusion**, you make a decision or form an opinion based on facts and details. The facts and details are stated directly, but the conclusion is not.

To draw a conclusion from something you have read, you use two or more stated ideas to lead to a decision or opinion that is not directly stated. So, to draw a conclusion, you must go beyond the information a passage contains. However, you must be sure that your conclusion fits with the facts and details that are given in the passage.

After reading the passage above, the reader might conclude that Hughes was not comfortable at Columbia University. Which two ideas help lead to this conclusion?

    a.   The university was too big and too cold. It was like being in a factory.

    b.   He had been in love with Harlem long before he got there.

    c.   Langston stopped studying and spent very little time on campus.

All the time, feeling out of place at Columbia, he kept writing poems. That winter he sent several to *The Crisis*, [a publication put out by the National Association for the Advancement of Colored People (NAACP)] and in January his "Negro" appeared, with these lines, which open and close the poem:

I am a Negro:
Black as the night is black,
Black like the depths of my Africa.

The editors of *The Crisis* awoke to the fact that the boy who had been sending them poems from Toluca was now in New York. They invited him to lunch. Langston panicked, imagining they were all so rich or remote that he wouldn't know what to say. Much as he admired Dr. Du Bois, he was afraid to show the great man how dumb he was. He went, anyhow, taking along his mother for **anchorage.** Although they tried to put him at ease, telling him how much the readers liked his work, he was too scared to see any more of them.

Despite the little amount of time he said he spent on the campus, he did not do badly at Columbia. His final grades show three Bs, a C, and a failing F in physical education. He was given no grade at all in mathematics because he was absent so often. He made no honors, but he didn't care, perhaps because it was honor enough to see his poems printed in *The Crisis* month after month. One of the staff even arranged for him to read his poems at the Community Church. These were signs that he was not standing still. But neither was he moving in the direction his father wanted him to go. So he wrote and said he was quitting college and going to work. He wouldn't ask for money any more.

His father never answered.

Langston was on his own. His mother had gone back to Cleveland. He took a room by himself in Harlem, and began to hunt for a job. It was June 1922, and business was booming. At least it looked like it from the number of help-wanted ads in the papers. Langston wasn't trained for much, so he followed up the unskilled jobs. But no matter what he applied for—office boy, busboy, clerk, waiter—the employer would always say he wasn't looking for a colored boy.

He turned to the employment agencies. It was no use here, either. Where was the job for a black man who wanted to work? Everyone was trying to prove Langston's father was right: the color line wouldn't let you live.

Drawing Conclusions To draw a conclusion, look for and analyze a variety of ideas that relate to the same topic. Which idea from the last two paragraphs helps lead to the conclusion that African-American men were not given a fair chance to make a living in the early 1920s?

   a.   Langston was on his own and looking for a job.
   b.   It was June 1922, and business was booming.
   c.   No matter what job Hughes applied for, the employer would always say he wasn't looking for a colored boy.

Thinking About the Story

Practice Vocabulary

The words below are in the passage in bold type. Study the context in which the words appear. Then write each word next to its meaning.

dazzled   **marquee**   **flurry**   **fraternity**   **anchorage**

1 a large, lighted sign _____

2 impressed by something shiny or fantastic _____

3 a means of feeling secure _____

4 a men's club on campus _____

5 a rush of activity _____

Understand What You Read

Write the answer to each question.

6 How did Hughes spend his first days in New York?

_____

_____

7 What did Hughes dream of doing when he went to Harlem?

_____

_____

8 What details support the conclusion that Hughes did not do badly at Columbia?

_____

_____

9 What are two reasons that Hughes had trouble finding a job?

_____

_____

10 What conclusion can you draw about the relationship between Langston and his father?

_____

_____

Check your answers on pages 234–235.

Apply Your Skills

Circle the number of the best answer for each question.

11 Which sentence best helps you understand the feelings and point of view Langston Hughes had about Columbia University?
   (1) Hughes had a week to himself before classes began.
   (2) The first week Hughes spent in Harlem was filled with new and wonderful insights.
   (3) Hughes spent hardly any time on campus and all the time he could in Harlem or downtown.
   (4) His final grades at Columbia were three Bs, a C and a failing F in physical education.
   (5) Langston went to an employment agency to look for a job.

12 Hughes had a meeting with the editors of *The Crisis*. Based on what you read in the passage, what can you conclude about *The Crisis?* It is
   (1) part of Columbia University.
   (2) a Negro musical hit.
   (3) a publication that included poetry.
   (4) a division of the public library.
   (5) a New York restaurant.

13 Think about everything you have learned about Langston Hughes in this passage. What do you conclude he'll do next? He will most likely
   (1) move back with his father.
   (2) go back to Columbia University.
   (3) go to Cleveland and live with his mother.
   (4) get a high-paying job in an office.
   (5) try to make a living writing poetry.

Connect with the Story

Write your answer to each question.

14 Why do you think Langston's father never answered the letter Langston sent?

_____

_____

15 From the passage, you can tell that Hughes loved Harlem. Is there any place that you feel this way about (even if you have never been there)? Explain why or why not.

_____

_____

_____

Biography

Setting the Stage

Remember that a biography is a person's life story. Many biographies are about people who have helped to change the world, such as inventors, explorers, or scientists. Often biographers show why a person is famous. To do this, the author gives information about the important things the person did. Readers find out about inventions and discoveries that have changed the way we live.

PREVIEW THE READING

Think about what you will be reading by looking at the title and reading the first few sentences of the passage.

1 Who is the biography about?

_____

2 What kind of work did this person do?

_____

RELATE TO THE TOPIC

This passage talks about the many inventions, theories, and accomplishments made by a famous nuclear scientist named Luis Alvarez. It also mentions some of the effects of his work.

3 What invention or event from the past do you think has had an important effect on society? How do you think the world might be different if this invention or event never happened?

_____

_____

VOCABULARY

radar	**nuclear**	**radiation**
inspire	**geologist**	**fossil**

Check your answers on page 235.

Luis W. Alvarez by Corinn Codye

In 1939, World War II broke out in Europe. In 1940, [Luis] Alvarez joined a group of scientists who were designing a way to guide airplanes through fog or darkness.

Alvarez and his group built a **radar** system called Ground-Controlled Approach, or GCA. In this system, a radio signal bounces off a lost plane and back to the sender of the signal. Then a flight controller on the ground can guide the plane safely to the ground.

Later during the war, Alvarez worked in Los Alamos, New Mexico, on a secret project for the government. **Nuclear** scientists there were searching for a way to make a powerful new weapon, the atom bomb.

It was a tricky job. The **radiation** given off by the atoms in such a bomb is deadly to living things. Also, an accidental explosion would cause a terrible disaster. The project to build the bomb was a top-secret race, because the first country to build an atom bomb would have the power to win the war.

Recognizing Supporting Details Supporting **details** help explain the **main idea** of a paragraph. The main idea of the second paragraph above is that Alvarez helped build a radar system. The fact that in the system a radio signal bounces off a lost plane is a detail that supports the main idea. Which two details support the main idea that making the bomb was a tricky job?

a. There was a race to build the bomb.
b. The radiation given off by the atoms in such a bomb is deadly.
c. An accidental explosion would cause a terrible disaster.

Finally, in July 1945, the atom bomb, which the scientists called the "Little Boy," was ready. The government planned to drop the bomb on Japan. Alvarez had the job of measuring the energy released by the bomb that would be dropped from the plane. Alvarez, the atom bomb, and a handful of others were taken to a tiny island in the Pacific Ocean.

On August 6, 1945, three planes took off toward Japan. One carried the bomb, and another carried photographers to film the blast. The third held Alvarez and his team with their blast-measuring instruments. They watched out of the window as the plane flew high over Japan, heading for the city of Hiroshima.

Suddenly they heard the "ready" signal from the plane that held the atom bomb. Alvarez and his team hurried to launch their measuring equipment. The bomb fell 30,000 feet (about 9,000 meters) in 45 seconds, while Alvarez's equipment, attached to parachutes, floated gently above it. The planes made a hard turn and sped away. As Alvarez and his team flew away from the bomb, a bright flash hit the airplane. On their electronic screens, they saw the blast being recorded by their measuring instruments. The screens showed two shock waves—one from the blast itself, then a second wave after the shock hit the ground and bounced back into the air.

A few seconds later, two sharp shocks jolted their plane, hard. A giant mushroom-shaped cloud filled the sky, from the ground all the way to where they flew at 30,000 feet.

They flew around the mushroom cloud once before returning to their tiny island base. Since Alvarez could see nothing but green forests below, he thought they had missed the target. The pilot explained that the city had been *entirely* destroyed.

Alvarez felt sad when he thought of all the people who had lost their lives. He later wrote a letter to his four-year-old son. In it he said that he hoped the powerful and destructive atom bomb would **inspire** people to prevent future wars.

After the war, Alvarez worked again at the Radiation Laboratory at Berkeley. There he built a device called a hydrogen bubble chamber. With this device, Alvarez discovered that atoms and other particles, when driven through liquid hydrogen, leave a track of bubbles. The larger the chamber, the easier it is to see particle tracks. Using bubble chambers, Alvarez's team discovered many new atomic particles.

In 1968, Alvarez received the Nobel prize, which recognizes the highest achievements in the world. The Nobel description of his important work and discoveries in physics was the longest in the prize's history.

Understanding Cause and Effect A **cause** is a situation or an event that makes something happen. The **effect** is what happens as a result of the cause. Sometimes words such as *since* and *because* can help you recognize a cause-and-effect relationship that is directly stated.

Read this sentence from the passage: "Since Alvarez could see nothing but green forests below, he thought they had missed the target." In this sentence, the cause is that Alvarez could see nothing but green forests. It comes first in the sentence and is introduced by the word *since.* The effect, or result, is that Alvarez thought they had missed the target.

Other cause-and-effect situations are not directly stated, or they do not have clue words to help you identify them. However, you can discover these unstated cause-and-effect relationships through careful reading.

Which item completes the sentence to make a cause-and-effect statement? There was a second shock wave after the bomb was dropped because
a.   a giant mushroom-shaped cloud filled the sky.
b.   the shock hit the ground and bounced back into the air.

Although his work with physics was very important, Alvarez may be best remembered for his work and "wild ideas" in a field he knew nothing about until age sixty-six. After retiring from the University of California, he began working with his son, Walter, who is a **geologist.** One day Walter gave his father a piece of layered rock from the mountains of Italy. The rock contained a mystery about the history of the earth.

The rock showed a clay layer that had formed 65 million years ago, the same time that the dinosaurs disappeared from the earth. The layer below the clay was filled with **fossil** shells. The layer above the clay also had shells, but they were almost entirely different. This showed that most of the animals living before the clay layer was formed had become extinct, or died out.

The two Alvarezes, father and son, studied the clay layer. They discovered large amounts of iridium, an element that comes mainly from outer space. They suggested that a body from outer space, 5 miles (about 8 kilometers) across, had hit the earth. Its crash set off a tremendous explosion, worse than all the atom bombs in the world put together. They suggested that the dust and smoke from the explosion covered the earth with a thick black cloud that blocked the sun. The dust settled after a few months, forming a ½-inch (about 1¼-centimeters) clay layer all the way around the earth. The Alvarezes suggested that without sunlight, most green plants died, and the animals—including the dinosaurs—starved and froze.

The Alvarez team tested their ideas carefully. For example, did the iridium come from erupting volcanoes instead of from outer space? They proved that the large amount of iridium in the clay layer could only have come from space.

Luis Walter Alvarez, one of the world's greatest nuclear scientists, died on August 31, 1988. Only a few months earlier, a newly discovered asteroid was named *Alvarez* in honor of his and Walter's work.

Drawing Conclusions A conclusion is a decision or opinion based on facts. Luis and Walter Alvarez drew some conclusions after analyzing the rock from Italy. They compared the layer above the clay to the layer below the clay. Because of the differences between these layers, they concluded that the animals who lived before and after the clay layer formed were very different.

What are two other conclusions they made after analyzing the rock?
a. Iridium found in the clay came from erupting volcanoes.
b. A large body from space hit the earth, setting off a huge explosion.
c. Dust and smoke from the explosion covered the earth.

Thinking About the Passage

Practice Vocabulary

The words below are in the passage in bold type. Study the context in which the words appear. Then write each word next to its meaning.

radar **nuclear** **radiation**

inspire **geologist** **fossil**

1 harmful particles given off by the nuclei (centers) of atoms

_____

2 the remains of a plant or animal preserved in the Earth's crust

_____

3 a system that uses radio waves to locate objects _____

4 having to do with the centers (nuclei) of atoms _____

5 a scientist who studies the Earth and how it was formed

_____

6 influence or motivate _____

Understand What You Read

Write the answer to each question.

7 According to the passage, Luis Alvarez may be best known for what accomplishment or idea?

_____

_____

8 What were two of Alvarez's other accomplishments?

_____

_____

9 What was Alvarez's role in the bombing at Hiroshima?

_____

_____

10 What were two ways in which Luis Alvarez was honored as a scientist?

_____

_____

Apply Your Skills

Circle the number of the best answer for each question.

11 What did Luis Alvarez hope would be the effect of dropping "Little Boy" on Japan?
(1) America would win the war.
(2) Future wars would be avoided.
(3) His son would be inspired to become a scientist.
(4) He would become famous.
(5) Scientists would stop nuclear research.

12 Luis and Walter Alvarez concluded that early animals died of starvation or froze to death during a short period in Earth's history. Which fact supports this conclusion?
(1) A large black cloud blocked off all sunlight.
(2) A clay layer formed on Earth at the same time that the dinosaurs disappeared.
(3) Fossil shells were found in both layers of the rock.
(4) The rock held a mystery about Earth.
(5) Dinosaurs no longer exist.

13 Which detail supports the statement that the Alvarez team tested their ideas carefully?
(1) The dust settled after a few months.
(2) The dust formed a clay layer around the earth.
(3) They proved that the large amount of iridium could not have come from erupting volcanoes.
(4) Alvarez received the Nobel prize.
(5) Alvarez was one of the world's greatest nuclear scientists.

Connect with the Story

Write your answer to each question.

14 How do you think the bombing of Hiroshima affected people's feelings about war? Give reasons for your opinion.

_____

_____

15 What discovery, invention, or accomplishment would you like to make? Why? How would it affect the way people live?

_____

_____

_____

10 Autobiography

Setting the Stage

In an **autobiography**, a person tells his or her own life story. An autobiography describes the important events, people, and decisions in a person's life. An autobiography is different from a biography because we learn about what happened in the person's life from the one who actually had the experiences.

PREVIEW THE READING

Begin to think about what you will be reading by looking at the title of the passage. Then read the first few paragraphs of the passage and answer the questions.

1 Who is this autobiography about?

_____

2 What is going on in the life of this person at this time?

_____

_____

RELATE TO THE CHARACTER

This passage is about Willie Mays, a legendary major league baseball player who joined the Army while he was still playing ball. At the end of this excerpt, Mays returns to baseball and goes on to become one of the greatest ball players of all time.

3 Have you ever left something and then gone back? What was it? How did you feel about going back?

_____

_____

_____

VOCABULARY

authority   ordeal   technicality   suspicious   morale

Check your answers on page 236.

Say Hey by Willie Mays with Lou Sahadi

I reported to Fort Eustis, Virginia. They discovered pretty quickly that I was a ball player. I went through the regular basic training, which didn't bother me, since I was in good shape. We played games against some other Army camps and colleges, and I came across other major-leaguers: Johnny Antonelli of the Braves, Vernon Law of the Pirates, and Lou Skizas of the Yankees. Although there were plenty of photographs showing me marching, they didn't take many of me playing ball, which is how the Army really used me most of the time. Of course, I enjoyed it. I was raised to say "Yes, sir," and I always respected **authority,** so the Army and I got along very well.

Meanwhile, Leo was looking after me even while I was in the service. Somehow, he would find out things that would disturb him. Once he found out that I sprained an ankle while I was playing basketball. He told me, "No more basketball, Willie." Another time he called me over an unnecessary chance I had taken—I tried to steal a base with my team leading. Leo couldn't stand dumb plays, even if he was a few hundred miles away and it wasn't even his team. When he got excited he would scream and talk so fast he sounded like Donald Duck. Leo used to send me a little money now and then, I think just to let me know he still cared.

Besides playing, I was also an instructor—not in how to use a hand grenade, but how to throw and catch and hit. One of the soldiers I was talking to suddenly said to me, "Try it my way," and he held his glove in front of his stomach, but with the palm up. I tried it and it felt more comfortable. My body was aligned correctly. I adopted that style. It came to be called my "basket" catch. What it allowed me to do was have my hands in the correct position to make a throw instantly. What's wrong with it, though, is that you tend to take your eyes off the ball at the last second. Still, I dropped only a couple of flies in my career that way.

Understanding Cause and Effect When something happens as the result of something else, the two events have a **cause-and-effect relationship**. The cause is what makes something happen. The effect is what happens.

In the passage above, Willie Mays sprains his ankle playing basketball. Playing basketball is the cause, and a sprained ankle is the effect. To find cause and effect when you read, first ask yourself what happened. Then look for what made it happen.

What happened when the Army found out that Mays was a baseball player?

a.   The Army had him play baseball while he was in the service.
b.   The Army had him teach soldiers how to throw hand grenades.

My worst time in the service came the day I heard my mother had died while giving birth to her eleventh child. I now had ten brothers and sisters, the oldest only eighteen. So there were a lot of younger ones to look after. I had always thought of them as my brothers and sisters. Now, certainly, the Army would let me out to be with them and take care of them. I always have believed that if a lesser-known soldier had gone through that **ordeal,** he would have been free to leave. I don't know whether the Army was concerned because the public thought it would be playing favorites, or whether there was just some **technicality.** All I knew then was that I was very sad. Even though my aunts had raised me, I had remained close to my mother and her new family. Now, although I wasn't much older than some of my brothers and sisters, I felt responsible for taking care of them. It didn't help my final months in the Army.

It was a cold late-winter day when I was discharged from Fort Eustis on March 1, 1954, and left immediately for the Giants' spring-training site in Phoenix. The Giants sent Frank Forbes from New York to meet me and send me off to Arizona. I didn't have an overcoat, so Frank took his off and gave it to me. It was two sizes too big, but I put it on anyway, probably looking like a scarecrow, or a panhandler. Frank stuffed some newspapers under his sports jacket for insulation. We must have been a sight when we arrived in Washington to catch a train for Phoenix. We had some time to kill, so naturally I suggested we go to the movies. When we got out, we were stopped by two F.B.I. agents. They must have thought they were arresting Dillinger, the way they grabbed us when we left the theater! . . . it turned out to be a case of mistaken identity. It turned out that they had been tipped off that two guys they were looking for might be in the same movie theater. I guess we did look sort of **suspicious,** after all.

I finally made my train, but I didn't stay on it for long. It made a stop in New Orleans, and I got off to get a sandwich and a soda. I didn't do it quickly enough, though, and when I got back to the track, the train had gone. I had to call Leo and tell him I was going to be late.

"Didn't they teach you about trains in the Army?" he said. He sounded exasperated, but I could tell he was probably laughing about the whole thing.

Understanding Cause and Effect Certain words and phrases can help you identify cause-and-effect relationships. Look for words such as *because, so, the reason for,* and *as a result.* These words are clues that lead to information about why something happened.

1 In the passage above, Willie arrives in New York in March without an overcoat. What is the effect of this action?
   a.   Frank gives Willie his overcoat.
   b.   Frank and Willie go to the movies.

2 What cause-and-effect clue word did you recognize in the first paragraph in the passage above? _____

Check your answers on page 236.

I couldn't wait to see all the guys, to be in the old locker room, to be on the same field again. I had heard that things hadn't been the same. There wasn't much joking around the clubhouse anymore. I guess when you finish fifth and aren't even playing .500 ball, there's not much to laugh about, especially when Leo is there every day kicking and screaming when things don't go the way he likes. I hoped that my return would make a difference in terms of **morale.** I always tried to keep things light, and I know the guys used to enjoy making fun of me and my squeaky voice. Even though I had played part of two seasons with the Giants, I was still three years younger than anyone else on the club.

I finally got to the ballpark. When I went into the clubhouse, Eddie Logan, the equipment manager, was the first person I saw. He didn't say anything to me. I thought maybe he didn't recognize me. I found my locker and changed into my uniform. I was alone. The players were already on the field when I walked onto the Arizona diamond for the first time in two years. Nobody said anything to me, and I was beginning to wonder what was going on. Then I remembered: the silent treatment. It's a way that ball players have of not showing emotion, of doing just the opposite of how they feel. We'd do that after someone hit a home run, say, a player who normally wasn't a long-ball hitter. He'd come back to the bench all excited, and we'd just sit there, yawning, or just looking out into space, and it would drive him crazy because he'd be looking for someone to say something nice, a pat on the back, anything at all.

Just when I was starting to get a little annoyed, someone yelled out, "Hey, Leo, here comes your pennant!" Leo turned around and with a big grin he rushed at me and grabbed me in a bear hug that took the wind out of me. The last time I had seen him do that to someone was when Thomson's homer won the pennant for us against Brooklyn. I couldn't even grab a bat and take some swings, though. Leo explained that I had to sign a contract first.

"Hey, give me the pen," I told him.

"Don't you even want to know how much we're paying you?" he asked.

"I'll sign for whatever they're offering me," I told him.

I trusted Leo, but I also loved playing baseball so much that I hardly cared what my salary was. I guess that always showed through. When I was in the Army, I once saw a tap dancer at a nightclub. He could make his feet fly, he was having so much fun. He'd laugh and say, "It's a shame to take the money." He said it for a laugh, but somehow I could tell that he really meant it. That's just how I always felt about baseball.

Understanding the Author's Purpose Sometimes authors include certain details to make a point. In the passage above, what was Mays' **purpose** for telling the story about the tap dancer?

    a.   Mays wanted to show that money was important to him.

    b.   Mays wanted to convey his joy in playing the game of baseball.

Check your answer on page 236.

Thinking About the Story

Practice Vocabulary

The words below are in the passage in bold type. Study the context in which the words appear. Then complete each sentence by writing the correct word.

| authority | ordeal | technicality | suspicious | morale |

1 A team that feels good about itself has good _____ .

2 Your boss has _____ over you and your coworkers.

3 A small detail that has meaning to only a certain group is called a

_____ .

4 You might be _____ if you noticed someone waiting around for several hours on a street corner late at night.

5 Getting through the _____ of the fire took courage and patience.

Understand What You Read

Write the answer to each question.

6 What did Mays want to do after his mother died?

_____

_____

7 Throughout this passage, Mays talks about "Leo." What kind of relationship do you think Mays and Leo had?

_____

_____

8 What do you think the player meant when he shouted, "Hey, Leo, here comes your pennant?"

_____

_____

9 From reading this passage, what kind of person do you think Willie Mays is?

_____

_____

_____

Check your answers on page 236.

Apply Your Skills

Circle the number of the best answer for each question.

10 What caused the FBI agents to think that Frank and Willie were criminals? Frank and Willie

(1) had tipped off the FBI.

(2) had sneaked into the movie without paying.

(3) were dressed in odd-looking clothes.

(4) were acting in an odd manner.

(5) had been meeting with the criminal Dillinger.

11 What caused Willie Mays to be late getting to spring training?

(1) The FBI agents had delayed him.

(2) He didn't know which train to take.

(3) He took too long getting his snack in New Orleans.

(4) Leo made him feel he wasn't wanted.

(5) The Army discharged him too late in the day.

12 Why does Mays describe getting the "silent treatment" from his teammates?

(1) To make the reader feel sorry for him.

(2) To illustrate how ball players treat each other.

(3) To show why everyone was scared of Leo's kicking and screaming.

(4) To explain why Eddie Logan didn't speak to him.

(5) To describe what it felt like to be the youngest ball player on the team.

Connect with the Story

Write your answer to each question.

13 If you were one of the New York Giants, how would you feel about having Mays back on the team? Give reasons for your opinion.

_____

_____

_____

14 What do you like to do as much as Willie Mays liked to play baseball? Is it something you would do whether or not you get paid?

_____

_____

_____

_____

_____

Autobiography

Setting the Stage

Some autobiographies take a look at a world that no longer exists. As an author writes about his or her own life, the reader gets the opportunity to discover what life was like in a different era from the eyes of someone who actually lived at that time.

This story is about Black Elk, a member of the Oglala Sioux who left his people to travel with Buffalo Bill's Wild West Show. Black Elk hoped to learn more about the "white man," whom his people called the *Wasichu*.

PREVIEW THE READING

Get some ideas about what you will be reading by looking at the title and reading the first two paragraphs of the passage. Then answer these questions.

1 What event is being described?

_____

2 How do you think the character feels about this event?

_____

RELATE TO THE CHARACTER

In this passage, Black Elk wanted to help his people find a peaceful way of living with the new settlers. He hoped that by living among the *Wasichu*, he would discover how to reach this goal. During his travels, Black Elk was very homesick.

3 Have you ever been away from your home for a period of time? Were you homesick? How did you feel?

_____

_____

_____

VOCABULARY

iron road	power of thunder	prisoner's house
big water	fire-boat	moons

Check your answers on pages 236–237.

Black Elk Speaks as told through
John G. Neihardt (Flaming Rainbow)

That evening where the big wagons were waiting for us on the **iron road,** we had a dance. Then we got into the wagons. When we started, it was dark, and thinking of my home and my people made me very sad. I wanted to get off and run back. But we went roaring all night long, and in the morning we ate at Long Pine. Then we started again and went roaring all day and came to a very big town [Omaha, Nebraska] in the evening.

Then we roared along all night again and came to a much bigger town [Chicago]. There we stayed all day and all night; and right there I could compare my people's ways with Wasichu ways, and this made me sadder than before. I wished and wished that I had not gone away from home.

Then we went roaring on again, and afterwhile we came to a still bigger town—a very big town [New York]. We walked through this town to the place where the show was [Madison Square Garden]. Some Pawnees and Omahas were there, and when they saw us they made war-cries and charged, couping us. They were doing this for fun and because they felt glad to see us. I was surprised at the big houses and so many people, and there were bright lights at night, so that you could not see the stars, and some of these lights, I heard, were made with the **power of thunder.**

We stayed there and made shows for many, many Wasichus all that winter. I liked the part of the show we made, but not the part the Wasichus made. Afterwhile I got used to being there, but I was like a man who had never had a vision. I felt dead and my people seemed lost and I thought I might never find them again. I did not see anything to help my people. I could see that the Wasichus did not care for each other the way our people did before the nation's hoop was broken.

Comparing and Contrasting   Remember that comparing two things means saying the ways they are alike. **Contrasting** means saying the ways they are different.

Which statement contrasts two things?
a.   The Pawnees and Omahas made war-cries when they saw Black Elk.
b.   The Wasichus did not take care of each other the way the Sioux did.

Both sentences are about two tribes, but only one sentence presents a contrast between the two. In the first sentence, the Pawnees and the Omahas are alike because they both made war-cries when they saw Black Elk. In the second sentence, the Wasichus and Sioux are different because one group, the Sioux, took care of each other and the other group, the Wasichus, did not. This sentence shows a contrast.

Check your answer on page 237.

They would take everything from each other if they could, and so there were some who had more of everything than they could use, while crowds of people had nothing at all and maybe were starving. They had forgotten that the earth was their mother. This could not be better than the old ways of my people. There was a **prisoner's house** on an island where the **big water** came up to the town, and we saw that one day. Men pointed guns at the prisoners and made them move around like animals in a cage. This made me very sad, because my people too were penned up in islands, and maybe that was the way the Wasichus were going to treat them.

In the spring it got warmer, but the Wasichus had even the grass penned up. We heard then that we were going to cross the big water to strange lands. Some of our people went home and wanted me to go with them, but I had not seen anything good for my people yet; maybe across the big water there was something to see, so I did not go home, although I was sick and in despair.

They put us all on a very big **fire-boat,** so big that when I first saw, I could hardly believe it; and when it sent forth a voice, I was frightened. There were other big fire-boats sending voices, and little ones too.

Afterwhile I could see nothing but water, water, water, and we did not seem to be going anywhere, just up and down; but we were told that we were going fast. If we were, I thought that we must drop off where the water ended; or maybe we might have to stop where the sky came down to the water. There was nothing but mist where the big town used to be and nothing but water all around.

We were all in despair now and many were feeling so sick that they began to sing their death-songs.

Identifying Point of View Looking at events through the eyes of another person can help you see the world in a new way. Often a person from another culture has a different point of view. Black Elk sees the white man's culture with the eyes of a Native American. It is not the same way the white men would see their own culture.

In the passage so far, Black Elk is describing his experiences in the Wasichu's world. Black Elk says, "They had forgotten that the earth was their mother." How do you think Black Elk feels about the white man?

    a.   He thinks that they are not kind to their mothers.

    b.   He thinks that they do not respect nature.

When evening came, a big wind was roaring and the water thundered. We had things that were meant to be hung up while we slept in them. This I learned afterward. We did not know what to do with these, so we spread them out on the floor and lay down on them. The floor tipped in every direction, and this got worse and worse, so that we rolled from one side to the other and could not sleep. We were frightened, and now we were all very sick too. At first the Wasichus laughed at us; but very soon we could see that they were frightened too, because they were running around and were

Check your answer on page 237.

very much excited. Our women were crying and even some of the men cried, because it was terrible and they could do nothing. Afterwhile the Wasichus came and gave us things to tie around us so that we could float. I did not put on the one they gave me. I did not want to float. Instead, I dressed for death, putting on my best clothes that I wore in the show, and then I sang my death-song. Others dressed for death too, and sang, because if it was the end of our lives and we could do nothing, we wanted to die brave. We could not fight this that was going to kill us, but we could die so that our spirit relatives would not be ashamed of us. It was harder for us because we were all so sick. Everything we had eaten came right up, and then it kept trying to come up when there was nothing there.

We did not sleep at all, and in the morning the water looked like mountains, but the wind was not so strong. Some of the bison and elk that we had with us for the show died that day, and the Wasichus threw them in the water. When I saw the poor bison thrown over, I felt like crying, because I thought right there they were throwing part of the power of my people away.

After we had been on the fire-boat a long while, we could see many houses and then many other fire-boats tied close together along the bank. We thought now we could get off very soon, but we could not. There was a little fire-boat that had come through the gate of waters and it stopped beside us, and the people on it looked at everything on our fire-boat before we could get off. We went very slowly nearly all day, I think, and afterwhile we came to where there were many, many houses close together, and more fire-boats than could be counted. These houses were different from what we had seen before. The Wasichus kept us on the fire-boat all night and then they unloaded us, and took us to a place where the show was going to be. The name of this very big town was London. We were on land now, but we still felt dizzy as though we were still on water, and at first it was hard to walk.

We stayed in this place six **moons;** and many, many people came to see the show.

Understanding Sequence The **sequence** of events is the order in which events happen in a story. Most writers tell the events in a story in sequence. They tell what happens first, what happens next, and what happens after that. Sometimes writers use clue words like *first* and *next*. Sometimes they just put the events in the order they occur, without using these time-order words.

Black Elk describes the trip from New York to London in sequence.

Which item describes the first main event on this trip?

a.   The ship passed through bad weather and high seas.

b.   The crew members became very ill.

c.   The ship left New York.

Check your answer on page 237.

Thinking About the Story

Practice Vocabulary

The words and phrases below are in the passage in bold type. Study the context in which each word or phrase appears. Then match each word or phrase with its meaning. Write the letter.

_____ **1** iron road

_____ **2** power of thunder

_____ **3** prisoner's house

_____ **4** big water

_____ **5** fire-boat

_____ **6** moons

a. ocean

b. months

c. electricity

d. railroad

e. prison

f. steamship

Understand What You Read

Circle the letter of the best answer to each question.

7 How did Black Elk feel after he left his people?
a. glad
b. homesick

8 What can you conclude about what the sailors thought of their Native American passengers?
a. The sailors looked down on them.
b. The sailors respected them.

Write the answer to each question.

9 Why did Black Elk decide to leave home?

_____

_____

10 How did Black Elk feel about New York City?

_____

_____

11 What was the ocean voyage like from New York to London?

_____

_____

Check your answers on page 237.

Apply Your Skills

Circle the number of the best answer for each question.

12 Black Elk feels like crying when he sees the bison and elk being thrown overboard. What do you think he compares this act to?
(1) the end of the Wild West Show
(2) the end of the railroad trip
(3) the end of the Wasichu way of life
(4) the end of the Native American way of life
(5) the end of the European way of life

13 Black Elk was a holy man of the Oglala Sioux. But when he was in New York, he felt like a man who "never had a vision." How would you describe his point of view in that statement?
(1) He felt like he could not see well.
(2) He felt like he was in a bad dream.
(3) He felt like he understood the Wasichu culture.
(4) He felt like he had no strength to face death.
(5) He felt like he had lost his spirit.

14 Which event happened last in the passage?
(1) Black Elk joined the Wild West Show.
(2) Black Elk traveled on the railroad.
(3) Black Elk performed for six months with the Wild West Show in London.
(4) Black Elk traveled from New York to London.
(5) Black Elk performed with the Wild West Show in Madison Square Garden.

Connect with the Story

Write your answer to each question.

15 Why do you think Black Elk was so unhappy living in the Wasichu's world?

_____

_____

16 Have you ever been in a situation where you seemed to be out of place? How did you feel? What did you decide to do?

_____

_____

_____

_____

Essay

Setting the Stage

Essays are short works of nonfiction in which the writer expresses an opinion about a specific topic. An essay can be about any topic, from everyday problems to major global issues. To get our interest, the author appeals to our common sense and emotions. The author's approach in an essay can be serious or humorous. Either way, the author's purpose is to express a certain point of view.

PREVIEW THE ESSAY

To get clues about the first essay you will be reading, read the title and author's name. Then read the first few sentences.

1 What is the general topic of the essay? What point do you think the author will make about this topic?

_____

_____

2 Read the title and first few sentences of the second essay. Then answer the same questions.

_____

_____

RELATE TO THE TOPIC

The essay "Back When a Dollar Was a Dollar" talks about how the value of a dollar has changed over the years.

3 Have you noticed a change in the value of the dollar since your childhood? How has that change affected your life?

_____

_____

VOCABULARY

| retain | abruptly | obligations |
| prior | realign | hierarchy |

Street Directions   by Andy Rooney

Where do streets go in a strange city and where do they come from?

If America wants to save gas, it ought to start over with its street signs and give everyone directions on how to give directions. It would not do this country any harm at all if there were college courses on the subject of direction giving.

Someone will say, "Go down here and turn left at the third traffic light. Keep going until you run into a dead end at Sixteenth Street, then bear right."

Those are simple enough, so you set out to follow directions. Within ten minutes you're at the corner of Broad and 4th streets, hopelessly lost. You never saw a Sixteenth Street. You feel either stupid and frustrated for not being able to follow simple directions or you feel outraged at the person who gave them to you.

I've often wanted to go back, find the guy and grab him by the throat. "All right, fella. You told me to turn left at the third traffic light and then keep going until I hit a dead end at Sixteenth. You were trying to get me lost, weren't you? Confess!"

It wouldn't be any use though. I know what he'd say. He'd say, "That's not counting this light right here. If you count this light, it's four."

Or he'd say, "Maybe it's Eighteenth Street where the dead end is . . ." or "You see, Sixteenth Street turns into Terwilliger Avenue after you cross Summit Boulevard."

Whatever his answer is, it's hopeless. He didn't mean to mislead you and you didn't mean to get lost, but that's what usually happens.

You can't lay all the blame on the people giving directions. People don't *take* them any better than they give them.

My own ability to **retain** directions in my head ends after the first two turns I'm given. Then I usually say to whomever I'm with, "Did he say right or left at the church on the right?" If there are seven or eight turns, including a couple of "bear rights" and a "jog left" or two, I might as well find a motel room and get a fresh start in the morning.

Understanding the Author's Tone   When people speak or tell a story, they use tone of voice to show how they feel. So, you not only need to listen to what they say, but also how they say it.

Authors use tone in their writing, too. The **tone** of a passage reflects the author's attitude or feelings about the topic. When you read, you must pay attention to what authors say as well as how they say it. An author's tone may be angry, humorous, sad, happy, or serious.

Which statement from the essay best shows the author's humorous tone?
a.   You can't lay all the blame on the people giving directions.
b.   My own ability to retain directions in my head ends after the first two turns I'm given.

Check your answer on page 237.

The superhighways that bisect and trisect our cities now aren't any help at all in finding your way around. Streets that used to lead across town in a direct fashion now end **abruptly** where the highway cut through. Finding the nearest entrance to the superhighway, so you can drive two miles to the next exit in order to get a block and a half from where you are, is the new way to go.

If they do start college courses in direction giving, I hope they devote a semester to arrow drawing for signmakers. It seems like a simple enough matter, but it is often not clear to a stranger whether an arrow is telling you to veer off to the right or to keep going straight.

Different towns and cities have different systems for identifying their streets with the signs they erect. Some have the name of the street you are crossing facing you as you drive past. Others identify the street with a sign that is parallel to it. This is more accurate, but you can't see it. And if you don't know which system they're using, it's further trouble.

There are cities in America so hard to find your way around that, unless you're going to live there for several years, it isn't worth figuring them out.

Many cities, like Washington, pretend to be better organized than they are. They have numbers and they use the alphabet just as though everything was laid out in an orderly fashion.

New York City, for example, has numbered avenues that run longitudinally up and down the island. What the stranger would never know is that in midtown the names go from Third Avenue to Lexington, to Park, and then to Madison before the numbers start again with Fifth Avenue. Where did Fourth Avenue go? Sorry about that, that's what we call "Park."

And then "Sixth Avenue" is next? Well, not actually. New Yorkers call it "Sixth," but the official name and the name on the signs is "Avenue of the Americas." No one calls it that but the post office.

I have long since given up asking for directions or reading maps. I am one of that large number of lost souls who finds that, in the long run, it's better simply to blunder on until you find where you're going on your own.

Understanding the Author's Tone One way to create a humorous tone is to use exaggeration. When authors exaggerate, they make a situation sound better or worse than it really is. Another way to exaggerate is by offering unlikely solutions to problems. For example, the author of this essay exaggerates the problem of giving directions by suggesting that colleges should offer courses on how to give directions.

Which two items are examples of exaggeration?
a.   The author suggests a course for signmakers on making arrows.
b.   The author suggests that superhighways don't help drivers find their way around.
c.   The author suggests that if directions are too complicated, he might as well get a hotel room and try again the next day.

Back When a Dollar Was a Dollar
by Diane C. Arkins

I remember dollars. When I was growing up in the not-so-distant '50s and '60s, dollars used to be wonderful things.

Just one of them could fund a month's worth of kindergarten milk-money **obligations**—with change to spare. You could buy 10 newspapers. You could mail a hundred post cards. You could easily top off the tank when you borrowed Dad's car. Why, even Malcolm Forbes used to throw himself a birthday bash for $49.95.

Yessir. Back then, with a shine on your shoes and a buck in your pocket, you could really go places. Yet Mom and Dad made certain that we understood the clear connection between the Work Ethic and spending those hard-earned $$$.

The American Way also meant a careful look **prior** to leaping with your signature on a dotted line of double-digit interest payments.

But somehow, some time, some*where* along the way, it happened. When we weren't looking, the feds managed to redefine the currency in which . . . we trusted. They seem far too eager to pencil in a few extra zeros on their growing mountains of red ink. And from Jane Taxpayer's point of view, Washington's current juggling—debt ceilings, capital gains, wage floorings—looks like a shotgun marriage between *Let's Make a Deal* and the old "new math."

It's time for Washington's creative accounting to be accountable. Perhaps instead of promoting a policy of dreaming up new prefixes to add to the word "million," the feds could benefit from a refresher course on the value of a buck. Here are some suggestions to help Washington **realign** its outlook and put a "punch" back into middle America's pocketbook.

Welcome to Money Management 101.

- Require all members of Congress to redecorate their homes by shopping at the Pentagon Specials Hardware Store, where toilet seats are always on sale for $795.

- Arrange for the Washington **hierarchy** to get back to basics and collect their vacation pay at minimum wage.

- Reorganize frequent-flier discounts. Whenever Donald Trump flies, 200 working stiffs fly free.

- Help Congress understand the true meaning of those extra budgetary zeros—make them collect a million-billion-zillion bottle caps just to see what that number actually represents before they agree to spend it.

Comparing and Contrasting Comparing two things means finding the ways they are alike. **Contrasting** means finding the ways they are different. You can contrast the two essays because the subject of one (money) is serious, while the subject of the other (directions) is not serious. You can also compare the two essays.

The two essays are alike because they both use a _____ tone.

Thinking About the Essays

Practice Vocabulary

The words below are in the passage in bold type. Study the context in which the words appear. Then complete each sentence by writing the correct word.

retain	abruptly	obligations
prior	realign	hierarchy

1 The _____ of a police officer are to serve and to protect.

2 The game stopped _____ when the thunder and lightning started.

3 It is sometimes hard to _____ information that you don't use often.

4 To keep the peace, both sides need to _____ their thinking.

5 _____ to getting the job, she spent several years in college.

6 Workers must move up the company _____ to get better-paying jobs.

Understand What You Read

Write the answer to each question.

7 After reading the first essay, what can you conclude about getting around in some cities in the United States?

_____

_____

8 What important point about the government does the author make in "Back When a Dollar Was a Dollar"?

_____

_____

9 How would you describe Diane Arkins' attitude toward the United States government?

_____

_____

Check your answers on page 237.

Apply Your Skills

Circle the number of the best answer for each question.

⑩ Which of the following is the best example of the humorous tone of "Street Directions"?

(1) "That's not counting this light right here. If you count this light, it's four."

(2) "Different towns and cities have different systems for identifying their streets with the signs they erect."

(3) "New York City, for example, has numbered avenues that run longitudinally up and down the island."

(4) "Those are simple enough, so you set out to follow directions."

(5) "If America wants to save gas, it ought to . . . give everyone directions on how to give directions."

⑪ Which of the following is the best example of exaggeration?

(1) A dollar used to be worth more in the '50s and '60s.

(2) Some city streets are not well organized.

(3) Government workers should be paid minimum wage for vacation time.

(4) Towns and cities use different systems for identifying streets.

(5) The government should consider the federal budget more carefully.

⑫ Which statement is the best example of a comparison?

(1) Our parents understood the connection between working hard and spending money.

(2) Both essays could be considered complaints.

(3) Some cities identify the street with a sign that is parallel to it.

(4) In the '50s and '60s, dollars used to do wonderful things.

(5) New Yorkers call it "Sixth Avenue," but the official name is "Avenue of the Americas."

Connect with the Story

Write your answer to the question.

⑬ These two essayists wrote about things that annoy them. Is there something that often annoys you? Tell what it is and write a brief suggestion about how to solve the problem.

_____

_____

_____

_____

Persuasive Essay

Setting the Stage

Some essayists want to do more than just describe a point of view. They want to persuade the reader to agree with that point of view. **Persuasive essays** often explain a situation and then suggest what can be done about it. The authors use both facts and opinions to persuade readers to believe that the suggested action will improve their own lives.

PREVIEW THE ESSAY

Begin to think about what you are going to read by looking at the title and reading the first paragraph of the passage. Then answer these questions.

1 What event is taking place?

_____

2 What point does the author make?

_____

RELATE TO THE EVENT

The author of this passage presents her opinions about peace and war. She tries to persuade the reader to agree with her ideas.

3 What are your thoughts about these issues? Do you believe that there will ever be peace on earth?

_____

_____

_____

VOCABULARY

disarmament   imperative   subdued

sterile   compensate

Check your answers on page 238.

Thoughts on Peace in an Air Raid
by Virginia Woolf

Up there in the sky young Englishmen and young German men are fighting each other. The defenders are men, the attackers are men. Arms are not given to the Englishwoman either to fight the enemy or to defend herself. She must lie weaponless tonight. Yet if she believes that the fight going on up in the sky is a fight for the English to protect freedom, by the Germans to destroy freedom, she must fight, so far as she can, on the side of the English. How far can she fight for freedom without firearms? By making arms, or clothes or food. But there is another way of fighting for freedom without arms; we can fight with the mind. We can make ideas that will help the young Englishman who is fighting up in the sky to defeat the enemy.

Distinguishing Fact from Opinion A **fact** is a statement that can be proved true. An **opinion** is a belief or judgment—a statement of what someone thinks. People can disagree with opinions, but they can't argue about the truth of facts.

An example of a fact in the passage is the statement that men are fighting in the sky. At the time the essay was written, anyone who looked up and listened could see that there was an air battle going on. The author's belief that the English were fighting to protect freedom is an opinion. People could have different ideas about why the English were fighting.

Which two of these statements from the passage are facts?

a. Englishwomen are not given weapons.

b. Englishwomen can fight with their minds.

c. The defenders are men, the attackers are men.

A bomb drops. All the windows rattle. The anti-aircraft guns are getting active. Up there on the hill under a net tagged with strips of green and brown stuff to imitate the hues of autumn leaves guns are concealed. Now they all fire at once. On the nine o'clock radio we shall be told "Forty-four enemy planes were shot down during the night, ten of them by anti-aircraft fire." And one of the terms of peace, the loudspeakers say, is to be **disarmament.** There are to be no more guns, no army, no navy, no air force in the future. No more young men will be trained to fight with arms. That rouses another mind-hornet in the chambers of the brain—another quotation. "To fight against a real enemy, to earn undying honour and glory by shooting total strangers, and to come home with my breast covered with medals and decorations, that was the summit of my hope. . . . It was for this that my whole life so far had been dedicated, my education, training, everything. . . ."

Those were the words of a young Englishman who fought in the last war. In the face of them, do the current thinkers honestly believe that by writing "Disarmament" on a piece of paper at a conference table they will have done all that is needful? Othello's occupation will be gone; but he will remain Othello. The young airman up in the sky is driven not only by the voices of loudspeakers; he is driven by voices in himself—ancient instincts, instincts fostered and cherished by education and tradition. Is he to be blamed for those instincts? Could we switch off the maternal instinct at the command of a table full of politicians? Suppose that **imperative** among the peace terms was: "Child-bearing is to be restricted to a very small class of specially selected women," would we submit? Should we not say, "The maternal instinct is woman's glory. It was for this that my whole life has been dedicated, my education, training, everything. . . ." But if it were necessary, for the sake of humanity, for the peace of the world, that child-bearing should be restricted, the maternal instinct **subdued,** women would attempt it. Men would help them. They would honour them for their refusal to bear children. They would give them other openings for their creative power. That too must make part of our fight for freedom. We must help the young Englishmen to root out from themselves the love of medals and decorations. We must create more honourable activities for those who try to conquer in themselves their fighting instinct, their subconscious Hitlerism. We must compensate the man for the loss of his gun.

Understanding Persuasion Remember that the purpose of persuasive writing is not only to get readers to agree with a point of view, but also to get them to act. However, authors of persuasive essays do not always state the actions they want the reader to take. Often they use words that will convince the reader that an action is necessary. Strong words such as *should, must,* and *necessary* suggest that something has to be done.

Which two of the following statements are examples of persuasion?
a.   There are to be no more guns, no army, no navy, no air force in the future.
b.   We must help the young Englishmen to root out from themselves the love of medals and decorations.
c.   We must compensate the man for the loss of his gun.

The sound of sawing overhead has increased. All the searchlights are erect. They point at a spot exactly above this roof. At any moment a bomb may fall on this very room. One, two, three, four, five, six . . . the seconds pass. The bomb did not fall. But during those seconds of suspense all thinking stopped. All feeling, save one dull dread, ceased. A nail fixed the whole being to one hard board. The emotion of fear and of hate is therefore **sterile,** unfertile. Directly that fear passes, the mind reaches out and instinctively revives itself by trying to create. Since the room is dark it can create only from memory. It reaches out to the memory of other Augusts—in Beyreuth, listening to Wagner; in Rome, walking over the Campagna; in London. Friends' voices come back. Scraps of poetry return. Each of those thoughts, even in memory, was far more positive, reviving, healing and creative than the dull dread made of fear and hate. Therefore if we are to **compensate** the young man for the loss of his glory and of his gun, we must give him access to the creative feelings. We must make happiness. We must free him from the machine. We must bring him out of his prison into the open air. But what is the use of freeing the young Englishman if the young German and the young Italian remain slaves?

The searchlights, wavering across the flat, have picked up the plane now. From this window one can see a little silver insect turning and twisting in the light. The guns go pop pop pop. Then they cease. Probably the raider was brought down behind the hill. One of the pilots landed safe in a field near here the other day. He said to his captors, speaking fairly good English, "How glad I am that the fight is over!" Then an Englishman gave him a cigarette, and an Englishwoman made him a cup of tea. That would seem to show that if you can free the man from the machine, the seed does not fall upon altogether stony ground. The seed may be fertile.

At last all the guns have stopped firing. All the searchlights have been extinguished. The natural darkness of a summer's night returns. The innocent sounds of the country are heard again. An apple thuds to the ground. An owl hoots, winging its way from tree to tree. And some half-forgotten words of an old English writer come to mind: "The huntsmen are up in America. . . ." Let us send these fragmentary notes to the huntsmen who are up in America, to the men and women whose sleep has not yet been broken by machine-gun fire, in the belief that they will rethink them generously and charitably, perhaps shape them into something serviceable. And now, in the shadowed half of the world, to sleep.

Understanding the Author's Purpose To persuade readers, authors must include facts and examples that support their opinions. The purpose of including these facts and examples is to help readers understand why these opinions make sense.

One opinion the author offers is that fear and hatred are sterile, unfertile emotions. The author supports this opinion with the example that all thinking stops during moments of great fear. Another opinion from the passage is that if men are freed from the machines of war, all sides in a conflict may become more caring. What fact or example supports this opinion?

a.   The fact that the pilot landed safely in a nearby field.

b.   The example that the pilot was given a cigarette and a cup of tea after he was captured.

Thinking About the Essay

Practice Vocabulary

The words below are in the passage in bold type. Study the context in which the words appear. Then complete each sentence by writing the correct word.

disarmament	imperative	subdued
sterile	compensate	

1 If a feeling is _____, it is reduced.

2 In a _____ agreement, all parties state that they will put down their weapons.

3 A _____ thought is one that lacks creativity.

4 If something is _____, it is usually urgent or necessary.

5 To _____, you must replace what is taken away.

Understand What You Read

Write the answer to each question.

6 How does the author describe the feelings she had while she waited for the bomb to drop?

_____

_____

_____

7 The author is concerned about the effects of disarmament. She thinks that we must help men overcome their desire to fight by giving them other creative outlets. Why does she think so?

_____

_____

_____

8 How does the author describe a person's state of mind after a feeling of fear has passed?

_____

_____

_____

Check your answers on page 238.

Apply Your Skills

Circle the number of the best answer for each question.

9 Which of the following is one of the author's opinions?
   (1) "Forty-four enemy planes were shot down during the night . . ."
   (2) ". . . that was the summit of my hope."
   (3) "All feeling, save one of dull dread, ceased."
   (4) "They point at a spot exactly above this roof."
   (5) "The young airman in the sky is driven by voices in himself."

10 Why does the author include the example of women giving up child-bearing if it were necessary for world peace?
   (1) to suggest that women are better than men
   (2) to make women aware of the overpopulation problem
   (3) to compare women's responsibilities with men's
   (4) to encourage Americans to stay out of the war
   (5) to urge women to have careers instead of families

11 Which statement from the passage is meant to convince the reader to take action?
   (1) "No more young men will be trained to fight with arms."
   (2) "We must free him from the machine."
   (3) "Those were the words of a young Englishman who fought in the last war."
   (4) "'It was for this that my life has been dedicated.'"
   (5) "'How glad I am that the fight is over!'"

Connect with the Story

Write your answer to each question.

12 What would you have been thinking about if you had been in the author's situation, waiting through an air raid? Explain.

_____

_____

_____

13 Have you ever felt strongly about an issue? Did you try to persuade someone to take action? Or has someone tried to persuade you? What was the issue? What was the action? Were you or the other person persuaded?

_____

_____

_____

_____

Setting the Stage

The purpose of a magazine article is usually to inform the reader about a topic. Articles can be written about a wide variety of topics. Authors write about people, places, and events. Topics could involve current issues or events from the past. A magazine article might even predict what life will be like in the future. Whatever the topic, a magazine article presents information that will interest the reader.

PREVIEW THE ARTICLE

You can get a good idea of what you will be reading by looking at the title of the passage and reading the first few paragraphs. Then answer these questions.

1 What are the names of the two athletes in these paragraphs?

_____

2 What event is described in the article?

_____

RELATE TO THE TOPIC

At the 1968 Olympics in Mexico City, two athletes made a silent protest against racial injustice in the United States. The protest was made on television for all the world to see.

3 Do you think this protest was appropriate? Why or why not? What are your thoughts about racial injustice?

_____

_____

_____

_____

VOCABULARY

| gesture | calculated | deprived |
| vindication | reprimanded | irrevocable |

A Courageous Stand by Kenny Moore

As the Olympics began, Smith was a man in search of a **gesture.** "It had to be silent—to solve the language problem—strong, prayerful and imposing," he says. "It kind of makes me want to cry when I think about it now. I cherish life so much that what I did couldn't be militant, not violent. I'll argue with you, but I won't pick up a gun.

"We had to be heard, forcefully heard, because we represented what others didn't want to believe. I thought of how my sisters cringed because they didn't want me to embarrass the family by describing how poor we were, when we *were* poor. No one likes to admit flaws, even though it's the first step to fixing them."

Symbols began to present themselves to him. He asked Denise [Smith's wife] to buy a pair of black gloves. A few days before his race, Smith knew what he would do. He did not tell Carlos. Until the race was over, Carlos was a competitor. . . .

After the semifinals of the 200 two days later, it appeared that Smith would not stand on any victory platform. Carlos won the first semi in 20.11, unbothered by running in the tight inside lane. Smith took the second semi in 20.13, but as he slowed, he felt a jab high in his left thigh. "It was like a dart in my leg. I went down, not knowing where the next bullet was coming from."

Using Context Clues To help understand the meaning of an unfamiliar word, look at the words and sentences around it for clues to its meaning. Such words and sentences give **context clues** that help show what the unfamiliar word means. This passage includes some sports terms that may be unfamiliar. The word *race* helps you figure out that *200* is probably the distance of the race.

Use context to help you figure out the meaning of these unfamiliar terms.

1 Reread the first paragraph. What do you think the word *militant* means?
  a. gentle and kind
  b. ready to fight

2 Find the terms *20.11* and *20.13* in the fourth paragraph. What do you think they refer to?
  a. The times at which the races occurred.
  b. How fast Carlos and Smith ran the races.

As he crouched on the track, he knew he had strained or torn an adductor muscle. All the work, he thought, was now useless. He raised his head and saw before him a familiar pair of hunting boots. They belonged to his San Jose State coach, Winter, who got him up, walked him to ice, packed his groin and then wrapped it.

The final was two hours later. "Thirty minutes before it, I went to the practice field," Smith says. "I jogged a straightaway, then did one at 30 percent. It was holding. I did one at 60 percent, then one at 90. It held. . . . Don't let there be any delays, I thought."

Check your answers on page 238.

As the eight finalists were led into the stadium, Carlos remembers saying to Smith, "I'm going to do something on the stand to let those in power know they're wrong. I want you with me."

Smith, Carlos recalls, said, "I'm with you."

"That made me feel good," says Carlos. "And it made the medal mean nothing. Why should I have to prove my ability when they'd just take it away somehow? I made up my mind. Tommie Smith gets a gift."

They were placed on their marks. "I took no practice starts," says Smith. John was in Lane 4. I was in 3. I **calculated** it this way: Come out hard but keep power off my inside leg on the turn with a short, quick stride. Then in the straightaway I'd maintain for four strides and attack for eight."

At the gun, Carlos was away perfectly. Smith ran lightly and with building emotion. He felt no pain. Carlos came out of the turn with a 1½-meter lead. Then, a man unto himself, he swiveled his head to his left and, he says, told Smith, "If you want the gold, . . . come on." Smith didn't hear him. Eighty thousand people were roaring as Smith struck with his eight long, lifting strides. They swept him past Carlos.

"I pulled back on the reins," Carlos says now. "America **deprived** our society of seeing what the world record would have been."

"If Carlos wants to say that," Smith says, "I applaud him for his benevolence."

"The medal meant more to Tommie," says Carlos. "Everyone got what he wanted, even Peter Norman." Carlos slowed so much that Norman, an Australian sprinter, caught him at the line for second.

When Smith knew he had won, he threw out his arms. He still had 15 meters to go. "I guess if I'd calculated a 12-stride attack, the time would have been 19.6," Smith says now. That record would have stood to this day.

Understanding Cause and Effect Remember that a cause is what makes something happen. The effect is what happens. In the passage, Smith showed that he supported Carlos. Smith's support had an important effect on Carlos. Carlos felt that winning the medal was no longer important since he had Smith's support.

During the race, Carlos slowed down. What two effects did that action have?
a. Smith came in first place.
b. Smith hurt his leg.
c. Norman came in second place.

He crossed the line with his arms outflung at the angle of a crucifix. His smile was of joy, relief and **vindication.** When he came to a stop, he felt resolve cool and strong in him.

The medalists were guided through a warren of stone tunnels under the stadium to a room that held their sweatsuits and bags. "It was a dungeon under there," says Smith.

Check your answers on page 238.

He went to Carlos. "John, this is it, man," he said. "All those years of fear, all the suffering. This is it. I'll tell you what I'm going to do. You can decide whether you want to."

"Yeah, man," said Carlos. "Right."

"I got gloves here. I'm going to wear the right. You can have the left." Carlos slipped it on.

Smith explained the symbolism of the gloves, the scarf, the stocking feet and the posture. "The national anthem is a sacred song to me," Smith said. "This can't be sloppy. It has to be clean and abrupt."

"Tommie, if anyone cocks a rifle," said Carlos, "you know the sound. Be ready to move."

Silver medalist Norman, who is white, overheard these preparations, and Carlos asked him if he would participate in the protest. Norman agreed, and Carlos gave him a large Olympic Project for Human Rights button. Norman pinned it to his Australian sweatsuit.

"I thought, In the '50s, blacks couldn't even *live* in Australia," says Smith. "And now he's going back there after doing this." (Norman would be severely **reprimanded** by Australian sports authorities.)

Smith, Norman and Carlos were placed behind three young Mexican women in embroidered native dress, each of whom carried a velvet pillow. Upon each pillow lay a medal. IOC vice-president Lord Killanin of Ireland, who would succeed Brundage [the president of the International Olympic Committee who had been accused of ignoring the civil rights issue] in four years, and the president of the International Amateur Athletic Federation, the Marquess of Exeter, led them to the ceremony.

"As Killanin hung the medal around my neck and shook my hand," says Smith, "his smile was so warm that I was surprised. I smiled back. I saw peace in his eyes. That gave me a two- or three-second relaxation there, to gather myself."

Along with his gold medal, Smith received a box with an olive tree sapling inside, an emblem of peace. He held the box in his left hand, accepting it into his own symbolism.

Then the three athletes turned to the right, to face the flags. *The Star-Spangled Banner* began. Smith bowed his head as if in prayer and freed his young face of expression. Then he tensed the muscles of his right shoulder and began the **irrevocable** lifting of his fist.

Predicting Outcomes You can use the information given in the passage and what you already know to **predict** the outcome of the story. The passage says that Peter Norman was severely reprimanded by Australian sports authorities, but it does not tell what else happened after the protest.

What do you predict happened as a result of Carlos' and Smith's protest?
a. Their protest caused people around the world to recognize the problem of racism.
b. Sports authorities in the United States praised their protest.

Thinking About the Article

Practice Vocabulary

The words below are in the passage in bold type. Study the context in which the words appear. Then write each word next to its meaning.

| gesture | calculated | deprived |
| vindication | reprimanded | irrevocable |

1 prevented from having or using something _____

2 unable to be changed _____

3 severely criticized _____

4 the act of being proved right _____

5 figured, estimated _____

6 an action that shows a feeling _____

Understand What You Read

Write the answer to each question.

7 What does Smith mean by "the language problem"?

_____

_____

8 How did Norman, the Australian sprinter, share in the protest?

_____

_____

9 Why wasn't Smith expected to win the final race?

_____

_____

10 Why did Smith and Carlos want to make a protest?

_____

_____

_____

_____

_____

Check your answers on pages 238–239.

Apply Your Skills

Circle the number of the best answer for each question.

⑪ What did Carlos mean when he said, "I pulled back on the reins"?
   (1) He was riding a horse in the race.
   (2) He slowed down.
   (3) He grabbed Smith's shoelaces.
   (4) He started to run faster.
   (5) He realized he couldn't win the race.

⑫ What did Carlos predict would have happened if he had not slowed down?
   (1) Norman would have won the race.
   (2) Smith would not have hurt himself.
   (3) Smith would have won the race anyway.
   (4) Carlos would have won the race and set a world record.
   (5) There would not have been a protest.

⑬ What do you predict happened to Smith and Carlos after their protest?
   (1) They won more races at the Olympic Games.
   (2) They received medals honoring them for their protest.
   (3) They were suspended from the rest of the Olympic Games.
   (4) They hosted a television program about racial injustice in America.
   (5) They became officials of the International Olympic Committee.

Connect with the Article

Write your answer to each question.

⑭ Why do you think the athletes decided to make their protest using gestures and not words?

_____

_____

_____

⑮ Is there anything you would like to make a strong protest about? Describe a way to protest that might make your point.

_____

_____

_____

_____

_____

Setting the Stage

Television is a popular form of entertainment and a good source of information. The number of shows offered on network, cable, and satellite channels is growing all the time. Because there are so many programs, it can be hard to decide what to watch.

Reading a TV review can help you decide if you are interested in a particular program. A **review** can tell what a program is about, how it is presented, and who the main characters are. Reviewers give their opinions about the quality of a program and sometimes even include behind-the-scenes information.

PREVIEW THE ARTICLE

Get an idea about what you will be reading by looking at the title and first sentence of the passage. Then answer these questions.

1 What television program is the review about?

_____

2 What actor is the review about?

_____

RELATE TO THE CHARACTER

This article talks about an actor's decision to leave a popular TV show. The show and the actor have received rave reviews, but the actor felt it was time to move on.

3 Have you ever made a decision to leave a job or a place? What helped you to make that decision? How did things work out?

_____

_____

_____

VOCABULARY

meticulous	**passive**	**turbulent**
subtler	**reinvigorated**	**improvise**

Check your answers on page 239.

Jimmy, we hardly knew ye—the real story behind Smits' departure from NYPD Blue by Bruce Fretts

Jimmy Smits stands beneath the Brooklyn Bridge and gives a simple explanation as to why he's leaving NYPD Blue. "My contract was up," says Smits, who's in Manhattan for his final week of location shooting. "I signed up for four years. I lived out the commitment like a gentleman, and now I just feel like it's time to move on."

Across the street in his hotel room, NYPD cocreator David Milch stretches out on a bed and offers a more complicated take. "My work process may have had something to do with Jimmy's feelings," he says. "He gets the material so late, and he's so **meticulous** a craftsman and takes such pride in his preparation that it became a little exhausting for him." As if to prove the point, Milch mentions that he hasn't yet finished writing new NYPD star Rick Schroder's first scene—which will begin shooting in only a few hours.

Summarizing When you **summarize**, you make a short statement that gives the main idea and the most important supporting details in a passage. It is helpful to summarize what you read. This shows that you understand what you are reading.

In the first paragraph, the main idea is that Jimmy Smits is leaving *NYPD Blue*. The most important detail is the reason he is leaving. A summary of this paragraph could be: Jimmy Smits' four-year contract for *NYPD Blue* was up. He decided that it was time to move on, so he's leaving the show.

The main idea of the second paragraph is that cocreator David Milch's work style may have influenced Smits' decision to leave the show. What important supporting detail would you include in a summary of this paragraph?
- a. Milch still hasn't finished writing Rick Schroder's first scene.
- b. Milch didn't allow Smits enough time to prepare the material as carefully as Smits likes.

What's more, Smits may have grown weary of playing such a **passive** character as Det. Bobby Simone, the calm counterpart to Dennis Franz's **turbulent** Det. Andy Sipowicz. "Jimmy felt that was constricting," explains Milch. Adds cocreator Steven Bochco: "As extraordinary as Dennis' work is, I always felt Jimmy's work was underestimated. You wouldn't want two guys banging off walls, so it fell to Jimmy to be the solid one, and that's always a **subtler** thing."

Check your answer on page 239.

Smits may not have the Emmys to show for it (Franz has won three), but it's exactly that quiet coiled power that kept the show on track, especially in the uncertain days after David Caruso's 1994 exit. "Jimmy's like a Ferrari," says Bochco. "You tap the pedal and get this instant burst of power. You haven't even begun to put your foot to the floor. You don't have to—there's always something in reserve."

In his final NYPD episodes, however, you might get to see Smits put the pedal to the metal. "He's been extraordinary," marvels Milch. But even though Simone gets stabbed by a suspect in the Oct. 20 season premiere, don't expect that to be the reason he's splitting. "What starts out looking like why he's going turns out to be a very different thing," teases the typically cryptic Milch. "People who look at the first episodes need to go to the end before they see what really happens."

Applying Ideas in a New Context When you understand an idea, you can figure out how you might use that idea in another situation. One important idea in the review is the quality of Smits' work. Steven Bochco compares his work to a Ferrari. A Ferrari is a powerful, high-performance car. This creates the image that Smits is an excellent performer. It also gives the reader the idea that Smits puts a lot of energy into his work without much pushing and suggests that his work is consistent and powerful.

Apply these ideas to a new context. Smits is leaving the show to pursue new roles. How do you suppose he would approach a completely different role, such as the role of a bad guy? Based on what you have learned about Smits' work habits, you would expect that he would dedicate the time and effort to create the best "bad guy" character possible.

1 Reread the second paragraph above. What is the main idea of the paragraph?
a. Simone gets stabbed by a suspect.
b. The ending will not be what viewers expect.

2 Which of the following statements shows that main idea being applied in a new context?
a. In many murder mystery novels, readers are led to believe that one or two characters are the main suspects. They are surprised to find out that the murderer is not who they expected.
b. In some television shows, characters are replaced with different actors. The viewers are surprised when they see a new actor playing a familiar character.

And even after Schroder joins the show in December, don't think you've seen the last of Smits, who might return for guest shots. "We're counting on it," says Milch. Kim Delaney lovers also needn't fret: Det. Diane Russell (Simone's spouse) is sticking around. When Smits announced his departure, the producers "immediately came up to me and said, 'You're taken care of,'" reports Delaney.

     Check your answers on page 239.

There's reason to be hopeful that NYPD, which fell into a bit of a creative slump last season, may be **reinvigorated** by the addition of Schroder. Milch certainly seems pumped: "If I can begin to **improvise** scenes in my head when I see two actors working together, then I know there's something there. And we wrote about four scenes in 10 minutes when Rick and Dennis started working together."

As for Smits, he'll move on to new dramatic challenges. "The thing I love about this business is you're moving from job to job," says the actor, who also left Bochco's L.A. Law before the show's run ended. "You're a cop one day and a lawyer another and a king another and a bum another. Change is good." Hope that holds true for NYPD Blue.

Summarizing Summarizing a whole passage can help you to understand it. First, think about what the main idea of the whole review is. Then look for details in each paragraph that support the main idea.

1 What should be the main idea of a summary of this review?
    a.   Jimmy Smits is leaving the show *NYPD Blue*.
    b.   Rick Schroder and Dennis Franz work well together.

2 Which four supporting details would you include in the summary?
    a.   Smits may have felt that the character of Det. Bobby Simone was too passive.
    b.   Dennis Franz has won three Emmys playing the role of Det. Andy Sipowicz.
    c.   The show's future was uncertain after David Caruso left in 1994, but Smits' tremendous effort kept *NYPD* on track.
    d.   Simone gets stabbed in the season premiere.
    e.   Rick Schroder will join the show once Smits leaves.
    f.   The creators are very hopeful that the show's success will continue with Schroder.

Now, summarize the review by putting together the answers you chose above. Write the main idea sentence first and then the four detail sentences.

Thinking About the Article

Practice Vocabulary

The words below are in the passage in bold type. Study the context in which the words appear. Then write each word next to its meaning.

meticulous	passive	turbulent
subtler	reinvigorated	improvise

1 less open or direct _____

2 extremely careful about details _____

3 full of commotion or disorder _____

4 offering no resistance; patient _____

5 to perform with no preparation _____

6 filled with energy again _____

Understand What You Read

Write the answer for each question.

7 After reading the review, how would you describe Jimmy Smits as an actor?

_____

_____

8 How do you think the cocreators of *NYPD Blue* feel about Smits?

_____

_____

9 From reading the review, how do you predict the show will be when Schroder replaces Smits?

_____

_____

10 Who are some of the other characters in the show?

_____

_____

Check your answers on page 239.

Apply Your Skills

Circle the number of the best answer for each question.

11 Which is the most important detail about Smits' departure from *NYPD Blue*?
  (1) Smits had a four-year contract for the show.
  (2) Jimmy had to be the solid one in the partnership with Dennis Franz.
  (3) The reason that Det. Simone leaves is a surprise.
  (4) Smits enjoys changes and he felt that it was time to move on.
  (5) Rick Schroder will join the show.

12 Which situation is the most similar to Smits' leaving *NYPD Blue*?
  (1) A woman leaves her job because she has a fight with a coworker and she feels that her boss is not doing anything about it.
  (2) A family moves out of state because the father got transferred to another branch of his company.
  (3) A man feels like he has done the best job possible but decides that it's time to look for a different job.
  (4) A worker takes a trip to promote a new product.
  (5) A worker gets fired for bad attendance and a bad attitude.

13 Which of the following is the best summary for this review?
  (1) Jimmy Smits was an important member of the *NYPD Blue* team for four years. He thrives on challenges and felt it was time to move on.
  (2) Smits made a commitment to the show, but he got tired of his role and decided that it was time to leave *NYPD Blue*.
  (3) Smits got so tired of Milch's work process that he decided to break his contract and leave *NYPD Blue* for good.
  (4) Smits' contract was up, so he decided to leave *NYPD Blue*. He wanted to give actor Rick Schroder a chance at success and fame.
  (5) The cocreators of *NYPD Blue* think that even without Smits, the show will continue to be successful.

Connect with the Article

Write your answer to each question.

14 If you were Smits, what would you have done when the contract was up? Why?

_____

_____

15 How do you feel about change? Do you think it's good, bad, necessary? Explain your ideas.

_____

_____

Book Review

Setting the Stage

A book review usually discusses the plot and the characters of a book, as well as the way the book is written. However, reviewers usually don't want to give away too much of the plot, so they try to make the characters sound as interesting as possible. Based mainly on the description of the characters, the reader must make a judgment about reading the book.

PREVIEW THE ARTICLE

To get a good idea of what you will be reading, look at the title and read a few sentences of the passage. Then answer these questions.

1 What is the name of the book being reviewed?

_____

2 What type of story is it?

_____

RELATE TO THE TOPIC

The reviewer states that the book seems to be saying that people who make movies are a lot like crooks—in other words, they are dishonest.

3 Have you ever heard about a business that didn't seem to be honest? What was it? How was it dishonest?

_____

_____

_____

VOCABULARY

cynic   acidic   moral

protagonist   villains   zinger

Get Shorty by Elmore Leonard, reviewed by Ralph Novak

A **cynic** might think old Elmore has revenge on his mind, getting back at what Hollywood has done to a few of his novels by writing this **acidic,** get-them-laughing-then-punch-them-in-the-gut, splendidly entertaining crime tale. Its **moral** seems to be that gangsters are a lot like the people who make movies, except crooks are more efficient and have a deeper sense of honor.

Understanding the Author's Tone How authors feel about a topic influences how they write about it. How an author writes about a topic—that is, the author's tone—influences how the reader feels about the topic. Tone is especially important in reviews, since the reviewer's main concern is to express an opinion.

Authors choose their words carefully to help develop the tone. If an author uses formal or technical words, the tone seems unemotional. The use of slang and humorous words creates a more informal tone. In the paragraph above, the slang word *gangsters* helps create the informal tone the reviewer wants.

The reviewer of *Get Shorty* sets an informal tone at once. The use of *old* is an informal way of referring to the author, Elmore Leonard. This word makes it seem like the author has been around a long time and the reviewer knows him well. Also, by using only the writer's first name, the reviewer makes it seem as if Elmore Leonard is a friend. Both word choices are intended to help the reader feel as comfortable with Elmore Leonard's work as the reviewer does.

1 Which of the following shows how the reviewer continues to set an informal tone?
   a. He describes the book as a "get-them-laughing-then-punch-them-in-the-gut" tale.
   b. He explains the moral of the story.

2 Here are two words the reviewer uses. Which one is a slang word that helps create an informal tone?
   a. people
   b. crooks

3 What purpose might the author have for using an informal tone?
   a. It makes the review fun to read.
   b. It is easier to write with an informal tone.

Leonard's **protagonist,** Chili Palmer, is an easy-going kind of loan shark, in semiretirement in Florida. But then one of his clients skips off to Las Vegas still owing him, so Chili dutifully takes off after him. It's not long before Palmer is in Los Angeles, hooking up with a has-been horror movie producer, Harry Zimm, a former B-movie actress, Karen Flores, and a current star, Michael Weir. Soon Chili is deciding he knows enough—which isn't all that much—to get into the filmmaking business.

It wouldn't be a Leonard novel without colorful **villains,** and this one has Ray Bones, an old enemy who has become Chili's boss in the Florida hierarchy, and Bo Catlett, a slick-dressing Angeleno who with his pal Ronnie is a jack-of-all-crimes, including murder.

In this company Chili comes off as a relatively nice guy, and one who knows how to use his expertise. "'What's the guy gonna do, Catlett, take a swing at me?'" he says to Harry. "'He might've wanted to, but he had to consider first, who is this guy? He don't know me. All he knows is I'm looking at him like if he wants to try me I'll . . . take him apart. Does he wanta go for it, get his suit messed up? I mean even if he's good he can see it would be work.'"

Understanding the Author's Tone To give the reader a feeling for the tone of the book being reviewed, the reviewer can include actual quotes from the story. This reviewer chose to feature a dialogue that shows some of the slang spoken by the characters. Slang is colorful language used in ordinary conversation but not in formal speech or writing.

❶ Which statement explains how the reviewer shows the tone of the book?
   a. The reviewer states that the book has colorful villains, including a murderer.
   b. The reviewer includes dialogue from the book, such as "'What's the guy gonna do, Catlett, take a swing at me?'"

❷ Write four examples of slang words from the passage above. Then choose one of them and write a word that has the same meaning but is more formal.

_____

_____

_____

_____

"'He could've had a gun,'" Harry said.

"'It wasn't a gun kind of situation.'"

Harry himself is on the hard-bitten side, recalling one unpleasant literary agent he had dealt with: "I asked him one time what type of writing brought the most money and the agent says, 'Ransom notes.'"

Things fall into place too easily for Chili at times, but Leonard compensates with nice twists, snappy action scenes and more than one blood-drawing **zinger.** You have to like a Hollywood novel in which a woman studio executive can say, "'Harry, I feel as if I know you. I've been a fan of yours ever since *Slime Creatures*. They remind me of so many people I know in the industry.'"

Recognizing Bias Bias is a strong preference for a particular point of view. A person can have a bias for or against something. You can recognize a reviewer's bias from words that emphasize either a negative or a positive view of something. For example, at the beginning of the review the writer describes *Get Shorty* as a "splendidly entertaining crime tale." You know he likes the book.

1 Here are three phrases from the review. Which two phrases help show the reviewer's bias in favor of this novel?
  a. "snappy action scenes"
  b. "colorful villains"
  c. "slick-dressing Angeleno"

2 How does the reviewer support his opinion of the novel?
  a. by using quotations from the novel
  b. by suggesting that it's the best book he has ever read

In this review, you can also tell that the writer has a bias against the film industry. At the beginning of the review he says that "gangsters are a lot like the people who make movies." And, at the end of the review he says "you have to like a Hollywood novel" with a character who says the movie title *Slime Creatures* reminds her of so many people she knows in the movie industry. This lets you know that he shares the character's opinion.

Reviewers may also show a bias when they tell only one side of a story. When you see clues that suggest a bias, be sure to read carefully to find out whether the reviewer supports his or her opinion with facts.

Thinking About the Review

Practice Vocabulary

The words below are in the passage in bold type. Study the context in which the words appear. Then complete each sentence by writing the correct word.

cynic	**acidic**	**moral**
protagonist	**villains**	**zinger**

1. The funny, surprise ending of the book was a real

   _____ .

2. You learn a lesson when you read a story with a _____ in it.

3. If you think that other people often behave selfishly, you might be

   called a _____ .

4. The main character, or _____ , of *Get Shorty* is Chili Palmer.

5. The salad dressing had a sharp, _____ flavor because it contained too much vinegar.

6. The _____ in a story are usually described in very negative ways.

Understand What You Read

Write the answer to each question.

7. What detail supports the conclusion that the reviewer has read many of Elmore Leonard's books?

   _____

   _____

8. Which two characters make Chili look like a nice guy?

   _____

   _____

9. Write one example of an opinion the reviewer gives about the book.

   _____

   _____

Check your answers on page 240.

Apply Your Skills

Circle the number of the best answer for each question.

10 Which of the following words best describes the tone of this review?
  (1) angry
  (2) sympathetic
  (3) humorous
  (4) serious
  (5) worried

11 The reviewer suggests that a cynic might think that Elmore Leonard writes with a bias against
  (1) crooks.
  (2) retired people.
  (3) horror films.
  (4) slick dressers.
  (5) the movie industry.

12 Which statement do you think represents this reviewer's bias?
  (1) The reviewer states that the protagonist is an easy-going kind of loan shark.
  (2) The reviewer tells that Chili Palmer moves to Las Vegas.
  (3) The author includes a dialogue from the book in his review.
  (4) The reviewer states that the story has nice twists.
  (5) The author mentions that Palmer gets into the film-making business.

Connect with the Story

Write your answer to each question.

13 If you were reviewing the book, what words would you use to describe the main character?

_____

_____

_____

14 Based on the review, would you like to read this book or one like it? Explain why or why not.

_____

_____

_____

_____

_____

Reading at Work

Real Estate: Property Manager

Some Careers in Real Estate

Property Valuer/ Appraiser
calculates value of properties by examining their condition and comparing them to similar buildings in the area

Real Estate Salesperson
helps people buy and sell homes, office buildings, and other types of structures

Real Estate Sales Assistant
helps real estate agent by making appointments and communicating with customers

Real Estate Receptionist
answers phone calls, handles correspondence, and makes appointments

Have you ever looked for an apartment or business space? If so, you've probably talked to a property manager. Property managers take care of office and apartment buildings. Some managers also act as the sales or rental agents for the property. They provide possible buyers or tenants with important information about the buildings and the surrounding community. Property managers must be able to read and present leases, brochures, and other written documents to their customers.

In addition to having strong reading skills, a property manager must also be a good writer, speaker, and listener. Property managers must communicate effectively with customers and with the workers and contractors who maintain the property.

Look at the chart of Some Careers in Real Estate.

- Do any of the careers interest you? If so, which ones?

- What information would you need to find out more about those careers? On a separate piece of paper, write some questions that you would like answered. You can find out more information about those careers in the *Occupational Outlook Handbook* at your local library.

Read the newspaper article. Then answer the questions.

Spring Meadows to Help Build New Community Center

CARVERTON Thursday the Spring Meadows Development Company announced that it will help the town of Carverton build a new community center. Carverton Mayor Kendra Clay said, "We're delighted for Spring Meadows' support of this exciting new facility for all of our residents."

The Carverton Community Center will have a gymnasium, a fitness center, an indoor track, an outdoor Olympic-size swimming pool, and an indoor pool. The center will also have meeting rooms and locker areas.

Spring Meadows is a large residential development in Carverton consisting of 200 single-family homes and 300 apartments. To date, 35% of the homes have been sold and 50% of the apartments have been rented.

As part of the agreement between the town and the development company, Mayor Clay announced that Spring Meadows residents would receive a discounted membership to the new community center.

1 The main idea of this article is that
   (1) Spring Meadows is a new residential development.
   (2) Kendra Clay is the mayor of Carverton.
   (3) There are more apartments than single-family homes in Spring Meadows.
   (4) Spring Meadows will help Carverton build its community center.
   (5) Already, 35% of the homes have been sold and 50% of the apartments have been rented.

2 As property manager of Spring Meadows, you would be most interested in this article because
   (1) Mayor Clay lives in Spring Meadows near the community center.
   (2) Spring Meadows residents are building the new community center.
   (3) There will be meeting rooms in the community center.
   (4) Spring Meadows residents will receive a discounted membership.
   (5) There will be swimming pools, a fitness center, and a running track.

3 As the property manager for Spring Meadows, you realize that this article contains several selling points. List three points that you could use to persuade people to buy or rent in Spring Meadows.

_____

_____

_____

Unit 2 Review: Nonfiction

Read the following passage from the autobiography _Stand by Your Man_ by Tammy Wynette with Joan Dew.

When I stepped inside the door, I saw a small-framed man with light brown hair, leaning back in a big leather chair with his feet propped up on his desk. He looked to be in his late twenties, not much older than me. He had on ordinary clothes—an open-collared shirt, casual pants and loafers—and he didn't appear very prosperous. He just sat there looking at me in a disinterested way, waiting for me to say something. He made me feel very uncomfortable; he seemed so cool and detached.

In my nervousness I blurted out, "My name is Wynette Byrd and I've recently moved here from Birmingham."

He said, "Well, I'm from Alabama myself, but you probably never heard of the place. It's a little town called Haleyville."

I said, "Yes, I have! That's the town where my father was born, and my grandparents still have a little house down there."

He almost smiled then and I thought, Well, at least the ice has been broken a little bit. He asked, "What can I do for you?"

I stammered, "I want a recording contract."

His expression didn't change at all. He said, "Do you have any tapes?"

I said, "No, but I'll sing for you if you'll loan me a guitar."

He reached over behind him and handed me his, then leaned back in his chair again. I sang a couple of songs I had written with Fred Lehner in Birmingham. Then I did a Skeeter Davis song and a George Jones song. His expression still didn't change, and he made no comment whatsoever about my singing. He didn't say anything at all for a minute or two, then spoke in a very matter of fact tone: "I don't have time to look for material for you, but if you can come up with a good song, I'll record you."

Just like that! At first I didn't believe I'd heard right. It couldn't be this easy, this casual, after a year of knocking on doors and facing one rejection after another. He didn't say _when_ he would record me and he didn't mention a thing about a contract, but I couldn't have been happier if I had just signed one for a million dollars. Even if this man didn't seem the least bit enthusiastic, someone had at least offered me a chance to record. Billy has never admitted it, but I think the only reason he made the offer was because he felt sorry for me. He once described his first impression of me to a reporter as "a pale, skinny little blond girl who looked like she was at her rope's end." And I guess he was right about that.

Items 1–6 refer to the passage on page 124.

Write the answer to each question.

1 Who is the narrator of this story?

_____

2 Why does Tammy Wynette think Billy let her record?

_____

_____

3 What is the main idea of the passage?

_____

_____

Circle the number of the best answer for each question.

4 Which of the following events happens first?

   (1) The woman enters the office and sees the man.

   (2) The woman feels uncomfortable.

   (3) The woman introduces herself.

   (4) The man asks the woman what she wants.

   (5) The man gives the woman a recording contract.

5 Why does the author repeat the fact that Billy had no expression on his face? To emphasize that this made her feel

   (1) hopeful

   (2) nervous

   (3) calm

   (4) relaxed

   (5) disinterested

6 Wynette was surprised by

   (1) the variety of songs she was able to remember.

   (2) how much she and Billy had in common.

   (3) how enthusiastic Billy was about her singing.

   (4) the casual way Billy offered to record her.

   (5) how much Billy knew about country music.

Read the following passage from "Star Time: James Brown" by David Hiltbrand.

Chuck Berry? Elvis? The Beatles?

When it comes down to who has had the most **profound** and lasting influence on pop music, no one can touch the Godfather of Soul.

This anthology (four CDs or cassettes) is the Fort Knox of funk. It chronologically traces Brown's **evolution** from a poor follow-the-crowd R&B singer from Georgia to the absolutely original, superbad superstar.

Disc No. 1 contains the greatest advances. On the earliest tracks, such as "Try Me" and "Bewildered" from the late '50's, Brown is trying to get over as a cookie-cutter pop singer. This smoothed-out doo-wop music isn't all that far from the Ink Spots. But even in this era, there were hints of genius. Mired in the **schmaltzy** ballad "I Know It's True," Brown still had a **flair** for using horns and drums.

By the time he recorded "Think" in 1960, James had discovered the funk, and he never **decamped.** He became a method singer, and that method was madness. His eruptive delivery was completely unpredictable. With "Bring It Up (Hipster's Avenue)" in 1966, lyrics had really become a **moot** point. A single phrase would **suffice.**

Brown was always a character. On "Papa's Got a Brand New Bag, Pts. 1, 2, 3," an extended, previously unreleased version of his 1965 hit, you hear the singer **exhorting** his longtime sax man, Maceo Parker, to play a solo. By the end of the jam, Brown is getting into a dialogue with the horns themselves. (If Brown was, as advertised, "the hardest working man in show business," the guys who worked in his backing bands were tied for second.)

The music is fast and furious the rest of the way. Disc Nos. 2 through 4 present a dizzying cavalcade of hits: "I Got You (I Feel Good)," "I Can't Stand Myself (When You Touch Me) Pt. 1," "Licking Stick-Licking Stick," "Give It Up or Turnit a Loose.". . .

There are many collections of Brown's work, but none so deep or well documented.

Items 7–18 refer to the passage on page 126.

Look in the passage for the numbered words below. They will be in bold type. Study the context in which each word appears. Then match each word with its meaning. Write the letter.

_____	**7**	profound	a.	of little importance
_____	**8**	evolution	b.	talent
_____	**9**	schmaltzy	c.	left or departed
_____	**10**	flair	d.	sentimental, mushy
_____	**11**	decamped	e.	change or development
_____	**12**	moot	f.	be enough
_____	**13**	suffice	g.	urging strongly
_____	**14**	exhorting	h.	deeply important

Write the answer to each question.

15 When a musician uses the word *jam*, it does not mean something that is put on bread. Reread the sixth paragraph on page 126. Based on the context, what does *jam* mean?

_____

_____

16 What is the reviewer's overall opinion of the music collection?

_____

_____

17 What statement in the review shows how the reviewer feels about James Brown's back-up musicians?

_____

_____

Circle the number of the best answer for the question.

18 Why does the reviewer describe the way James Brown encouraged his sax player to do a solo?
(1) To give an example of how unusual James Brown is
(2) To show that James Brown knows how to play a horn
(3) To suggest that James Brown is selfish
(4) To criticize James Brown's style
(5) To give an example of method singing

Read the following passage from the speech "I Have a Dream" by Martin Luther King, Jr.

I have a dream today. I have a dream that one day every valley shall be exalted and every hill and mountain shall be made low, the rough places will be made plain and the crooked places will be made straight, and the glory of the Lord shall be revealed, and all flesh shall see it together.

This is our hope. This is the faith that I go to the South with. And with this faith we will be able to hew out of the mountain of despair a stone of hope. With this faith we will be able to transform the jangling discords of our nation into a beautiful symphony of brotherhood. With this faith we will be able to work together, to play together, to struggle together, to go to jail together, to stand up for freedom together, knowing that we will be free one day.

And this will be the day—this will be the day when all of God's children will be able to sing with new meaning:

My country, 'tis of thee,
Sweet land of liberty,
Of thee I sing;
Land where my fathers died,
Land of the Pilgrims' pride,
From every mountainside
Let freedom ring.

And if America is to be a great nation, this must become true.

And so let freedom ring from the prodigious hilltops of New Hampshire. Let freedom ring from the mighty mountains of New York. Let freedom ring from the heightening Alleghenies of Pennsylvania. Let freedom ring from the snow-capped Rockies of Colorado. Let freedom ring from the curvaceous slopes of California.

But not only that. Let freedom ring from Stone Mountain of Georgia. Let freedom ring from Lookout Mountain of Tennessee. Let freedom ring from every hill and molehill of Mississippi. "From every mountainside let freedom ring."

And when this happens—when we allow freedom to ring, when we let it ring from every village and every hamlet, from every state and every city—we will be able to speed up that day when all of God's children, Black men and white men, Jews and Gentiles, Protestants and Catholics, will be able to join hands and sing in the words of the old Negro spiritual: "Free at last! Free at last! Thank God Almighty. We are free at last!"

Items 19–23 refer to the passage on page 128.

Write the answer to each question.

19 What two words in the passage have almost the same meaning as *slopes*?

_____

_____

20 What does the writer mean by a "beautiful symphony of brotherhood"?

_____

_____

Circle the number of the best answer for each question.

21 Which of these words means the same as the word *dream*?
(1) hope
(2) despair
(3) thought
(4) struggle
(5) glory

22 Which sentence best states the main idea of this passage?
(1) Life is unfair.
(2) Freedom cannot be achieved.
(3) Good things come to those who wait.
(4) People feel more free in the mountains.
(5) By working together, all people can become free.

23 After reading the passage, you might conclude that Martin Luther King, Jr., was working to help make people free. Which three details from the passage help lead to this conclusion?
(1) ". . . we will be able to work together. . ."
(2) "I have a dream today."
(3) "This is the faith that I go to the South with."
(4) "Sweet land of liberty, of thee I sing;"
(5) ". . . the snow-capped Rockies of Colorado."

Nonfiction Extension

Look through a news magazine or a newspaper for an article about a recent event. Write a brief summary of the article that includes the main idea of the article and details that support this main idea. List several examples of facts and opinions from the article. What conclusions can you draw from the ideas presented in the article? What details did you use to draw these conclusions?

Reading Connection: Nonfiction and Letter Writing

August 6

Dear William:

Life can be good. I hope I've taught you that. Watching your child being born. Helping him take his first steps. Hearing him speak his first words. Catching his first throw. Teaching him to be responsible and seeing him take responsibility for himself and his own family. To me, these simple pleasures have been life's greatest gift.

I am grateful to have experienced them all. I am grateful to you for having been such a willing student. Most of all, I am grateful for having such a remarkable son.

When we leave Earth, our lives will be judged by those left behind. That is not as important as how you judge your own life. Be sure you try to achieve all that you are capable of. Be sure you bring happiness to those around you.

These are the goals I set for myself. I have tried my hardest to achieve them. I believe I have, for I am fortunate to have had so many good people in my life. I hope you will be equally fortunate.

We all know that things have a beginning and an end. My end is drawing near. Don't be sad for me; I'm not sad for myself. I know that I am leaving behind a wonderful son and a good person, capable of bringing joy into the lives of all who walk the path of life with you.

I love you,
Dad

Writing Skills: Letters

Letters are one form of written communication. However, they are often among the most expressive, as in the letter above. Letters give information or express personal ideas.

Letters have four basic components.
- The **date** tells when the letter was written.
- The **salutation,** or greeting, tells to whom the letter is written.
- The **body** includes an introductory paragraph, all the important information the reader needs to know, and a closing paragraph.
- A common **closing** for letters is *Sincerely* or *Yours Truly.* Many people use the closing *Love* to someone very close. The writer's signature follows a closing.

Use the letter on page 130 to answer the questions.

1 Which sentence best states the main idea of the letter from the father to the son?

(1) Take advantage of every chance to get ahead.

(2) Make your life something to be proud of.

(3) Be sad when a loved one passes away.

(4) Set goals and stick to them.

(5) Don't judge yourself.

2 The father wrote this letter because he

(1) wants his son to know how much he loves and respects him.

(2) wants his son to have direction for how to lead a good life.

(3) needs to tell his son that he is at the end of his life.

(4) needs to tell his son how to raise his own children.

(5) wants his son to become a caring, responsible person.

3 The style and tone of the father's letter could best be described as

(1) funny and calm.

(2) informal and joyful.

(3) distant and angry.

(4) serious and loving.

(5) unhappy and disappointed.

4 Using a separate piece of paper, write a personal letter about something important in your life. Write your letter in the style and tone most appropriate for your reader and purpose.

A formal style and tone are used for people you don't know very well or for work-related situations. An informal style and tone are generally used for letters to friends and relatives.

● As the writer of the letter on page 130 did, make specific points to the reader.

● Be sure to include all four parts of a personal letter.

Check your answers on page 242.

UNIT 3

Poetry and Drama

Plays are stories written to be acted out. They are written as conversations among the characters. A play can be funny, serious, or both, but a good play will hold our attention, perhaps make us laugh or cry, and make us think.

Poetry is one of the oldest types of storytelling. Centuries ago in many cultures poetry was spoken, not written. In later times, many of these poems were written down. Poems can tell us stories, create strong images in our minds, and make us feel a variety of emotions.

○ Think about a play you have seen on a stage or have watched on television. This play likely affected your emotions in some way. How? Did it make you think about something in a new way? If so, what was it?

○ Think about the words to a song you particularly like. They are a kind of poetry. What kinds of images and emotions do they create? How did the writer use words to create these images and emotions?

SECTIONS

Popular Drama

Setting the Stage

Many **plays** are written to make the audience laugh. A play that is meant to be funny is called a **comedy.** Sometimes the characters in a comedy have serious problems or conflicts, but the way they behave makes the play funny. In most comedies, the characters overcome their problems and there is a happy ending.

PREVIEW THE PLAY

To get an idea of what the play is about, read the title and the first few lines. Then answer these questions.

1 What are the names of the characters?

_____

2 What are the characters doing at the beginning of the play?

_____

RELATE TO THE TOPIC

In this play, the characters are planning a birthday surprise. Meg and Babe are lighting the candles on a cake to surprise Lenny.

3 Have you ever been to a surprise party? Who was the party for? How did the person feel about the surprise?

_____

_____

VOCABULARY

improvising	**spontaneous**	**superstition**
ravenously	**glimmer**	

Check your answers on page 242.

Crimes of the Heart by Beth Henley

MEG: But, Babe, we've just got to learn how to get through these real bad days here. I mean, it's getting to be a thing in our family. *(Slight pause as she looks at Babe)* Come on, now. Look, we've got Lenny's cake right here. I mean, don't you wanna be around to give her her cake, watch her blow out the candles?

BABE: *(Realizing how much she wants to be here)* Yeah, I do, I do. 'Cause she always loves to make her birthday wishes on those candles.

MEG: Well, then we'll give her her cake and maybe you won't be so miserable.

BABE: Okay.

MEG: Good. Go on and take it out of the box.

BABE: Okay. *(She takes the cake out of the box. It is a magical moment.)* Gosh, it's a pretty cake.

MEG: *(Handing her some matches)* Here now. You can go on and light up the candles.

BABE: All right. *(She starts to light the candles.)* I love to light up candles. And there are so many here. Thirty pink ones in all, plus one green one to grow on.

MEG: *(Watching her light the candles)* They're pretty.

BABE: They are. *(She stops lighting the candles.)* And I'm not like Mama. I'm not so all alone.

MEG: You're not.

BABE: *(As she goes back to lighting candles)* Well, you'd better keep an eye out for Lenny. She's supposed to be surprised.

MEG: All right. Do you know where she's gone?

BABE: Well, she's not here inside—so she must have gone on outside.

MEG: Oh, well, then I'd better run and find her.

BABE: Okay; 'cause these candles are gonna melt down. *(Meg starts out the door.)*

MEG: Wait—there she is coming. Lenny! Oh, Lenny! Come on! Hurry up!

Making Inferences When you make an **inference**, you figure out something that the author suggests but does not state directly. To make an inference, use the facts that are given and what you already know to decide what the suggestion is.

The author does not tell us that Meg, Babe, and Lenny are sisters. Instead she gives clues to help us make this inference. Meg says "it's getting to be a thing in our family." Babe mentions how much Lenny always loves to make birthday wishes. Both of these ideas plus the familiar way the characters talk to each other lead the reader to believe that the characters are sisters.

At the beginning of the play, it seems as though Babe had been planning to leave before the birthday surprise. Which idea supports this inference?

a. Meg asks Babe whether she wants to be around to give Lenny the cake.

b. Meg tells Babe to light the candles.

BABE:	*(Overlapping and **improvising** as she finishes lighting the candles)* Oh, no! No! Well, yes—Yes! No, wait! Wait! Okay! Hurry up! *(Lenny enters. Meg covers Lenny's eyes with her hands.)*
LENNY:	*(Terrified)* What? What is it? What?
MEG/BABE:	Surprise! Happy birthday! Happy birthday to Lenny!
LENNY:	Oh, no! Oh, me! What a surprise! I could just cry! Oh, look: *Happy Birthday, Lenny—A Day Late!* How cute! My! Will you look at all those candles—it's absolutely frightening.
BABE:	*(A **spontaneous** thought)* Oh, no, Lenny, it's good! 'Cause—'cause the more candles you have on your cake, the stronger your wish is.
LENNY:	Really?
BABE:	Sure!
LENNY:	Mercy! *(Meg and Babe start to sing.)*
LENNY:	*(Interrupting the song)* Oh, but wait! I—can't think of my wish! My body's gone all nervous inside.
MEG:	. . . Lenny—Come on!
BABE:	The wax is all melting!
LENNY:	My mind is just a blank, a total blank!
MEG:	Will you please just—
BABE:	*(Overlapping)* Lenny, hurry! Come on!
LENNY:	Okay! Okay! Just go! *(Meg and Babe burst into the "Happy Birthday" song. As it ends, Lenny blows out all the candles on the cake. Meg and Babe applaud loudly.)*
MEG:	Oh, you made it!
BABE:	Hurray!
LENNY:	Oh, me! Oh, me! I hope that wish comes true! I hope it does!
BABE:	Why? What did you wish for?
LENNY:	*(As she removes the candles from the cake)* Why, I can't tell you that.
BABE:	Oh, sure you can—
LENNY:	Oh, no! Then it won't come true.

Identifying Conflict in Drama   Plays are often based on a **conflict** or problem between characters. Sometimes the conflict comes from the situation that is occurring. This type of conflict may last for only a short time before it is quickly resolved. A brief conflict can create a feeling of suspense or excitement.

In the passage above, a minor conflict happens when Lenny is supposed to blow out the candles on the cake. The reader is briefly left in suspense. Which of the following describes the conflict in the passage?

a.   Lenny is upset because her sisters are celebrating her birthday a day late.

b.   Meg and Babe become impatient with Lenny when she can't decide what to wish for.

Check your answer on page 242.

BABE: Why, that's just **superstition!** Of course it will, if you made it deep enough.

MEG: Really? I didn't know that.

LENNY: Well, Babe's the regular expert on birthday wishes.

BABE: It's just I get these feelings. Now, come on and tell us. What was it you wished for?

MEG: Yes, tell us. What was it?

LENNY: Well, I guess it wasn't really a specific wish. This—this vision just sort of came into my mind.

BABE: A vision? What was it of?

LENNY: I don't know exactly. It was something about the three of us smiling and laughing together.

BABE: Well, when was it? Was it far away or near?

LENNY: I'm not sure; but it wasn't forever; it wasn't for every minute. Just this one moment and we were all laughing.

BABE: Then, what were we laughing about?

LENNY: I don't know. Just nothing, I guess.

MEG: Well, that's a nice wish to make.

(Lenny and Meg look at each other a moment.)

MEG: Here, now, I'll get a knife so we can go ahead and cut the cake in celebration of Lenny being born!

BABE: Oh, yes! And give each one of us a rose. A whole rose apiece!

LENNY: *(Cutting the cake nervously)* Well, I'll try—I'll try!

MEG: *(Licking the icing off a candle)* Mmmm—this icing is delicious! Here, try some.

BABE: Mmmm! It's wonderful! Here, Lenny!

LENNY: *(Laughing joyously as she licks icing from her fingers and cuts huge pieces of cake that her sisters bite into **ravenously**)* Oh, how I do love having birthday cake for breakfast! How I do!

*(The sisters freeze for a moment laughing and eating cake. The lights change and frame them in a magical, golden, sparkling **glimmer;** saxophone music is heard. The lights dim to blackout, and the saxophone continues to play.)*

Determining Plot   The **plot** of a story or drama is the series of events that create the action. The events of a plot can be described in the order in which they happen. A scene in a play has a plot. The first event of the plot for this scene is Meg and Babe planning a birthday surprise for Lenny. Which two items are also events in the plot of this scene?

    a.   Lenny is surprised by the birthday cake.

    b.   Babe is an expert on birthday wishes.

    c.   Lenny is persuaded to tell her wish.

Thinking About the Play

Practice Vocabulary

The words below are in the passage in bold type. Study the context in which the words appear. Then complete each sentence by writing the correct word in the blank.

improvising	spontaneous	superstition
ravenously	glimmer	

1 The young man ate _____; it was as if he hadn't eaten for days. (ravenously, improvising)

2 We saw a soft _____ of light shining down on the water. (glimmer, superstition)

3 I made up the story as I went along because I enjoy

_____. (superstition, improvising)

4 Knocking on wood for good luck is a _____. (glimmer, superstition)

5 The audience was so surprised that they broke into

_____ applause. (ravenously, spontaneous)

Understand What You Read

Write the answer to each question.

6 What wish does Lenny make as she blows out her birthday candles?

_____

_____

7 What does Babe mean when she says "keep an eye out for Lenny"? Why do you think she says this?

_____

_____

8 What is the superstition that is mentioned in the passage?

_____

_____

9 What do you think helped make the birthday celebration such a surprise?

_____

_____

Check your answers on page 242.

Apply Your Skills

Circle the number of the best answer for each question.

10 You can infer from the scene that Babe seems to make up "facts" as she goes along. Which detail supports this inference?
(1) She loves to light up candles.
(2) She thinks the cake is pretty.
(3) She says that Lenny's wish will come true if she makes it deep enough.
(4) She wants everyone to get a piece of cake with a rose on it.
(5) She says that she's not like her mother.

11 Which line from the passage best shows that there is a conflict among the sisters?
(1) "Well, she's not inside—so she must have gone on outside."
(2) ". . . we've just got to learn how to get through these real bad days here."
(3) "My mind is just a blank, a total blank!"
(4) "Why, I can't tell you that."
(5)   "Why that's just a superstition!"

12 Based on the information in the passage, what do you think might have happened earlier in the plot?
(1) The family has always gotten along well.
(2) Meg was causing problems in the family.
(3) Lenny said she hated birthday celebrations.
(4) Babe was taking saxophone lessons.
(5) All the sisters were having problems.

Connect with the Play

Write your answers in the space provided.

13 Do you think Lenny's wish has been granted? Why or why not?

_____

_____

14 You have probably made a wish at some time. What was it? Did it come true? Did you do anything that helped it come true?

_____

_____

15 Have you ever felt nervous and unable to think the way Lenny did at first when she had to make a birthday wish? When was it? What happened?

_____

_____

Social Drama

Setting the Stage

Some plays known as **social dramas** deal with major social issues. Social dramas describe conflicts, but the problems are not always solved.

One common theme in social dramas is prejudice. A drama might deal with unfair treatment of a minority group, or it could deal with prejudice against individuals who have trouble fitting into society. A play can use a humorous or a serious approach to the issue, or a combination of both.

PREVIEW THE PLAY

You can get a good idea about the play by looking at the title and reading a few lines. Read until you can identify the four characters in the play. Then answer these questions.

1 Who are the characters in the play?

_____

2 Which characters are members of the same family? How are they related?

_____

RELATE TO THE THEME

The title of the play, *A Raisin in the Sun,* comes from a protest poem by the African-American poet Langston Hughes. The play deals with a possible neighborhood conflict .

3 Has there ever been any kind of conflict between neighbors where you live? What was done about it? What do you think should have been done?

_____

_____

VOCABULARY

consulting	expectantly	labored
deplore	quizzical	affirmation

A Raisin in the Sun by Lorraine Hansberry

BENEATHA:	Sticks and stones may break my bones but . . . words will never hurt me! *(Beneatha goes to the door and opens it as Walter and Ruth go on with the clowning. Beneatha is somewhat surprised to see a quiet-looking middle-aged white man in a business suit holding his hat and a briefcase in his hand and **consulting** a small piece of paper.)*
MAN:	Uh—how do you do, miss. I am looking for a Mrs.—*(He looks at the slip of paper.)* Mrs. Lena Younger?
BENEATHA:	*(Smoothing her hair with slight embarrassment)* Oh—yes, that's my mother. Excuse me. *(She closes the door and turns to quiet the other two)* Ruth! Brother! Somebody's here. *(Then she opens the door. The man casts a curious quick glance at all of them.)* Uh—come in please.
MAN:	*(Coming in)* Thank you.
BENEATHA:	My mother isn't here just now. Is it business?
MAN:	Yes . . . well, of a sort.
WALTER:	*(Freely, the Man of the House)* Have a seat. I'm Mrs. Younger's son. I look after most of her business matters. *(Ruth and Beneatha exchange amused glances.)*
MAN:	*(Regarding Walter, and sitting)* Well—My name is Karl Lindner . . .
WALTER:	*(Stretching out his hand)* Walter Younger. This is my wife—*(Ruth nods politely.)*—and my sister.
LINDNER:	How do you do.
WALTER:	*(Amiably, as he sits himself easily on a chair, leaning with interest forward on his knees and looking **expectantly** into the newcomer's face)* What can we do for you, Mr. Lindner!
LINDNER:	*(Some minor shuffling of the hat and briefcase on his knees)* Well—I am a representative of the Clybourne Park Improvement Association—
WALTER:	*(Pointing)* Why don't you sit your things on the floor?

Drawing Conclusions About Characters   Unlike stories, plays don't usually include descriptions of the **characters.** Stage directions and characters' words and actions give clues about what the characters are like.

The stage directions describe Walter's attitude. They also describe the way he greets the guest and how the women react. Walter states that he looks after his mother's business matters. From these clues, the reader gets the sense that Walter sees himself as the head of the household, the one in control. Which stage direction gives the reader a clue about what Ruth and Beneatha think of Walter's attitude?

   a.   *Ruth and Beneatha exchange amused glances.*

   b.   Beneatha (*Smoothing her hair with slight embarrassment*)

Check your answer on page 243.

LINDNER: Oh—yes. Thank you. (*He slides the briefcase and hat under the chair.*) And as I was saying—I am from the Clybourne Park Improvement Association and we have had it brought to our attention at the last meeting that you people—or at least your mother—has bought a piece of residential property at—(*He digs for the slip of paper again.*)—four o six Clybourne Street . . .

WALTER: That's right. Care for something to drink? Ruth, get Mr. Lindner a beer.

LINDNER: (*Upset for some reason*) Oh—no, really. I mean thank you very much, but no thank you.

RUTH: (*Innocently*) Some coffee?

LINDNER: Thank you, nothing at all.
(*Beneatha is watching the man carefully.*)

LINDNER: Well, I don't know how much you folks know about our organization. (*He is a gentle man; thoughtful and somewhat **labored** in his manner.*) It is one of these community organizations set up to look after—oh, you know, things like block upkeep and special projects and we also have what we call our New Neighbors Orientation Committee . . .

BENEATHA: (*Drily*) Yes—and what do they do?

LINDNER: (*Turning a little to her and then returning the main force to Walter*) Well—it's what you might call a sort of welcoming committee, I guess. I mean they, we, I'm the chairman of the committee—go around and see the new people who move into the neighborhood and sort of give them the lowdown on the way we do things out in Clybourne Park.

BENEATHA: (*With appreciation of the two meanings, which escape Ruth and Walter*) Un-huh.

LINDNER: And we also have the category of what the association calls—(*He looks elsewhere.*)—uh—special community problems . . .

Recognizing Theme A **theme** is an idea that runs through the entire passage. It is a general truth about life, or human nature, suggested in a story. In the passage Lindner wants to discuss something with the Youngers. His words and actions indicate that he seems very uncomfortable.

❶ Which two items support the idea that Lindner is uncomfortable talking to the Youngers?
   a. He shuffles his hat and briefcase.
   b. He uses words like *oh, uh,* and *well* often.
   c. The Youngers offer him coffee.

❷ From what you have read so far, you know that Lindner is white and you can infer that the Youngers are African Americans. What do you think the author is trying to suggest about human nature by the way he writes about Lindner's behavior?
   a. People often feel uncomfortable when meeting new neighbors.
   b. People can become uncomfortable with people they see as different.

Check your answers on page 243.

BENEATHA:	Yes—and what are some of those?
WALTER:	Girl, let the man talk.
LINDNER:	(*With understated relief*) Thank you. I would sort of like to explain this thing in my own way. I mean I want to explain to you in a certain way.
WALTER:	Go ahead.
LINDNER:	Yes. Well. I'm going to try to get right to the point. I'm sure we'll all appreciate that in the long run.
BENEATHA:	Yes.
WALTER:	Be still now!
LINDNER:	Well—
RUTH:	(*Still innocently*) Would you like another chair—you don't look comfortable.
LINDNER:	(*More frustrated than annoyed*) No, thank you very much. Please. Well—to get right to the point I—(*A great breath, and he is off at last*) I am sure you people must be aware of some of the incidents which have happened in various parts of the city when colored people have moved into certain areas—(*Beneatha exhales heavily and starts tossing a piece of fruit up and down in the air.*) Well—because we have what I think is going to be a unique type of organization in American community life—not only do we **deplore** that kind of thing—but we are trying to do something about it. (*Beneatha stops tossing and turns with a new and **quizzical** interest to the man.*) We feel—(*gaining confidence in his mission because of the interest in the faces of the people he is talking to*)—we feel that most of the trouble in this world, when you come right down to it—(*He hits his knee for emphasis.*)—most of the trouble exists because people just don't sit down and talk to each other.
RUTH:	(*Nodding as she might in church, pleased with the remark*) You can say that again, mister.
LINDNER:	(*More encouraged by such **affirmation***) That we don't try hard enough in this world to understand the other fellow's problem. The other guy's point of view.

Summarizing It is sometimes helpful to **summarize** speeches by leaving out unnecessary information and including only the main idea and the most important supporting details. This will help you understand what the speaker is really trying to say.

In Lindner's long speech on this page, he mentions incidents that have happened when African-American families move into white neighborhoods, the fact that his association is trying to do something about it, and that people should sit down and talk to each other. What main idea is supported by these details?

    a. Lindner wants new people to join committees to help keep the neighborhood clean.

    b. He thinks that an African-American family moving into Clybourne Park is a "special community problem."

    c. Lindner wants the Youngers to help plan a neighborhood party.

Check your answer on page 243.

Thinking About the Play

Practice Vocabulary

The words below are in the passage in bold type. Study the context in which the words appear. Then complete each sentence by writing the correct word.

consulting	expectantly	labored
deplore	quizzical	affirmation

1 If you give an _____, it shows that you agree.

2 A person with a _____ look is likely to be curious about something.

3 He's _____ a mechanic before buying a used car.

4 If you _____ an action, you strongly dislike it.

5 A patient who has _____ breathing has difficulty inhaling and exhaling.

6 The student was _____ awaiting the results of the test.

Understand What You Read

Write the answer to each question.

7 Which character seems to be suspicious of Lindner? Give one clue that supports your answer.

_____

_____

8 At first how do the Youngers treat their visitor?

_____

_____

9 What do you think Lindner refers to when he mentions special community problems?

_____

_____

10 Why do you think Lindner is uncomfortable?

_____

_____

Apply Your Skills

Circle the number of the best answer for each question.

11 Based on Lindner's approach to the Younger family, what do you think he probably will do to solve the problem?
(1) threaten them
(2) ask them to join the association
(3) suggest in a nice way that they sell the house
(4) learn to accept the family
(5) have them arrested for disturbing the peace

12 Lindner suggests that racial problems exist because people are quick to judge, without thinking about the other person's point of view. Which statement supports this theme?
(1) Lindner's organization includes a welcoming committee.
(2) Lindner went to talk to the family about the property Mrs. Younger bought.
(3) There have been race riots in Clybourne Park.
(4) Lindner suggests that people should sit down and talk to each other.
(5) The Youngers have protested against African-American people.

13 In the passage, Lindner says the purpose of the Clybourne Park Improvement Association is to ensure that the neighborhood is properly maintained and that new people understand and follow the "rules." Which detail does not support this main idea?
(1) The organization is set up to look after upkeep and special projects.
(2) Mrs. Younger bought property in the neighborhood.
(3) The organization has a New Neighbors Orientation Committee.
(4) The association includes a category called special community problems.
(5) The association is trying to do something about racial conflicts.

Connect with the Play

Write your answer to each question.

14 If you were a member of the Younger family, how would you respond to Lindner's speech? Explain why.

_____

_____

15 Have you or someone you know had an experience with some kind of prejudice? Was the prejudice suggested or was it stated directly? Was the problem resolved? Explain.

_____

_____

Popular Poetry

Setting the Stage

Poetry uses language in a special way. **Poets** want the reader to use their senses to experience a scene. They often use vivid words that bring a picture, or an image, to the reader's mind. Poets do not just give facts or information. Instead they choose words carefully to convey feelings or experiences.

Popular poetry includes works that have been recently written. The poems are about events in modern-day life. They may be about the ordinary things people do in their day-to-day life or about ideas that people can imagine.

PREVIEW THE POEM

To get an idea of what you will be reading, look at the title of the first poem. When a poet uses words like *my* and *I* in a poem, the speaker is the main character, not the poet. Read the first stanza of this poem. Then answer these questions.

1 Who is the main character?

_____

2 How does the character describe herself?

_____

RELATE TO THE CHARACTER

The character in the first poem is thirty-eight years old and somewhat disappointed with her life. She expected to be more than she is.

3 How do you feel about your own life? Are you doing what you expected to be doing? Is there anything more that you feel you should do?

_____

_____

VOCABULARY

countenance	awkward	mantel
extend	precious	embrace

Check your answers on pages 243–244.

The Thirty Eighth Year
by Lucille Clifton

the thirty eighth year
of my life,
plain as bread
round as a cake
an ordinary woman.

an ordinary woman.

i had expected to be
smaller than this,
more beautiful
wiser in Afrikan ways,
more confident,
i had expected
more than this.

i will be forty soon.
my mother once was forty.

my mother died at forty four,
a woman of sad **countenance**
leaving behind a girl
awkward as a stork.
my mother was thick,
her hair was a jungle and
she was very wise
and beautiful
and sad.

Identifying Figurative Language **Figurative language** is a way of using words in different and unusual ways to make a strong point. One type of figurative language occurs when poets compare two things that are very different. In the passage above, the poet compares her mother's hair to a jungle. The word *jungle* creates the image of wild and untamed things. By using figurative language, she forcefully makes the point that her mother's hair was wild, or hard to control.

In this passage the poet describes herself as "plain as bread." What point is she making about herself?

    a.   She thinks that she is a good cook.
    b.   She thinks that she is not very pretty or special in any way.

Check your answer on page 244.

i have dreamed dreams
for you mama
more than once.
i have wrapped me
in your skin
and made you live again
more than once.
i have taken the bones you hardened
and built daughters
and they blossom and promise fruit
like Afrikan trees.
i am a woman now.
an ordinary woman.

in the thirty eighth
year of my life,
surrounded by life,
a perfect picture of
blackness blessed.
i had not expected this
loneliness.

if it is western,
if it is the final
Europe in my mind,
if in the middle of my life
i am turning the final turn
into the shining dark
let me come to it whole
and holy
not afraid
not lonely

out of my mother's life
into my own
into my own.

i had expected more than this.
i had not expected to be
an ordinary woman.

Summarizing   You can summarize a poem by finding the main idea and supporting details. Which statement best summarizes the feelings of the speaker in this poem?

    a.   She feels disappointed that she is getting older and is no longer young and beautiful.

    b.   She feels disappointed that she is not as wise and beautiful as her mother was.

A Picture on the Mantel

by James Lafayette Walker

All he knew about his mom
Was the picture of her face
That always seemed to have been on
The **mantel** by a vase.
He didn't have the love that every
Child of five should know
That only mothers can **extend**
Mixed with a warming glow.
One day while shopping with his dad
He stopped and gave a stare
"Look, Dad, look, can't you see
That's mother over there?"
"That isn't mother," said the dad
"Your mother's now with God."
"Are you sure, Dad, are you sure?"
Dad gave a knowing nod.
The dad said "Please excuse my son"
As tears welled in his eyes
"He's too young to understand
when someone **precious** dies."
The child said to the lady,
"But you have my mother's face."
He longed for her to hold him
In a mother's fond **embrace.**
"Are you a mother?" He then asked
"Why yes," she sadly smiled
"Will you hold me close?" he begged
The mother held the child.

Identifying Details   **Details** that support the main idea can help you understand what the characters are thinking and feeling. The little boy in this poem is unsure about what happened to his mother. The father understands how confused his son feels. He explains this to the woman in the store. The father shows his understanding in two ways. The details that show this are the knowing nod and the tears in his eyes. Which two details show that the boy in the poem is confused?

   a.   He asks his father if he is sure his mother is with God.
   b.   He wonders if a stranger might be his mother.
   c.   He has a picture of his mother on the mantel.

Check your answers on page 244.

Thinking About the Poems

Practice Vocabulary

The words below are in the passage in bold type. Study the context in which the words appear. Then write each word next to its meaning.

countenance	awkward	mantel
extend	precious	embrace

1 a hug _____

2 the shelf above a fireplace _____

3 very valuable _____

4 offer _____

5 clumsy _____

6 face _____

Understand What You Read

Write the answer to each question.

7 What four things had the speaker in "The Thirty Eighth Year" expected to be at the age of 38?

_____

_____

8 In what way are the speaker in "The Thirty Eighth Year" and the boy in "A Picture on the Mantel" alike?

_____

_____

9 What is the boy in "A Picture on the Mantel" looking for? Does he find it?

_____

_____

10 The woman in "A Picture on the Mantel" was not the boy's mother. Why do you think she gave him a hug?

_____

_____

Check your answers on page 244.

Apply Your Skills

Circle the number of the best answer for each question.

11 The speaker in "The Thirty Eighth Year" says "I have wrapped me in your skin." What does she mean by this?
(1) Her mother bothered her.
(2) She wore her mother's clothes.
(3) She has tried to be like her mother.
(4) She looks exactly like her mother.
(5) She misses her mother very much.

12 Which detail would you not include in a summary of "A Picture on the Mantel?"
(1) The child's mother died when he was very young.
(2) The child doesn't understand what it's like to have a mother's love.
(3) The mother's picture was placed next to the vase.
(4) The child doesn't understand what happened to his mother.
(5) The child is searching for someone who can give him a mother's love.

13 The speaker in "The Thirty Eighth Year" wants to live the rest of her life on her own terms. Which detail supports this idea? She says,
(1) "I am now an ordinary woman."
(2) "I have dreamed dreams for you more than once."
(3) "I had expected to be smaller than this."
(4) "I will be forty soon."
(5) ". . . out of my mother's life into my own."

Connect with the Poems

Write your answer to each question.

14 If you were the boy's father in "A Picture on the Mantel," what would you tell your son? How would you help him understand the situation?

_____

_____

_____

15 Both poems are about people who have lost someone close to them. Have you ever lost someone you felt very close to? If not, imagine what it would be like. What do you (would you) miss most about that person?

_____

_____

_____

Setting the Stage

Classical poems have stood the test of time. Although they were written years ago, they are still read and enjoyed by millions of people today. These poems appeal to people of all ages. They speak about experiences and emotions that are common to everyone.

PREVIEW THE POEM

To get an idea of what you will be reading, look at the title and read the first six lines of "The Road Not Taken." Then answer these questions.

1 What choice is the speaker trying to make?

_____

2 Does this seem to be a difficult choice or an easy one?

_____

RELATE TO THE TOPIC

We are faced with important choices and decisions every day. The poem "The Road Not Taken" is about choosing what direction to take in life.

3 What is an important choice that you have had to make? What helped you to decide? Do you feel now that you made the right choice?

_____

_____

_____

_____

VOCABULARY

diverged	**claim**	**trodden**
arrayed	**fluttered**	**minuet**

The Road Not Taken by Robert Frost

Two roads **diverged** in a yellow wood,
And sorry I could not travel both
And be one traveler, long I stood
And looked down one as far as I could
To where it bent in the undergrowth;

Then took the other, just as fair,
And having perhaps the better **claim,**
Because it was grassy and wanted wear;
Though as for that the passing there
Had worn them really about the same,

And both that morning equally lay
In leaves no step had **trodden** black.
Oh, I kept the first for another day!
Yet knowing how way leads on to way,
I doubted if I should ever come back.

I shall be telling this with a sigh
Somewhere ages and ages hence:
Two roads diverged in a wood, and I—
I took the one less traveled by,
And that has made all the difference.

Using Context Clues   Sometimes you will see an unfamiliar word or phrase when you read a passage. Study other related words and phrases near the unfamiliar word or phrase. These surrounding words are the context. The context contains clues that can help you figure out the meaning of an unfamiliar word.

The word *undergrowth* appears in the fifth line of the poem. The clues *yellow wood, grassy,* and *in leaves* suggest that this scene takes place in a forest. Now look at the two words that make up the compound word *undergrowth*. These clues help you to guess that *undergrowth* means "the plants that grow close to the ground in a forest."

Find the phrase *wanted wear* in the second stanza. Can you figure out from the context what this phrase means? *Wanted wear* means "had not been used much." Which two context clues from the rest of the poem could help a reader figure out the meaning of *wanted wear*?

a.   no step had trodden
b.   Two roads diverged in a wood
c.   the one less traveled by

Richard Cory by Edwin Arlington Robinson

Whenever Richard Cory went down town,
We people on the pavement looked at him:
He was a gentleman from sole to crown,
Clean favored, and imperially slim.

And he was always quietly **arrayed,**
And he was always human when he talked;
But still he **fluttered** pulses when he said,
"Good-morning," and he glittered when he walked.

And he was rich—yes, richer than a king—
And admirably schooled in every grace:
In fine, we thought that he was everything
To make us wish that we were in his place.

So on we worked, and waited for the light,
And went without the meat, and cursed the bread;
And Richard Cory, one calm summer night,
Went home and put a bullet through his head.

Recognizing Theme   The **theme** of a piece of writing is an idea that states a general truth about life or an insight into human nature. The theme is usually not stated directly. Readers have to analyze all the events and look for supporting details in order to decide for themselves what the theme is. Some stories or poems have more than one theme.

Reread the lines "We people on the pavement . . . " and " . . . wish that we were in his place." This shows that the ordinary people on the street admired Richard Cory and wished that they were in his place. These lines support one theme of the poem—that people often want to be something they are not.

❶   Which other line also supports the theme that people often want to be something they are not?
   a.   "And he was always human when he talked;"
   b.   "In fine, we thought that he was everything. . . "
   c.   "Went home and put a bullet through his head."

❷   Another theme in this poem could be that wealth or money doesn't necessarily make a person happy. What detail supports this theme?
   a.   Richard Cory was richer than a king and schooled in every grace.
   b.   Even though Richard Cory seemed to have everything, he killed himself.
   c.   Richard Cory glittered when he walked.

                          Check your answers on page 244.

The Minuet by Mary Mapes Dodge

Grandma told me all about it,
Told me so I couldn't doubt it,
How she danced, my grandma danced; long ago—
How she held her pretty head,
How her dainty skirt she spread,
How she slowly leaned and rose—long ago.

Grandma's hair was bright and sunny,
Dimpled cheeks, too, oh, how funny!
Really quite a pretty girl—long ago.
Bless her! why, she wears a cap,
Grandma does, and takes a nap
Every single day: and yet
Grandma danced the **minuet**—long ago.

"Modern ways are quite alarming,"
Grandma says, "but boys were charming"
(Girls and boys she means, of course) "long ago."
Brave but modest, grandly shy;
She would like to have us try
Just to feel like those who met
In the graceful minuet—long ago.

Restating the Main Idea   Remember that the main idea is an important idea in a paragraph, passage, or stanza. This important idea is supported by details. All forms of literature, including poems, have one or several main ideas. Sometimes the author tells us directly what the main idea is. Other times we have to think about the events and details in a section of writing in order to figure out the main idea.

After you have figured out the main idea in a section of writing, you can **restate** it. To restate a main idea, you figure out how to put the main idea into different words. The main idea of the first six lines of the poem is that Grandma described how she danced. This main idea can be restated. One way to restate it would be to say that Grandma paid a lot of attention to how she danced.

Reread the last seven lines of the poem. One way to state the main idea of this section is that Grandma would like her grandchildren to experience the things she experienced as a young girl. How could you restate this main idea?

a.   Grandma is living in the past. She needs to realize that times have changed and today things are different.

b.   Grandma thinks that the old ways were good, and she wishes that today's young people could feel the way she did.

Thinking About the Poems

Practice Vocabulary

The words below are in the passage in bold type. Study the context in which the words appear. Then complete each sentence by writing the correct word.

diverged	**claim**	**trodden**
arrayed	**fluttered**	**minuet**

1 More than a century ago, a popular dance was the

_____.

2 Over the summer, hikers have _____ this path through the woods.

3 The road _____ at the fork, and we didn't know which way to go.

4 When people have dressed up for a special occasion, they have

_____ themselves in nice clothing.

5 The butterfly _____ its wings and flew away.

6 If you say you have a right to something, you are making a

_____.

Understand What You Read

Write the answer to each question.

7 What did the speaker in "The Road Not Taken" do before he chose which road to take?

_____

_____

8 In "The Minuet," why did the speaker say that the way Grandma looked long ago was "funny"?

_____

_____

9 Why is it a surprise to find out that Richard Cory killed himself?

_____

_____

Check your answers on page 244.

Apply Your Skills

Circle the number of the best answer for each question.

10 Use context clues to figure out the meaning of the phrase *just as fair* from "The Road Not Taken." It means

(1) just as long.

(2) just as attractive.

(3) just as important.

(4) just as traveled.

(5) just as dark.

11 To the townspeople, Richard Cory appeared to have everything, including wealth and happiness. At the end we find out this is not true. Which of the following sayings best states this theme in "Richard Cory"?

(1) A bird in the hand is worth two in the bush.

(2) An apple a day keeps the doctor away.

(3) You can't judge a book by its cover.

(4) You can't change a sow's ear into a silk purse.

(5) Money is the root of all evil.

12 The main idea of "The Road Not Taken" could be stated as follows: the speaker took the road less traveled, and it turned out to be the better choice. How could this main idea be restated?

(1) If you do what everyone else does, you can get in trouble.

(2) It is not always a good idea to break away from the pack and do your own thing.

(3) When you travel, it's a good idea to take the route that most people follow.

(4) People don't always make the best decisions in life.

(5) Sometimes you can get more out of life if you do something different and don't just follow the crowd.

Connect with the Poems

Write your answer to each question.

13 If you were the speaker in "The Road Not Taken," how would you feel about the choice you made? Give reasons for your answer.

_____

_____

14 Richard Cory killed himself even though he seemed to have everything. What reasons might explain why Richard Cory killed himself?

_____

_____

Reading at Work

Service: Childcare Provider

Some Careers in Service

Library Assistant
helps librarians and patrons by locating and delivering requested materials

Lunchroom Attendant/ Recess Aide
monitors students in lunchrooms or cafeterias and in indoor and outdoor play areas

Preschool Aide
helps children and teachers with the day's functions, lessons, and activities

Teacher Aide
provides clerical and instructional support for classroom teachers and students

If you enjoy caring for young children, you may be interested in becoming a childcare provider. Childcare providers can work in a variety of settings—preschools, day care centers, and private homes.

Most providers care for infants, toddlers, preschoolers, or elementary grade students after school. Providers who work with very young children devote much of their time to caring for the children's basic health, social, emotional, and play needs. Providers working with preschoolers and kindergartners may find themselves spending more time on the social and educational development of the children.

Childcare providers should have patience, a basic knowledge of child development, good listening and reasoning skills, and a strong interest in nurturing and teaching children.

Look at the Some Careers in Service chart.

- Do any of the careers interest you? If so, which ones?

- What information would you need to find out more about those careers? On a separate piece of paper, write some questions that you would like answered. You can find out more information about those careers in the *Occupational Outlook Handbook* at your local library.

Read the passage. Then answer the questions.

Happy Lands Day Care Center
Guidelines for Selecting Poems and Stories for Children

At Happy Lands Day Care Center, we believe in building a love of reading and literature in the children in our care. We believe that children of all ages benefit from being read to. We encourage our providers to share a wide variety of stories, songs, and poems with the children.

Please be responsible about the types of stories, poems, and songs you choose to share with the children. Keep in mind the following suggestions when selecting your material:

- Select materials with vocabulary that is appropriate for the ages of the children in your class.
- Evaluate the content of the material. Make sure the material will not frighten or confuse the children. Material with adult themes of violence, abuse, and disaster is not appropriate for children.
- Vary the types of material you share with the children. Expose them to different rhythms in songs and poetry and to different kinds of stories.
- Use good judgment. If you have a question about the material, don't use it or ask the Center Director if it is appropriate.

1 The guidelines above encourage providers to
　(1)　let the children choose which materials should be read aloud.
　(2)　share stories, poems, or songs with adult themes with the children.
　(3)　let the Center Director select all material for the children.
　(4)　expose the children to a wide variety of stories, poems, and songs.
　(5)　select materials that have an appeal to a wide range of ages.

2 Happy Lands Day Care Center believes providers should read to children because
　(1)　it helps keep them quiet and well behaved.
　(2)　otherwise, children become violent and abusive.
　(3)　the center wants children to develop a love of reading and literature.
　(4)　children don't hear stories, poems, and songs anywhere else.
　(5)　providers need activities to fill up the children's time at the center.

3 According to the descriptions, which selection would not be appropriate for children at the Happy Lands Day Care Center?
　(1)　"Merrily We Roll Along," a happy song with a catchy melody
　(2)　"Greedy Dog," a delightful poem about a dog who will eat anything
　(3)　"The Old Field," a sad poem about a field abandoned by children and animals
　(4)　"The Turkey," a funny poem about a turkey's bad luck on Christmas
　(5)　"The Wild Hog," a poem about a mean hog who kills many men

4 What is your favorite children's story or song? Write the name of the story or song. Then explain why you like it.

_____

_____

Read the following passage from the play *The Tomorrow Radio* by Robyn Reeves.

NARRATOR: Marcos and Adela Perez, a husband-and-wife team of scientists, are working on a project in their lab at home. For several years they have been trying to discover evidence of life on other planets by picking up radio signals from deep outer space. Their work has been expensive, however, and their money is about to run out. . . .

ADELA: Marcos, wait a minute. . . . I'm not sure. It sounds like—words.

NARRATOR: The sounds become clearer, and Marcos and Adela are able to make out a voice. . . .

RADIO VOICE: . . . And now, a weather forecast for tomorrow.

ADELA: What next? I never thought we'd be crossing sound waves with an ordinary radio broadcast. . . .

RADIO VOICE: Today's rain will turn into light showers tonight. Tonight will be slightly cooler. Sunday will be mostly cloudy. The high will be in the low fifties. . . .

ADELA: That's odd. It's not raining here. The announcer said "tomorrow's weather" and then talked about the weather for Sunday. But tomorrow is Saturday.

RADIO VOICE: Here are today's football scores. Dartmouth beat Yale in New Haven, 20 to 17. And here's a big upset. Indiana stunned Ohio State, 35 to 7! In the South . . . *(Static)*

ADELA: This is incredible! How could he have these football scores now? None of these games will be played until tomorrow. . . . This is no ordinary broadcast. . . .

MARCOS: *(Looking over her shoulder)* What are you doing?

ADELA: I'm writing down the football scores. If this thing is as good as it seems to be, we may never have to worry about money again!

RADIO VOICE: And that's the last of the football scores. This completes our broadcast day. Join me tomorrow, Sunday, at 10:00 AM for a sports and weather update. Until then . . . *(Music plays, then static)*

MARCOS: I still can't believe it. A radio that tells the future! . . . Think of all the good that people could do if they knew what was going to happen a day early. . . . And think of all the bad that could be done too. If this radio ever got into the wrong hands. . . .

NARRATOR: The radio suddenly crackles to life once more.

RADIO VOICE: I've just been handed a special news bulletin. The River Bridge in Sommerville has just collapsed. So far, one person is known dead. Stay tuned for more details. *(Static again then silence)*

Items 1–7 refer to the passage on page 160.

Write the answer to each question.

1 How are Adela and Marcos trying to discover evidence of life on other planets?

_____

2 The action of the play takes place on what day of the week?

_____

3 Why does Adela say, "if this thing is as good as it seems to be, we may never have to worry about money again"?

_____

4 What is the relationship between Adela and Marcos?

_____

Circle the number of the best answer for each question.

5 Why were Adela and Marcos surprised by the broadcast? They
  (1) didn't expect the radio to ever receive anything.
  (2) were trying to contact scientists in other countries.
  (3) were expecting to receive signals from outer space.
  (4) expected to receive ordinary radio broadcasts.
  (5) had turned the radio off.

6 The news bulletin about the collapse of the bridge could be a chance to use the radio to
  (1) make money.
  (2) fool people.
  (3) prove there's life on other planets.
  (4) do something good.
  (5) hear an ordinary broadcast.

7 After hearing the last broadcast, what do you predict Adela and Marcos will do next? They will
  (1) say nothing and continue their research.
  (2) try to sell the radio to make money for their lab.
  (3) wait to see if the bridge collapses before they tell anyone.
  (4) go to the authorities and try to convince them that the bridge will collapse.
  (5) try to find out where the broadcast is coming from.

Read the poem "Getting Out" by Cleopatra Mathis.

That year we hardly slept, waking like inmates
who beat the walls. Every night
another refusal, the silent work
of tightening the heart.
Exhausted, we gave up; escaped
to the apartment pool, swimming those laps
until the first light relieved us.

Days were different: FM and full-blast
blues, hours of guitar "you gonna miss me
when I'm gone." Think how you tried
to pack up and go, for weeks stumbling
over piles of clothing, the unstrung tennis rackets.
Finally locked into blame, we paced
that short hall, heaving words like furniture.

I have the last unshredded pictures
of our matching eyes and hair. We've kept
to separate sides of the map,
still I'm startled by men who look like you.
And in the yearly letter, you're sure to say
you're happy now. Yet I think of the lawyer's bewilderment
when we cried, the last day. Taking hands
we walked apart, until our arms stretched
between us. We held on tight, and let go.

Items 8–13 refer to the poem on page 162.

Write the answer to each question.

8 The poem describes how the couple acted during one particular year. What happened after that year?

_____

9 What is the first thing the speaker talks about?

_____

10 What can you conclude that the speaker has done with most of the couple's photographs?

_____

Circle the number of the best answer for each question.

11 What does the phrase *heaving words like furniture* suggest the couple was doing?
(1) arguing bitterly
(2) throwing chairs at each other
(3) rearranging the furniture
(4) moving out of the apartment at the same time
(5) throwing books at each other

12 What is the best meaning of the phrase *kept to separate sides of the map*?
(1) They kept a map in the middle of the apartment.
(2) They needed a map to find their way around.
(3) They lived in different parts of the country.
(4) They had an apartment that was laid out like a city street.
(5) They always argued about where to live.

13 The speaker seems sad but sure that the divorce was right. Which of the following phrases from the poem best expresses this feeling?
(1) "tightening the heart"
(2) "relieved us"
(3) "you gonna miss me"
(4) "paced that short hall"
(5) "held on tight, and let go"

Poetry and Drama Extension

Think about a movie, play, or television show that you have seen recently. Write a brief summary of it, including a description of the main characters, the main idea, and supporting details.

Reading Connection: Poetry and Life Science

Waking Up by Eleanor Farjeon

Oh! I have just had such a lovely dream!
And then I woke,
And all the dream went out like kettle-steam,
Or chimney-smoke.

My dream was all about – how funny, though!
I've only just
Dreamed it, and now it has begun to blow
Away like dust.

In it I went – no! in my dream I had –
No, that's not it!
I can't remember, oh, it is *too* bad,
My dream a bit.

But I saw something beautiful, I'm sure –
Then someone spoke,
And then I didn't see it any more,
Because I woke.

Native Americans thought dreamcatchers would catch bad dreams in the web and let good dreams pass through the center hole.

Life Science: A Good Night's Sleep

What do we do every night, whether we know it or not? We dream. Researchers have found that we dream about the same amount on nights that we remember our dreams as on the nights that we don't. The amount of time we sleep is broken into cycles and states. There are two states of sleep:

1. The first state is called NREM, or non-rapid eye movement. It consists of four stages:

   - Stage 1 is when we feel relaxed and sleepy.
   - Stage 2 is when we move into a light sleep. We don't dream in these two stages.
   - Stages 3 and 4 are called slow-wave sleep. In these stages, we are in a deep sleep and the dreams we have are ones we don't usually remember.

2. The second state is called REM, or rapid eye movement. This is when we dream the most and have the dreams we remember the most. For many people, their REM dreams are the most meaningful and visually exciting.

Approximately three-fourths of our total sleep time is spent in the NREM state and one-fourth in the REM state. We sleep by cycling through these states. Throughout the night, we experience four to six NREM/REM cycles.

Use the poem and the information on the previous page to answer the questions.

1 The poet compares her dream to kettle-steam because
(1) kettle-steam is hot and noisy, like her dream.
(2) people tend to drink tea in the evening to help them dream.
(3) kettle-steam is hard to hold on to, like her dream.
(4) the whistle from the kettle woke her from her dream.
(5) the noise from the kettle helped her remember her dream.

2 Many people remember nothing about their dreams when they awake. The person in the poem
(1) remembered she had a dream, but did not remember the specifics.
(2) thought she should have had a dream, but could not remember what she dreamed.
(3) had a dream about kettles steaming, chimneys smoking, and dust blowing.
(4) was upset because someone woke her before she had a chance to dream.
(5) had one dream about a burning house and another about someone beautiful.

3 Which of the following statements is <u>not</u> true?
(1) We dream even when we don't remember it.
(2) Dreams experienced during stages 3 and 4 are the most memorable.
(3) Most of our sleep time is spent in the non-rapid eye movement state.
(4) REM dreams tend to be more exciting than NREM dreams.
(5) We spend more time in NREM sleep than in REM sleep.

4 The dream experienced in the poem most likely occurred during
(1) stage 1 of NREM.
(2) stage 2 of NREM.
(3) stage 3 of NREM.
(4) stage 4 of NREM.
(5) the REM state.

5 Many people like to try to remember their dreams by keeping a dream log or journal. They put a notepad and pen by their bed. When they wake up, they immediately write down all that they remember about their dream. They write about where the dream took place, who was in it, what happened, and how it made them feel.

Using a separate piece of paper, write about a dream you once had. If you can't remember any dreams, use a dream log for the next few nights to record your dreams.

UNIT 4

Prose and Visual Information

We read and interpret prose, pictures, and diagrams all the time. **Prose** is ordinary language used to communicate information. Job manuals use prose to tell employees what will be expected of them on the job. Forms use prose to give directions and organize data.

Sometimes words alone are not enough for clear communication. Imagine trying to hook up a new VCR without a diagram showing where to plug in each cord. We need pictures and diagrams to learn how to use new products. Charts, graphs, and diagrams can help us make sense of the information we need at home, in our communities, and on the job.

○ Have you ever read a book or an article to learn a new skill? What did you learn how to do? Do you enjoy learning by reading?

○ Have you ever asked a friend for directions? Did the directions include a drawing or a map? When you read directions, do you rely more on the words or the pictures?

SECTIONS

Brochures and Advertisements

Setting the Stage

Brochures and **advertisements** are designed to persuade people to accept certain ideas or to buy certain products. Should you believe everything you read in an advertisement or brochure? Certainly not. However, if you read carefully and use common sense, advertisements and brochures can be good sources of information.

PREVIEW THE BROCHURES AND THE ADVERTISEMENT

You can get a feeling for the main idea of a brochure or an advertisement right away. Read the titles and headings of the brochures and advertisement on pages 169–171. Then answer these questions.

1 Does the author of the brochure on page 169 believe that watching television will harm a child's ability to learn? How do you know?

_____

2 Look at the advertisement on page 171. At first glance, do you think the product will be an expensive one? Why or why not?

_____

RELATE TO THE BROCHURES AND THE ADVERTISEMENT

The purpose of the brochure on page 170 is to help people make good choices about which medications to take.

3 Have you ever used information in brochures or advertisements to make health care decisions? What did you learn? Was the information helpful?

_____

_____

VOCABULARY

hypnotized	**antibiotics**	**symptoms**
allergic	**enhanced**	**clarity**

Check your answers on page 246.

This brochure might be sent home by a school to help parents improve their parenting skills. As you read, try to figure out the main idea of the brochure.

Too Much Television and Your Child's Ability to Learn

Television shortens a child's attention span.

Have you watched television with your child recently? If you have, you know that children's television shows are filled with visual images that usually last two or three seconds. Loud music, explosions, and other sound effects grab your child's attention. Many children seem **hypnotized** by the bright colors and quick cuts.

The story itself is broken up into short segments separated by commercials. Children who watch a lot of television lose the ability to concentrate for long periods of time. In school, they may have difficulty listening to the teacher read a simple story from start to finish.

Television weakens a child's language skills.

Try this experiment. Spend 15 minutes listening to, not watching, a children's television show. What do you hear? When you take out the visual images, sound effects, and music, you will find that the characters speak in short phrases and incomplete sentences. To learn language, children need to hear a rich vocabulary and clear sentence structure. They also need to be able to ask and answer questions. Children's television shows usually don't provide these important requirements for learning language.

Television weakens a child's reading skills.

In a way, watching television is the opposite of reading. Reading a good book requires a long attention span, a rich vocabulary, and the ability to understand complex sentences. Reading encourages children to ask questions and use their imagination. Television attempts to do all the imagining for the viewer. If children spend too much time watching television, they may lose the ability to make a written story come to life in their minds.

Finding the Main Idea   The main idea in a brochure is the most important idea. Often, the main idea is suggested by the title and the headings of the sections. Figuring out the main idea can help you understand the author's point of view. The main idea of each section should support the overall main idea.

The author of this brochure has a certain opinion about how television affects a child's ability to learn. Which statement best expresses the main idea of the brochure?

a.   Watching too much television may make it difficult for a child to learn.

b.   Watching too much television may cause a child to forget how to read.

c.   Watching television can help a child learn how to read.

Facts About Antibiotics

Brochures are often used to educate the public. You have probably seen health care brochures like the one below at the pharmacy or in your doctor's office.

Have you ever taken **antibiotics** for an earache? After a few doses, your ear probably stopped hurting. After a few more doses, you may have felt completely cured. Perhaps you stopped taking the medicine, thinking that you could save the rest for another illness. Although this decision seems to make sense, doctors tell us that it could ruin our health.

Antibiotics are prescribed to fight infections. Sore throats, earaches, and other **symptoms** may be caused by the growth of bacteria in your body. As the antibiotics fight to destroy the bacteria, the bacteria struggle to become stronger. When you do not take all your medication, the bacteria may not be completely destroyed. In a short time, the infection may return, much stronger than before.

Always follow your doctor's instructions. Ask your doctor or pharmacist about the purpose of your medication. Find out exactly what you must do for the treatment to work. Antibiotics can help you only when you take them at the right time and in the right amounts.

Follow these tips:

• Take all the prescribed doses even after you begin to feel better.

• Take the medicine at the same time each day. Make a schedule. If you forget a dose, take it as soon as you remember. Then get back on schedule.

• Follow special instructions. Some antibiotics must be taken with food or milk. Others must be taken on an empty stomach.

• Find out what other medications, foods, or drinks to avoid while taking your prescription.

• Some people may be **allergic** to certain antibiotics. Ask your doctor or pharmacist what side effects to look for. Notify your doctor immediately if you get a rash or have difficulty breathing.

Locating Factual Details The details in a brochure support the main idea or purpose of the brochure. Details are facts about the subject. Factual details answer questions about who, what, when, where, why, and how. The brochure on this page gives details about why it is important to follow instructions carefully when taking antibiotics.

1 Reread the second paragraph. Why should you take all the medicine your doctor prescribed even after you feel better?
   a. Antibiotics can kill the bacteria that cause sore throats and earaches.
   b. The bacteria may not all be destroyed if you don't take all your medication.

2 Reread the list of tips. What should you do if you forget to take a dose of medicine?
   a. Take two doses of medicine next time.
   b. Take it as soon as you remember.

Check your answers on page 246.

Advertisements are everywhere. We see them on billboards and at bus stops. You have probably seen advertisements like the one below in magazines. As you read, think about how the author tries to persuade you to buy the product.

Don't You Deserve the Best Technology Money Can Buy?

Introducing the Award-Winning Enhanced WAVE-AUDIO Player from MicroTech!

It's Unlike Anything You'd Expect From a CD Player.
It's Exactly What You'd Expect From MicroTech.

It's finally arrived: the new **Enhanced** WAVE-AUDIO Player from MicroTech. When it's high-quality sound that counts, you can count on MicroTech. You told us that you wanted clear high tones and deep, warm bass tones—all in an elegant, slim, space-age design. We took your suggestions back to our Sound Laboratory and produced the Enhanced WAVE-AUDIO Player. Our compact design of radio and CD player with built-in speakers takes up only 18 by 22 inches of table space, yet its sound can fill a concert hall.

With our unique CD400 audio engine, you'll never want to listen to music on any other CD player again. Be the first among your friends to own the CD player that Music World called the "Invention of the Year."

Experience the Enhanced WAVE-AUDIO Player at your local dealer or visit us today at www.microtech.com. We know you'll be delighted with **clarity** of sound never before possible from a small CD player.

Understanding Persuasive Techniques   An advertisement is a type of **persuasive writing.** In persuasive writing, authors often use strong emotional words to convince you to accept a certain point of view. Advertisements make claims that may not be true. Read advertisements carefully to separate facts from emotional claims about the product.

1 Which two phrases try to appeal to the reader's emotions?
   a.   Don't you deserve the best?
   b.   Be the first among your friends to own one.
   c.   Our compact design takes up very little space.

2 Which of these claims is probably not true?
   a.   *Music World* called this CD player the "Invention of the Year."
   b.   You'll never want to listen to music on any other CD player again.

Thinking About the Brochures and the Advertisement

Practice Vocabulary

The words below are in the passages in bold type. Study the context in which the words appear. Then complete each sentence by writing the correct word.

hypnotized	**antibiotics**	**symptoms**
allergic	**enhanced**	**clarity**

1 After sneezing several times, your friend decides that she may be

_____ to cats.

2 The new, improved laundry detergent has _____ cleaning power.

3 The patient's _____ are a fever and a sore throat.

4 With my new glasses, I could see with greater _____ .

5 The crowd seemed _____ by the flashing lights of the police cars.

6 Medicines that fight infections are called _____ .

Understand What You Read

Write the answer to each question.

7 Look at the brochure on page 169. What are two reasons to limit the amount of time a child watches television?

_____

8 What will you hear when you listen to a children's television show without watching it?

_____

9 Look at the brochure on page 170. How do antibiotics get rid of some sore throats and earaches?

_____

10 Look at the advertisement on page 171. What are two claims made about the CD player in the advertisement?

_____

                        Check your answers on pages 246–247.

Apply Your Skills

Circle the number of the best answer for each question.

11 Look at the brochure on page 169. Which statement best expresses the main idea of the third paragraph?
(1) Most television shows have too many loud sound effects.
(2) Watching television may weaken a child's language skills.
(3) Children often speak in short phrases and incomplete sentences.
(4) Television encourages children to use their imagination.
(5) Children who watch television usually have long attention spans.

12 Look at the brochure on page 170. Based on the list of tips, which of these statements about antibiotics is true?
(1) Antibiotics are mainly used to treat allergies.
(2) You should never take antibiotics with milk.
(3) You should stop taking antibiotics once your sore throat is better.
(4) If you get well quickly, always throw away any pills that are left.
(5) For antibiotics to work well, you need to take them on a schedule.

13 Look at the advertisement on page 171. Which of these claims about the CD player may not be true?
(1) The CD player has built-in speakers.
(2) The CD player also includes a radio.
(3) The CD player won an award.
(4) The CD player will delight you.
(5) The CD player is a new design.

Connect with the Brochures and the Advertisement

Write your answer to each question.

14 Think of a product such as clothing, shampoo, or car wax that you have bought based on information you read or heard in an advertisement. What was it about the advertisement that convinced you to try the product? Do you think the claims made in the advertisement were true? Why or why not?

_____

_____

15 Do you think that watching a lot of television is bad for adults? Why or why not?

_____

_____

Setting the Stage

Calendars and **schedules** are designed to help us organize our time at work and at home. On the job, employers often use calendars and schedules to communicate work assignments and daily tasks to their employees.

PREVIEW THE CALENDAR AND THE SCHEDULES

You can often get an idea of the kind of information you will find on a calendar or schedule by reading the title and the headings for the columns and rows. Read the titles and the column headings for the schedules on pages 176 and 177. Then answer these questions.

1 Name one kind of information you would expect to find on the Shipping and Receiving Schedule on page 176.

_____

2 What kind of information do you think you will find on the work schedule on page 177?

_____

RELATE TO THE CALENDAR AND THE SCHEDULES

The purpose of the calendar on page 175 is to communicate which classes and events will be offered at the recreation center during the spring.

3 Have you ever used a calendar of events for school, work, or a community group? What kind of information was on the calendar? Was the calendar helpful?

_____

_____

VOCABULARY

intermediate	**international**	**destination**
punctuality	**personnel**	

Check your answers on page 247.

The calendar below shows the classes and events offered at a community recreation center. You may have seen calendars like this at schools and other public buildings.

Gardner Park Recreation Center
Spring Calendar of Events

All classes begin Monday, March 8, and end Friday, June 11.
All other events occur weekly unless otherwise noted.

Monday	Tuesday	Wednesday	Thursday	Friday
Preschool Fun Time Ages: 3–4 9 A.M. to noon	Preschool Fun Time Ages: 3–4 9 A.M. to noon	Preschool Fun Time Ages: 3–4 9 A.M. to noon	Fitness Club Ages: Adult 10–11 A.M.	Preschool Fun Time Ages: 3–4 9 A.M. to noon
Beginning Gymnastics Ages: 5–12 4–4:45 P.M.	**International** Foods Ages: 6–8 3:30–4:15 P.M.	Beginning Acting Ages: 7–10 3:30–4:15 P.M.	Beginning Tap Dancing Ages: 6–Adult 2–3 P.M.	Yoga Ages: Adult 10–11 A.M.
Used Book Drop-off March 15 and April 12 4:15–5:15 P.M.	Beginning Cartooning Ages: 8–9 3:30–4:30 P.M. Ages: 10–12 4:30–5:30 P.M. Ages: 13–Adult 5:30–6:30 P.M.	Mad Scientist Club Ages: 5–7 4–4:45 P.M.	Teen Drop-in Center 3–6 P.M.	2-Person Basketball Competition Ages: 16–Adult 4–6 P.M.
Intermediate Gymnastics Ages: 5–12 4:45–5:30 P.M.		Advanced Gymnastics Ages: 5–12 5:30–6:15 P.M.	Gardening Club Ages: Adult 7–9 P.M.	Hip Hop Dancing Ages: 11–15 5:30–6:30 P.M.

Using the Format   The **format** of a calendar is the way the information is arranged and presented. **Columns** put information in vertical form. Reading the column headings and titles of events is a good way to find out what information you will find in a calendar. The columns in this calendar show which classes, activities, and events occur each day.

1. Suppose you want to find a class for your ten-year-old child on either Tuesday or Wednesday. Which class is not available then?
   a.   Intermediate Gymnastics
   b.   Beginning Cartooning
   c.   Advanced Gymnastics

2. You want to sign up for a class or activity for adults on Thursday. How many choices do you have?
   a.   1   b.   2   c.   3

How well we do a job often depends on how well we use our time. For jobs that require many people to work together, a schedule of tasks is often prepared before the work is to take place. The schedule below might be used by a shipping clerk to oversee the loading and unloading of goods at a shipping dock.

Shipping and Receiving Schedule

Loading Dock 3   **Thursday, June 9**

Time	Task
7:30–8:15 A.M.	Unload shipment from Garth Paper Supplies
8:15–9:15 A.M.	Unload shipment from Williams Electronics
9:15–9:30 A.M.	Break
9:30–11:00 A.M.	Load Truck 6 for Route 7B **Destination:** Redwood City
11:00 A.M.–12 noon	Lunch break
12 noon–12:30 P.M.	Complete schedule for June 10 Submit paperwork for day's shipments to supervisor
12:30–1:45 P.M.	Load Truck 9 for Route 3 Destination: Freemont
1:45–2:30 P.M.	Unload shipment from Jensen Office Supplies
2:30–2:45 P.M.	Break
2:45–3:30 P.M.	Load Truck 4 for Route 6A Destination: Local
3:30–4:30 P.M.	Unload shipment from A&S Computer Warehouse

Finding Relevant Information   A schedule is a collection of specific facts that tells who, what, when, and where. To find the information you need, look down the appropriate column to find important words or numbers. Once you find the location of the information, slow down and read carefully to make sure you understand the facts.

1 What time will the shipment from Jensen Office Supplies be unloaded?
   a.   7:30–8:15 A.M.
   b.   1:45–2:30 P.M.

2 How many shipments are scheduled to be loaded between 11 A.M. and 4:30 P.M.?
   a.   2
   b.   4
   c.   7

3 According to the schedule, what is the destination of Truck 6?
   a.   Route 7B
   b.   Freemont
   c.   Redwood City

On many jobs, employees may not work the same hours each day. Managers often post work schedules for the upcoming week on a bulletin board to help employees plan their time.

Mayfair Appliances

Work Schedule for Floor **Personnel**: Week of July 6

Punctuality is important. When you are late to work, your fellow workers must perform your duties until you arrive. As a general rule, all personnel should report to work at least 10 minutes before the start of their shift.

	Employees					
	Max	**Brad**	**Kina**	**Gayla**	**Lamar**	**Silas**
Mon. July 6	8:30 A.M.– 5 P.M.	1 P.M.– 9:30 P.M.	8:30 A.M.– 5 P.M.	10:30 A.M.– 7 P.M.	1 P.M.– 9:30 P.M.	OFF
Tues. July 7	8:30 A.M.– 5 P.M.	OFF	10:30 A.M.– 7 P.M.	1 P.M.– 9:30 P.M.	1 P.M.– 9:30 P.M.	OFF
Wed. July 8	OFF	1 P.M.– 9:30 P.M.	8:30 A.M.– 5 P.M.	1 P.M.– 9:30 P.M.	OFF	10:30 A.M.– 7 P.M.
Thurs. July 9	OFF	1 P.M.– 9:30 P.M.	10:30 A.M.– 7 P.M.	OFF	1 P.M.– 9:30 P.M.	8:30 A.M.– 5 P.M.
Fri. July 10	10:30 A.M.– 7 P.M.	1 P.M.– 9:30 P.M.	8:30 A.M.– 5 P.M.	OFF	1 P.M.– 9:30 P.M.	10:30 A.M.– 7 P.M.
Sat. July 11	8:30 A.M.– 5 P.M.	OFF	OFF	1 P.M.– 9:30 P.M.	10:30 A.M.– 7 P.M.	1 P.M.– 9:30 P.M.
Sun. July 12	8:30 A.M.– 5 P.M.	1 P.M.– 9:30 P.M.	OFF	1 P.M.– 9:30 P.M.	OFF	10:30 A.M.– 7 P.M.

Applying Information to a New Situation   Schedules contain information about time in an easy-to-use form. Managers and employees often refer to schedules to plan, solve problems, and make decisions.

1   On Thursday, July 9, the manager needs to send an employee to a customer service workshop at 2 P.M. Which employees will be at work on the day and time of the workshop?
a.   Brad, Kina, Gayla, Lamar
b.   Brad, Lamar, Silas
c.   Brad, Kina, Lamar, Silas

2   The company would like to have a one-day sale on a day when at least five of the six employees are scheduled to work. Which days would be the best for the sale?
a.   Friday and Saturday
b.   Monday and Sunday
c.   Monday and Friday

Thinking About the Calendar and the Schedules

Practice Vocabulary

The words below are in the passages in bold type. Study the context in which the words appear. Then complete each sentence by writing the correct word.

intermediate	international	destination
punctuality	personnel	

1. At the festival, I especially enjoyed the _____ music from Central and South America.

2. Mike's _____ has improved since he started setting his alarm clock 30 minutes earlier.

3. Since I have already completed a year of martial arts, I think I will sign up for the _____ class.

4. The airplane reached its _____ in a little less than three hours.

5. All _____ who work 40 hours per week will be able to join the new retirement plan.

Understand What You Read

Choose the best answer to each question.

6. Look at the calendar on page 175. Which of the following is a true statement about the classes offered on Tuesday?
    a. The class International Foods is offered at three different times.
    b. The only class open to 4-year-olds is Preschool Fun Time.

7. Look at the shipping and receiving schedule on page 176. Which truck is scheduled to make deliveries in the local community?
    a. Truck 3 delivers in the local area.
    b. Truck 4 delivers in the local area.

8. Look at the work schedule on page 177. According to the schedule, when should workers report to work?
    a. Workers should report at least 10 minutes before their shifts begin.
    b. Workers should report at least 20 minutes before their shifts begin.

Apply Your Skills

Circle the number of the best answer for each question.

9 Look at the calendar on page 175. Which classes are available for five-year-old children after 3 P.M. on Wednesday?
- (1) Advanced Gymnastics only
- (2) Mad Scientist Club only
- (3) Advanced Gymnastics and Mad Scientist Club
- (4) Mad Scientist Club and Beginning Acting
- (5) Advanced Gymnastics and Beginning Acting

10 Look at the shipping and receiving schedule on page 176. Which is a true statement about the shipments that will be unloaded?
- (1) Two shipments will be unloaded after the lunch break.
- (2) The shipment from Garth Paper Supplies will arrive at 8:15 A.M.
- (3) The paperwork for each shipment is given to the supervisor after each shipment is unloaded.
- (4) The last shipment will arrive at 1:45 P.M.
- (5) The shipment from Jensen Office Supplies will arrive on Truck 9.

11 Look at the work schedule for Mayfair Appliances on page 177. The assistant manager needs to help Lamar and Max learn more about the product line. He would like to plan a training session for Tuesday. At which time on Tuesday will both Lamar and Max be at work?
- (1) 9:30 A.M.
- (2) 11:30 A.M.
- (3) 3:30 P.M.
- (4) 5:30 P.M.
- (5) 7:30 P.M.

Connect with the Calendar and the Schedules

Write your answer to each question.

12 On a busy day, how do you keep track of everything you need to do at home or at work? Does your system work? How could you improve it?

_____

_____

_____

13 Many families use a calendar to write down appointments and to make sure everyone knows what chores to do. Invent the perfect system for keeping track of all the things the people in your household need to do. Describe your system, and explain why it works well for you.

_____

_____

_____

23 Forms and Documents

Setting the Stage

Forms provide a way to gather and organize important information. There are many different kinds of forms. You use them frequently as an employee, a citizen, and a consumer.

Documents are designed to communicate official or legal information. If you read and sign a document, you are agreeing to the terms in the document. Always read documents carefully before you sign them.

PREVIEW THE FORMS AND THE DOCUMENT

Most forms and documents are divided into small sections. You can quickly get a sense of the purpose and organization of a form or document by reading the headings for all the sections. Read the section headings on the forms and documents on pages 181–183. Then answer these questions.

1 Read the column headings under Section 2 of the form on page 181. What seems to be the purpose of this part of the form?

_____

2 Read the title of the form on page 182. Then look at the words in the first few boxes. What type of company do you think uses this form?

_____

RELATE TO THE FORMS AND THE DOCUMENT

Common legal agreements include leases, loan documents, and credit card agreements. Look at the credit card agreement on page 183.

3 Have you ever entered into a legal agreement such as this one? Did you read the entire document? How could you get help understanding it?

_____

VOCABULARY

specify	**references**	**authorize**
certify	**constitute**	**introductory**

When you apply for a job, you are asked to fill out a common form, an employment application. The application makes it easier for the people who make hiring decisions to find the information they need.

Employment Application

Section 1: General Information Use black ink. Be accurate and complete.

Name (First) (Middle) (Last)		Social Security #	Date

Address (Street, City, State, Zip)	Home Telephone #	Message Telephone

Are you at least 18 years of age? Yes ☐ No ☐   Do you have proof of U.S. citizenship or a
If no, do you have a work permit? Yes ☐ No ☐   U.S. permanent resident visa? Yes ☐ No ☐

Position Desired   Check One:
Full-time ☐   Part-time ☐   Short term ☐   Other ☐

Available for Work:
Any hour ☐   Any day ☐   Other ☐   Please **specify:**

Section 2: Work Experience List your previous employment in order. Start with your most recent employer first. Write additional work experience on a separate page.

Dates From	To	Name and Address of Employer	Job Title	Wage or Salary	Reason for Leaving
		Company: Address: Supervisor:			
		Company: Address: Supervisor:			

Section 3: References List two **references.** Do not include relatives, persons employed by this company, or previous employers.

Name	Telephone #	Occupation
Name	Telephone #	Occupation

Understanding Organization To fill out any form, you need to understand its organization. Most forms are divided into sections. Each section has its own subject or purpose. Look for headings and instructions. Use the lines or boxes that separate sections to understand how a form is organized.

1 Read the section titles. In which section would you expect to write your home telephone number?

    a.   Section 1: General Information   b.   Section 3: References

2 Read the headings and instructions for Sections 2 and 3. In which section would you list your brother?

    a.   Section 2: Work Experience   c.   neither section
    b.   Section 3: References

If you have health or dental insurance, you may have to fill out claim forms. These forms are often provided by your employer. Always read insurance forms carefully. Your claim may not be paid if the form is filled out incorrectly.

Group Dental Claim Form

Instructions to the Employee

1. Please type or print clearly using black ink.
2. Please answer questions in boxes 1 through 12 completely.
3. Sign and date the "Authorization to Release Information" on Line 13.
4. If you wish to have your benefits paid directly to the dentist, sign and date Line 14.
5. Sign and date the certification statement on Line 15.
6. Attach this form to your dental bill and mail to Dental Health, Inc.

1. Patient Name	2. Relationship to Employee Self ☐ Spouse ☐ Child ☐ Other ☐	3. Sex M ☐ F ☐	4. Patient Birthdate (m/d/y)
5. Employee Name (First, Middle, Last)	6. Employee Social Security #		7. Employee Birthdate (m/d/y)
8. Employee Address (Street Address, City, State, Zip)			
9. Account / Policy #	10. Employer's Name and Address		
11. Is patient covered by another dental plan? Yes ☐ No ☐	12. If yes, please indicate: Dental Plan Name: Group #:		

13. *Authorization to Release Information* — I hereby **authorize** the release of any information about my dental history or this treatment to the Insurer for the purpose of determining the benefits payable.	Signature of Patient or Parent	Date
14. *Authorization to Pay Benefits to Dentist* — I hereby authorize payment of benefits directly to my dentist.	Signature of Employee	Date
15. *Certification* — I **certify** the information I have provided is true and correct.	Signature of Employee	Date

Understanding Directions   Always read the directions before you begin filling out a form. The directions may be written at the top or bottom of the form or even on the back of the page. When directions refer to a specific line or box on the form, find that place on the form and think about what information you will put there.

Some directions are contained within the form. Box 5 on this form asks for the employee's name. The instructions in parentheses tell how to write the name. Some instructions use abbreviations. In Box 3 the letter *M* stands for *male* and *F* stands for *female*. In Box 4 the letters *m/d/y* stand for *month, day,* and *year*.

1 Look at Box 4. What date do you write?
   a.   today's date   b.   the patient's date of birth

2 Review the instructions at the top of the form. Should every patient sign lines 13, 14, and 15?
   a.   Yes   b.   No

Credit card companies send all kinds of offers through the mail. Once you accept an offer, the company will send you a legal document that tells exactly what your responsibilities are to the credit card company. Read these documents carefully before you sign them. Make sure that you understand what you are agreeing to do.

CREDIT CARD AGREEMENT: I understand that the use of the enclosed credit card will **constitute** my acceptance of the terms and conditions listed below.

TERMS AND CONDITIONS

A. Annual Percentage Rate

With a balance transfer from another credit card account: I agree to pay a 5.9% **introductory** rate for purchases and balance transfers for the first six months the account is open; after that, a 12.9% rate on purchases and balance transfers.

Without an initial balance transfer: I agree to pay a fixed 12.9% rate for purchases and balance transfers; the rate for cash advances is 19.9%.

B. Late Payments

If payment is received late once during the introductory period, the rate will adjust to 12.9% on purchases and balance transfers. If payment is received late twice within any six-month period, a 19.9% annual rate will immediately take effect.

C. Grace Period

Provided your previous balance was paid in full, you have a grace period of 20 to 25 days from the date of the statement to pay any balance arising from purchases. If the payment is made within the grace period, no interest will be charged.

D. Annual Fee

None.

E. Transaction Fee for Cash Advances

If you use your card to borrow cash, you will be charged a fee of 3% of the amount of each cash advance, but not less than $5 nor more than $45.

Using Context Clues to Understand Meaning   Legal documents often contain unfamiliar terms. When you come across an unfamiliar word, first look at the words and phrases around it. These surrounding words are the context. The context contains clues that can help you figure out the meaning of the unfamiliar word.

1 Reread Section C. Based on the context, what is the meaning of the term *grace period*?

   a.   A period of time in which the customer will not be charged interest

   b.   A period of time in which the customer will pay a lower rate of interest

2 Reread Section A. Based on the context clues in the section, what is a *balance transfer*?

   a.   Switching an amount of money owed to one credit card over to another

   b.   Changing the amount of interest owed after the introductory period is over

Thinking About the Forms and the Document

Practice Vocabulary

The words below are in the passages in bold type. Study the context in which the words appear. Then complete each sentence by writing the correct word.

authorize	certify	constitute
introductory	references	specify

1 Breaking a rule of the club will _____ an end to your membership.

2 When she applied for the job, Pat listed two friends

as _____ .

3 A customer complained that there was an incorrect amount on her bill.

Please ask her to _____ which amount is incorrect.

4 After you receive your new credit card, you will have a three-month

_____ period when you will not pay any interest.

5 You can _____ a money transfer over the telephone by giving your account number and social security number.

6 Maria signed the job application form to _____ that the information in the form was true.

Understand What You Read

Write the answer to each question.

7 Read Section 1 of the Employment Application on page 181. Who would need to answer the question "Do you have a work permit?"

_____

8 Look at the form on page 182. What is the purpose of Box 2?

_____

9 Why does Box 13 in the Group Dental Claim Form require a signature?

_____

10 Read Section B of the Credit Card Agreement on page 183. What will cause the cardholder's interest rate to increase to 19.9%?

_____

Check your answers on page 248.

Apply Your Skills

Circle the number of the best answer for each question.

11 Look at the Employment Application form on page 181. Read the headings for Section 2. Which of the following information is <u>not</u> needed to fill out Section 2?
(1) The name of the position you held on your last job
(2) The position you are applying for
(3) The date that you started your last job
(4) The name of your supervisor on your last job
(5) The amount you were paid on your last job

12 Look at the Group Dental Claim Form on page 182. According to the instructions, what should an employee do in order to tell the insurance company to send payment directly to the dentist?
(1) The employee should fill out Boxes 1 through 4.
(2) The employee should leave Line 15 unsigned.
(3) The employee should sign and date Line 14.
(4) The employee should check "Yes" in Box 11.
(5) The employee should attach the form to the dental bills.

13 Look at Section E in the Credit Card Agreement on page 183. Which words provide a context clue for the meaning of the term "cash advance"?
(1) "not less than $5 nor more than $45"
(2) "you will be charged a fee"
(3) "for the first six months the account is open"
(4) "if the payment is made within the grace period"
(5) "if you use your card to borrow cash"

Connect with the Forms and the Document

Write your answer to each question.

14 Suppose you have a friend who is beginning a job search. What advice could you give about filling out employment applications?

_____

_____

15 Do you believe that companies should try harder to write documents in everyday language? Or, would everyday language cause confusion since words can mean different things to different people? Explain.

_____

_____

Manuals and Handbooks

Setting the Stage

Manuals and **handbooks** are usually not read from cover to cover. Instead they are used to find specific information. To find out your company's dress code, you would look in the employee handbook for that particular topic. To find out how to set the clock on your VCR, you would consult the owner's manual for that particular procedure.

PREVIEW THE MANUAL AND THE HANDBOOKS

Manuals and handbooks often use **heads** and **subheads** to make information easy to find. Preview the heads and subheads for the manuals and handbooks on pages 187–189. Then answer these questions.

1 Look at the Personnel Policies on page 187. Write a question that you think you could answer from the information on the page.

_____

2 Look at the Microwave Oven Manual on page 188. Which section would you go to in order to find out where to get your microwave oven repaired?

_____

RELATE TO THE MANUAL AND THE HANDBOOKS

The procedure on page 189 tells how to clean up dangerous spills to prevent the spread of disease.

3 Have you ever been in an emergency situation? If so, what did you do? If not, imagine an emergency that might happen at work or at home. How would you know what to do?

_____

_____

VOCABULARY

probationary	**reinstated**	**eligible**
precautions	**technicians**	**contaminated**

Most workplaces have an employee handbook to explain the company's personnel policies. Employees are usually given a copy of the handbook when they begin work.

Personnel Policies

Probationary Period

Your first six months of employment are a **probationary** period. During this time, your supervisor works closely with you to help you learn your duties. After six months, your supervisor will give you a written evaluation. If your work is satisfactory for this six-month period, you become a permanent employee with health care and retirement benefits.

Health Care Benefits

As a permanent employee, you are entitled to sign up for a medical and dental health care plan. Your supervisor will give you a booklet explaining the various group insurance plans available to permanent employees. Please select a health care plan and go to the Human Resources Office, Room 201, to fill out the necessary paperwork.

Types of Leave

1. **Sick Leave:** Each full-time permanent employee earns eight hours of sick leave per month. For part-time employees, sick leave is based on the number of regular hours you are assigned to work. You may use sick leave for any illness, for pregnancy, or for visits to a doctor or dentist. You may also use sick leave when there is illness in your immediate family (parent, brother, sister, husband, wife, or child).

2. **Maternity Leave:** You may be granted maternity leave if you plan to return to work as soon as your doctor permits. By law, if you return to work within four months of the start of your leave, you must be **reinstated** in the position you held before the leave.

3. **Family Leave:** After one year of employment, you are **eligible** for family leave to handle urgent family matters. Family leave is limited to four months during a twenty-four-month period.

4. **Vacation Leave:** Full-time employees receive ten hours of vacation leave for each month worked with a maximum of 15 days per year. Part-time vacation leave is based upon the average number of hours worked per month. Vacation leave must be cleared with your supervisor.

Using Heads and Subheads   Information in manuals and handbooks is often organized using heads and subheads. A head is the title of a section. It gives you an idea of the main idea of the section. Subheads are used to break the main section into smaller parts. Before you begin reading, preview the heads and subheads. Think about how the subheads are related to the main head.

1. Which of these is a kind of leave described in this policy manual?
   a. Family Leave
   b. Unpaid Leave

2. Which heading would you look under to find out more about your dental benefits?
   a. Sick Leave
   b. Health Care Benefits

Most household appliances come with manuals. These manuals provide the operating instructions and explain the safety guidelines for the appliance.

Microwave Oven Operating Guide

Using the Timer—Use the built-in timer to keep track of parts of the cooking process. The timer operates without microwave energy.
- Push the Timer button.
- Enter the time in minutes and seconds using the Number Pad.
- Then press Start. The timer will beep when the time is up.

Using the MicroTime Feature—MicroTime allows you to microwave for a set amount of time. Use this feature for regular microwave cooking.
- Place the food or beverage on the turntable. Push the MicroTime button.
- Enter the time to cook in minutes and seconds using the Number Pad.
- Push the Power Level button and select a power from 1 (low) to 10 (high).
- Then press Start. When the time is up, the oven will beep and flash the word "Done" in the display window. Open the door and remove your food or beverage.

Important Safety Precautions—Make sure you read and understand these safety **precautions** before using your oven. Keep this manual in a convenient location for future reference.
- Closed jars and tightly sealed containers may explode. Do not heat them in the microwave oven.
- Cookware may become very hot. Use potholders to remove cookware from the oven.
- Liquids may start to boil after removal from the microwave oven. To prevent burns, stir the liquid briefly before removing it from the oven.
- Hot foods may have steam, which can cause burns. When opening bags and containers of hot food, direct the steam away from your hands and face.

If You Need Service—We hope you will never need assistance with your Microwave Oven, but if you do, qualified **technicians** are ready to help at a Service Center near you.
- Turn to the Repair Services list on page 87 of this manual or call 1-800-555-OVEN.
- Call the nearest Service Center in your area. Be prepared to give the serial number on the back of the oven and the date of purchase. A service representative will help you.

Skimming and Scanning to Find Information   When you need to get the general idea of a manual or handbook, **skim**, or read quickly, through the information. Look for heads and subheads as you read. When you need to find specific information, **scan** the material. To scan, read quickly to find numbers, amounts, and important words.

1 What is the purpose of the Power Level button? Skim the material to find the answer.
   a.   The Power Level button is used to choose how long to cook the food.
   b.   The Power Level button is used to choose how much power to use in cooking the food.

2 What telephone number should you call to find a Service Center? Scan the material to find the answer.
   a.   1-800-555-OVEN
   b.   1-800-555-FOOD

Check your answers on page 249.

Every job site, even an office, has safety procedures to help employees handle emergency situations. Safety procedures may be posted on bulletin boards or kept in special notebooks for employee use. The safety procedures below might be found in a handbook of emergency procedures for a health care facility, a community center, or a school office.

CLEANUP OF SPILLS RELATED TO ILLNESS AND INJURY

Goal: To prevent the spread of disease in the workplace

General Information: Special handling and cleanup procedures are required for fluids that may contain blood or blood products. After contact with blood or other dangerous material, trained personnel must clean all equipment and work surfaces.

Use the following cleaning procedures:

Step 1: Put on appropriate protective clothing and equipment, including vinyl gloves, filter mask and/or face shield, and plastic apron or disposable coveralls.

Step 2: Wipe up any fluids with paper towels and dispose of them in a red trash bag with the biohazard warning symbol (shown here to the right).

Step 3: Clean all **contaminated** areas and materials first with soap and water.

Step 4: Follow with a freshly made bleach solution (1 part bleach to 9 parts cold water).

Step 5: Allow the bleach solution to remain on the contaminated surface for 5 to 10 minutes. Then rinse the area thoroughly with water to prevent damage to the surface from the bleach.

Note: If the spill occurs outside, use a hose with the water turned on at full force to wash down the area completely.

Step 6: If mops, brooms, dustpans, or other equipment have been used in the cleanup, rinse these items with the bleach solution.

For more information, call the Environmental Health and Safety Department.

Following a Sequence of Steps   A procedure is a way to do something. Most procedures have a series of steps that must be done in order to reach a desired outcome. When you read a procedure, make sure you understand the **sequence** of steps. Some steps may contain one or more related tasks. As you read, picture yourself performing each action. Try to understand why the sequence is the way it is.

❶ Which statement describes the correct sequence to use in cleaning up a spill related to illness or injury?
 a. After wiping the contaminated surface with paper towels, put on protective clothing.
 b. After putting on protective clothing, wipe the contaminated surface with paper towels.

❷ When should you use the bleach solution?
 a. Before cleaning the area with soap and water.
 b. After cleaning the area with soap and water.

Thinking About the Manual and the Handbooks

Practice Vocabulary

The words below are in the passages in bold type. Study the context in which the words appear. Then complete each sentence by writing the correct word.

contaminated	eligible	precautions
probationary	reinstated	technicians

1. Wearing gloves is one of the important _____ for working with dangerous cleaning supplies.

2. The new employee's work during the _____ period was good.

3. Our skilled _____ will help repair problems with your dishwasher.

4. Bacteria in raw chicken _____ surfaces in the kitchen.

5. After two years, you will be _____ for our retirement plan.

6. After taking time off to care for his elderly father, Kyle was

   _____ to his former work assignment.

Understand What You Read

Write the answer to each question.

7. Look at the Personnel Policies handbook on page 187. After six months, how will a supervisor give a new employee feedback about his or her work?

   _____

8. According to the Personnel Policies handbook, when can an employee use sick leave?

   _____

   _____

9. Look at the Operating Guide on page 188. After microwaving food in a closed container, why should you point it away from your face as you open it?

   _____

Check your answers on page 249.

Apply Your Skills

Circle the number of the best answer for each question.

10 Look at the Personnel Policies on page 187. Your friend needs to help her mother move to a nursing home. She wants to find out how much time she can take off work without losing her job. Which heading would you tell your friend to look under to find the information she needs?
(1) Probationary Period
(2) Health Care Benefits
(3) Maternity Leave
(4) Family Leave
(5) Vacation Leave

11 Scan the Operating Guide on page 188. What is the purpose of the MicroTime button on the microwave oven? Its purpose is
(1) to allow you to cook food for a certain amount of time.
(2) to allow you to operate the built-in timer.
(3) to allow you to set the cooking temperature.
(4) to help prevent burns from hot liquids and steam.
(5) to allow you to heat closed jars and containers.

12 Look at the safety procedures on page 189. A young child at a day care center cuts her lip. She gets a small amount of blood on a table. After the day care worker puts on gloves and wipes the table with paper towels, what should she do next?
(1) Clean the table with soap and water
(2) Take the table outside and wash it with a garden hose
(3) Make a fresh bleach solution
(4) Rinse the table with clean water
(5) Dispose of the paper towels in a red trash bag

Connect with the Manual and the Handbooks

Write your answer to each question.

13 Suppose you are starting a new job. Your supervisor gives you a 100-page employee handbook. Should you read the entire handbook? Explain.

_____

_____

14 If you were writing the perfect instruction manual, what features (such as drawings or steps) would you include?

_____

_____

Drawings and Diagrams

Setting the Stage

Drawings and **diagrams** can often communicate what words cannot. When drawings are combined with words, they can help us learn how to operate new pieces of equipment or how to repair or build things. They can also improve our understanding of how to solve problems and do our jobs.

PREVIEW THE DRAWING AND THE DIAGRAMS

When you see a drawing or a diagram, think about how the words and pictures work together to help you understand something. Look at the first few captions or phrases on the drawings and diagrams on pages 193–195. Then answer these questions.

1 Look at the drawing of the computer printer on page 193. Name one thing you think this drawing might help you learn.

_____

2 Look at the chart on page 195. What does it show you how to do?

_____

RELATE TO THE DRAWING AND THE DIAGRAMS

Many instructions have both words and drawings. Look at the instructions for wrapping an injured wrist on page 194.

3 Have drawings ever helped you make sense of written instructions? How? If not, can you think of some instructions that need drawings? Explain.

_____

_____

VOCABULARY

connection	**irregular**	**anchor**
ascend	**implement**	**inventory**

Check your answers on page 250.

Instructions often make more sense when they are accompanied by a drawing. Many owner's manuals and operator's guides have drawings to help you become familiar with the parts of the machine you are learning to use.

Identifying the Parts of Your LaserPro Printer

The illustration on this page will help you locate the parts of your LaserPro Printer. Take a few minutes to become familiar with these parts.

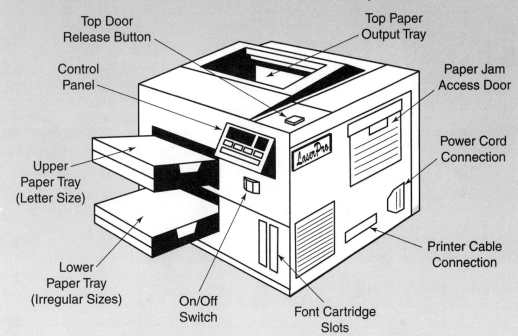

Getting Started With Your LaserPro Printer—Begin by plugging the power cord into the power cord **connection** on the printer. Then connect the other end to the electrical outlet. Use the printer cable to connect the printer port on your computer to the printer cable connection on your printer.

Adding Paper—Your LaserPro Printer has two paper trays. Load up to 250 sheets of regular $8 \frac{1}{2} \times 11$ inch paper in the upper paper tray. You can print on **irregular** sizes of paper by changing the settings on the control panel to match the length and width of the paper, which is put in the lower paper tray.

Understanding the Main Idea   The main idea of a drawing or diagram is its purpose. Reading the title can help you understand the main idea. To understand a drawing, read everything on it. Study the details. Ask yourself: Why have I been given this drawing? What is it supposed to help me understand?

Which of the following gives the main idea of the drawing above? In other words, what can you expect to learn from the drawing?

   a.   The parts of a LaserPro Printer

   b.   How to clear paper jams in a LaserPro Printer

Step-by-step instructions use words and diagrams together to help readers understand how to perform each step. The instructions below could be found in a first-aid manual.

HOW TO WRAP AN INJURED WRIST

Use an elastic bandage, 2 to 3 inches wide. Stretch the bandage slightly to provide support to the injured wrist. The bandage should not cause discomfort. Do not stretch the bandage so tightly that you reduce the flow of blood to the hand.

Step 1. Anchor the end of the bandage by loosely making one complete turn around the wrist.

Step 2. Stretch the bandage as you bring it across the back of the hand and through the web space between the thumb and index finger.

Step 3. Bring the bandage across the palm of the hand to the wrist.

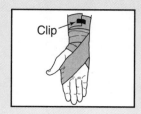

Step 4. Bring the bandage around the back of the wrist, across the palm to below the base of the little finger, and once more through the web space and back to the wrist.

Step 5. Begin wrapping the wrist. Gradually, **ascend** the wrist to the lower arm. Leave the final 4 to 6 inches of the bandage unstretched. Then fasten the end of the bandage to the layer beneath with a clip.

Using Text and Diagrams Together   Whenever text refers to a drawing or diagram, take time to study the illustration. Think about the connection between the words and the pictures before you go on to the next step. To understand what takes place in each step, study how the pictures change from step to step.

1 Where should you place the end of the bandage to begin the wrapping?
   a.   Place the end of the bandage on the front (palm side) of the wrist.
   b.   Place the end of the bandage on the back of the wrist.

2 How many times does the bandage wrap through the web space between the thumb and index finger?
   a.   The bandage wraps three times through the web space.
   b.   The bandage wraps twice through the web space.

   Check your answers on page 250.

The diagram below is called a **flow chart.** It shows a process that is used in the workplace. Employers use diagrams like this to help their workers do their jobs efficiently.

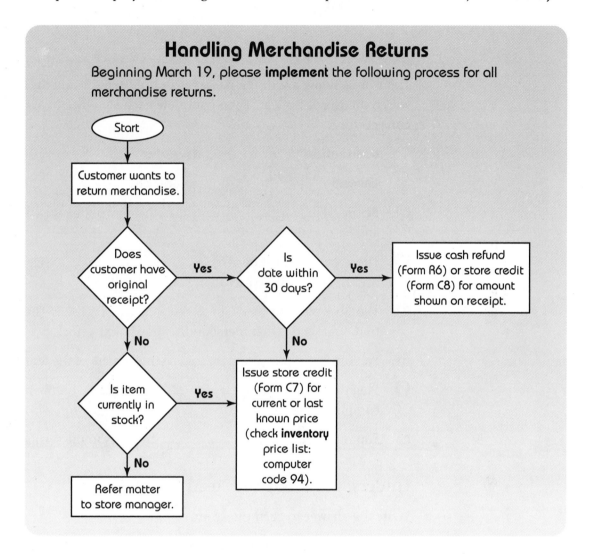

Handling Merchandise Returns

Beginning March 19, please **implement** the following process for all merchandise returns.

Start

Customer wants to return merchandise.

Does customer have original receipt? — **Yes** → Is date within 30 days? — **Yes** → Issue cash refund (Form R6) or store credit (Form C8) for amount shown on receipt.

Does customer have original receipt? — **No** ↓

Is date within 30 days? — **No** ↓ Issue store credit (Form C7) for current or last known price (check **inventory** price list: computer code 94).

Is item currently in stock? — **Yes** → Issue store credit (Form C7)...

Is item currently in stock? — **No** ↓ Refer matter to store manager.

Following a Process In a flow chart, different shapes are used for the steps in the process. Arrows show in what order the steps must be taken. To use a flow chart, begin at the shape marked "Start." Then follow the arrows. When you come to a decision step, answer the question and follow the appropriate path.

1 A customer wants to return a pair of shoes. The customer gives the employee the original receipt. What should the employee do next?
   a. Check to make sure the item is still in stock.
   b. Check the date on the receipt.

2 A customer wants to return a shirt that she received as a gift. The customer doesn't have the receipt, and the store no longer sells the shirt. What should the employee do?
   a. Refer the matter to the store manager.
   b. Check the inventory price list.

Thinking About the Drawing and the Diagrams

Practice Vocabulary

The words below are in the passages in bold type. Study the context in which the words appear. Then complete each sentence by writing the correct word.

connection	irregular	anchor
ascend	implement	inventory

1 Before we _____ the new policy, we will meet to answer questions.

2 Those pillows must be a(n) _____ size because I couldn't find pillowcases that would fit well.

3 The store plans to check the _____ Thursday night to find out exactly what merchandise they have in stock.

4 You must _____ the corners of the tent firmly.

5 Plug this cable into the _____ on the back of the computer case.

6 You must _____ the stairs to the second floor.

Understand What You Read

Write the answer to each question.

7 Look at the drawing of the computer printer on page 193. How would you explain to someone where the On/Off Switch is located?

_____

8 Look at the instructions on how to wrap an injured wrist on page 194. When should you begin stretching the elastic bandage?

_____

9 After you have wrapped the injured wrist, how do you fasten the bandage?

_____

10 Look at the flow chart diagram on page 195. How can an employee find out the last known price for an item?

_____

Apply Your Skills

Circle the number of the best answer for each question.

11 Look at the drawing of the printer on page 193 and the information under it. What is the printer cable connection used for?
(1) It opens the printer in case paper gets stuck.
(2) It connects to an electrical outlet.
(3) It connects to the computer.
(4) It counts the number of pages that are printed.
(5) It changes the settings so that irregular paper can be used.

12 Look at the instructions on page 194. Based on the drawings and the text, where should the end of the bandage be?
(1) The bandage should end at the fingertips.
(2) The bandage will usually end on the back of the hand.
(3) The bandage should end just below the base of the little finger.
(4) The bandage should end at the base of the hand.
(5) The bandage should end part of the way up the lower arm.

13 Look at the flow chart diagram on page 195. A customer wants to return a coat and receive store credit to make another purchase. The employee believes the coat was not purchased at this store. What is the first thing the employee should do?
(1) Talk to the manager about the situation.
(2) Examine the coat to see if it has any sales tags.
(3) Check to see if the coat is currently in stock.
(4) Ask the customer for the sales receipt.
(5) Ask if the coat was purchased within the last 30 days.

Connect with the Drawing and the Diagrams

Write your answer to each question.

14 When would a flow chart be most helpful in learning a new procedure?

_____

_____

_____

15 Have you ever had to learn how to use an unfamiliar piece of equipment? How did you go about it? Would drawings and diagrams have made the task easier?

_____

_____

Charts and Graphs

Setting the Stage

Charts are designed to make it easy to find important information. **Graphs** create pictures of information. Companies use charts and graphs to see whether they are meeting their goals. Newspapers and magazines print charts and graphs to inform the public. By studying a chart or graph, you can figure out the main idea of the information and draw your own conclusions.

PREVIEW THE CHART AND THE GRAPHS

You should be able to see the main idea of a chart or graph at a glance. Read the titles and labels for the chart and the graphs on pages 199–203. Then answer these questions.

1 Look at the chart on page 199. What might you use this chart for?

_____

2 Look at the graph on page 202. Why do you think the hospital might have created this graph?

_____

RELATE TO THE CHART AND THE GRAPHS

Graphs can help us see information in new and useful ways. They can help us make decisions and draw conclusions.

3 Have you ever used the information in a chart or a graph to make a decision? What was it? If not, what kind of information would you like to see in a chart or a graph?

_____

_____

VOCABULARY

overdraft	projections	bimonthly
priorities	allocated	

Charts are used to organize information. The organization makes it easier to find the facts you need. Charts are everywhere. You see them in newspapers, in magazines, in stores, and on the Internet. The chart below is given to new banking customers.

Universal Bank Checking Accounts

Note: Unless your plan offers **overdraft** protection, any check written for an amount greater than your account balance will be returned unpaid. With overdraft protection, your check (up to an amount of $500) will be paid and you will have five days to deposit the required funds. There is a $25 fee for each overdraft.

Plan Name	Minimum Balance Required	Monthly Service Charge	Fees Per Check	Interest Earned	Special Banking Services
Personal Checking	None	$6.50	$0.10	None	Pay bills by phone for only $3.95 per month
Direct Deposit Checking	None	None	$0.10	None	Pay bills by phone free
Standard Checking	$1,000	$5.50	None	None	• Pay bills by phone free • Overdraft protection
Star Checking	None	$10.00	None	None	• No-fee regular savings account • 3 free money orders or cashier's checks per month
Silver Checking	$2,000	None	None	1%	• No-fee regular savings account • Overdraft protection • Bank debit card
Gold Checking	$10,000	None	None	4%	• Low-interest credit card • No-fee regular savings account • Check printing at no charge • Safe deposit box
Student Checking	None	$6.50	$0.50	None	None

Understanding Organization   Charts organize information in **columns** and **rows**. The information in each column is similar. It belongs in the same category. The heading for each column tells you the category of information in the column. The first column usually provides a name for each row on the chart. To find a specific fact on a chart, find the appropriate row, then read across until you come to the column you want.

1 Suppose you want a checking account that does not require you to keep a minimum balance in your account. Which column should you look in for this information?

  a.   Monthly Service Charge   b.   Minimum Balance Required

2 Use the Special Banking Services column. Which plans offer overdraft protection?

  a.   Standard Checking and   b.   Silver Checking and
       Silver Checking   Gold Checking

Businesses often use **bar graphs** to display financial information. The bar graph below shows the projected sales for each department in the store for the month of April.

To: Family SuperStore Department Managers

This graph shows our sales **projections** for next month. We have made these predictions based on our sales last April and our sales totals for January and February of this year. Please use this information to set individual sales goals for April.

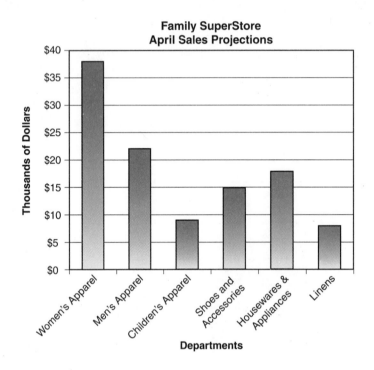

Family SuperStore April Sales Projections

Understanding Graphs Bar graphs use bars to represent data. To understand the main idea of the graph, read the title of the graph. Also, scan the labels along the sides and bottom of the graph.

The lengths of the bars will help you understand what numbers they represent. The bars extend along a scale, much like a ruler. Read the labels on the scale to understand the size of the numbers. For example, a scale may be marked with the numbers 1 to 10, but the numbers may represent millions of dollars.

To figure out the number that a bar represents, draw an imaginary line from the top of the bar to the scale. Then figure out what number would lie at that point on the scale.

1 Which department is projected to have between $20,000 and $25,000 in sales in April?
  a. Women's Apparel
  b. Men's Apparel

2 Which department is projected to have more sales in April?
  a. Shoes and Accessories
  b. Housewares & Appliances

Graphs are often created by businesses or research organizations to help the public understand data. But graphs can also be used by families to make financial decisions. Some families use a computer program to keep track of their income and expenses. These programs can produce graphs and charts to make it easier to see changes in the family's financial picture. This graph compares the Gallindo family's gas bills for two different years. The **bimonthly** organization of the graph shows how much they spent for each two-month period.

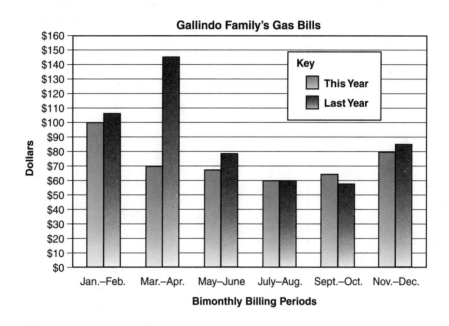

Understanding Graphs   A **double-bar graph** has two bars for each label along the base of the graph. Each bar is a different color. A **key** explains the meaning of the colors of the bars.

You can **compare** and **contrast** information on the graph by looking at the lengths of the bars. A longer bar represents a greater amount and a shorter bar represents a lesser amount.

1 In which bimonthly billing period last year did the Gallindo family have the highest gas bill?
   a.   January–February
   b.   March–April

2 In which bimonthly billing period did the Gallindo family spend the same amount this year as they did last year on their gas bill?
   a.   May–June
   b.   July–August

3 In which bimonthly billing period did the Gallindo family spend more this year than they did last year?
   a.   March–April
   b.   September–October

Government and health agencies sometimes prepare graphs to help us understand how our life choices affect our safety. You might see this type of graph in a newspaper article.

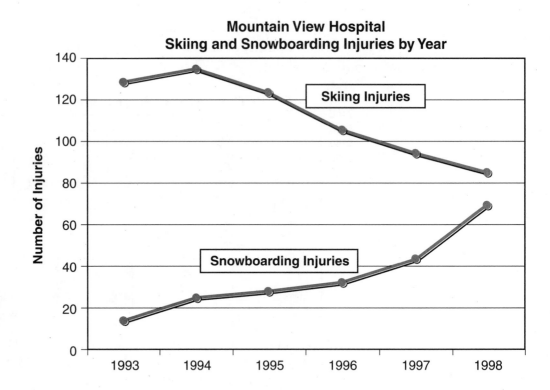

**Mountain View Hospital
Skiing and Snowboarding Injuries by Year**

Understanding Graphs Line graphs are useful for showing how something changes over time. Sometimes we are able to see a **trend,** or tendency, in the movement of the line. In other words, the line seems to move in the same direction over a period of time. This suggests that it will continue to do so. Seeing a trend can help us make predictions about what will happen in the near future. The line graph above has two lines, each representing a different trend.

❶ In which year were there about 40 snowboarding injuries?
   a.   1997
   b.   1998

❷ Which statement best describes the trend in skiing injuries from 1993 to 1998?
   a.   Except for a slight rise in 1994, skiing injuries have declined steadily.
   b.   Skiing injuries have remained about the same for the years shown on the graph.

❸ Based on the trends shown on the graph, which of these conclusions makes more sense?
   a.   There will always be more skiing than snowboarding injuries.
   b.   Eventually, there will be more snowboarding injuries than skiing injuries.

                    Check your answers on page 251.

Circle graphs are often used to communicate information about finances. Government agencies sometimes create **circle graphs** to show the public how their tax dollars are spent. Charities sometimes make circle graphs to show supporters how their donations are spent. You can find circle graphs in newspaper articles and brochures.

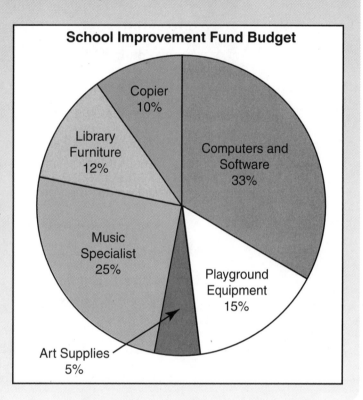

Riverdale Public Schools

Dear Parents,

The School Council has determined the following spending **priorities** for the coming school year. The Council has **allocated** amounts from the School Improvement Fund Budget to cover the expenses that we have determined to be most important. Our School Council meets on the second Thursday of each month. Please feel free to attend.

School Improvement Fund Budget

- Copier 10%
- Library Furniture 12%
- Computers and Software 33%
- Music Specialist 25%
- Playground Equipment 15%
- Art Supplies 5%

Understanding Graphs   Circle graphs, also called pie charts, usually show information about finances. The whole circle represents the total amount. The sections of the circle represent parts of the total amount.

To understand a circle graph, read the labels and percents written in the sections. For example, a section labeled 50% is half the size of the total circle because 50% is half of 100%. You can also compare the sizes of the sections to draw conclusions about the amounts of money the sections represent.

❶ What does the School Council plan to spend more money on?
a.   Computers and Software
b.   Library Furniture

❷ On what item does the School Council plan to spend 25% of its money?
a.   Playground Equipment
b.   Music Specialist

Thinking About the Chart and the Graphs

Practice Vocabulary

The words below are in the passages in bold type. Study the context in which the words appear. Then complete each sentence by writing the correct word.

overdraft	**projections**	**bimonthly**
priorities	**allocated**	

1 The _____ magazine is published six times a year.

2 The check was considered a(n) _____ because the writer of the check did not have enough money in his account to cover it.

3 Based on our high profits for the first quarter of this year, I am raising my _____ for the rest of the year.

4 The city council _____ $212,000 to street repairs.

5 The library committee agreed that the top _____ were buying new books and lighting the parking lot.

Understand What You Read

Write the answer to each question.

6 Look at the chart of checking account plans on page 199. What is the monthly service charge for a customer who has the Silver Checking plan?

_____

7 Look at the bar graph on page 200. Which department at the store is expected to have the lowest sales? How much is it projected to sell?

_____

8 Look at the line graph on page 202. About how many patients were treated at Mountain View Hospital in 1995 for skiing injuries?

_____

9 Look at the circle graph on page 203. On what item does the School Council intend to spend the least amount? What percent will be spent on this item?

_____

Check your answers on page 251.

Apply Your Skills

Circle the number of the best answer for each question.

10 Look at the chart on page 199. Which checking account plan requires a minimum balance and charges a monthly service fee?
(1) Personal Checking
(2) Direct Deposit Checking
(3) Standard Checking
(4) Star Checking
(5) Silver Checking

11 Look at the double-bar graph on page 201. Compare the bars for this year and last year for each billing period. In which period was there the greatest difference between the amounts of the two bills?
(1) March–April
(2) May–June
(3) July–August
(4) September–October
(5) November–December

12 Look at the line graph on page 202. If the trends for both skiing and snowboarding injuries continue, which statement best describes what you would expect to see in 1999?
(1) There will be no snowboarding or skiing injuries.
(2) There will be more than 300 skiing and snowboarding injuries.
(3) There will be more snowboarding injuries than skiing injuries.
(4) The numbers of both types of injuries will increase.
(5) The numbers of both types of injuries will decrease.

Connect with the Chart and the Graphs

Write your answer to each question.

13 Look at the line graph on page 202. Why do you think the number of snowboarding injuries is increasing? Based on the graph, can you conclude that skiing is safer than snowboarding? Explain your thinking.

_____

_____

14 Look at the circle graph on page 203. Does your household have a budget? How could a circle graph help your household understand its spending?

_____

_____

Reading at Work

Communications: Desktop Publishing

Desktop publishing workers use computers to design pages.

You see the results of their work everywhere—in catalogs, magazines, menus, ads, and brochures. You find them working at advertising agencies, newspapers and magazines, book publishers, and graphic design studios. They are desktop publishers. If you like to work with computers and you have a flair for design, then desktop publishing may be a job for you.

Desktop publishing workers use computers to create a wide range of visual communications. To do their work, they follow directions (called specifications) developed by an art director or a designer. These specifications tell the desktop publisher how to present the text and the pictures (called graphics) on a project. Desktop publishers should have a good eye for detail and an ability to follow the written and visual directions in a manual or on a computer screen.

Look at the chart on Some Careers in Graphic Communications.

- Do any of the careers interest you? If so, which ones?

- What information would you need to find out more about those careers? On a separate piece of paper, write some questions that you would like answered. You can find out more information about those careers in the *Occupational Outlook Handbook* at your local library.

Use the desktop publishing directions below to answer the questions. Circle the correct answer for each question.

Using Text Design to Communicate Effectively

Good design helps a reader get the most out of information. Practice using these effective design techniques to lay out a section of text.

1. Place all heads or titles in **bold** type and capital letters.
2. Number each direction or step in a process.
3. Put all specialized terms or vocabulary words in **bold** type.
4. Use *italic* type when you want to emphasize a word.
5. When working with a list, use the following set of rules:
   - insert a bullet (a small circle) before *every* rule.
   - capitalize the first letter of the first word after the bullet.
   - put each rule on its *own* line.

① According to the directions, how should a title or heading be treated?
   (1) numbered
   (2) capitalized and bold type
   (3) on its own line
   (4) italic type
   (5) preceded by a bullet

② According to the rules, which words in number 5 above are being emphasized to the reader?
   (1) design techniques
   (2) bold type
   (3) number each direction
   (4) every, own
   (5) capitalize the first letter

③ Which of the following rules is <u>not</u> being followed in the directions?
   (1) Place all heads or titles in bold type and capital letters.
   (2) Number each direction to keep track of your work.
   (3) Insert a bullet (a small circle) before *every* rule.
   (4) Capitalize the first letter of the first word after a bullet.
   (5) Put each rule on its own line.

④ Below is a specialized vocabulary word that might be used in desktop publishing directions. Based on the directions, which form is correct?
   (1) **font**
   (2) FONT
   (3) *Font*
   (4) font
   (5) <u>font</u>

Read the schedule and registration form for a summer camp for children.

Summer Day Camp Registration Form

Child's Name: Last _____ First _____

Parent's Name: Last _____ First _____

Child's Birthdate _____ Age _____ Grade in Fall _____ Gender M ☐ F ☐

Address _____ City _____ State _____ Zip _____

Home Phone _____ Work Phone _____ Cellular Phone/Pager _____

Camp Schedule
All Camps–Regular Hours–Monday through Friday: 9:30 A.M.–3:30 P.M.

Summer Camps	Ages	Dates	Fees
Summer Day Camp	5–12	June 21–August 27	$115/week
Sports Camp I	7–10	June 21–July 23	$130/week
Sports Camp II	11–14	July 12–August 27	$140/week
Performing Arts Camp	8–14	June 14–July 16	$120/week

Emergency Contacts (other than parent)

I authorize only these additional persons to pick up my child:

Name _____ Phone (____) _____ Relation _____

Name _____ Phone (____) _____ Relation _____

If your child becomes ill, we will attempt to reach you by telephone. If we cannot reach you and your child's medical situation seems urgent, we will call for emergency services to take your child to the hospital. Please provide the name of your child's doctor and any necessary insurance information so that your child can be treated promptly.

Is your child on any medications? _____ Allergies? _____

Insurance Company Name _____ Medical Group/Policy # _____

Doctor's Name _____ Doctor's Phone # _____

I have read and agree to the policies and procedures listed on page 14 of the Summer Camp Guide. Children not signed out of any camp by 3:30 P.M. will automatically be placed in Extended Care and will be charged $10 per 30 minutes or any portion thereof.

Note: Please have your child wear a camp T-shirt each day.

Signature of Parent/Guardian _____ Date _____

Items 1–8 refer to the form and schedule on page 208.

Write the answer to each question.

1 What must parents read and agree to?

_____

2 How can you authorize a friend to pick up your child?

_____

3 How old must your child be in order to attend the Performing Arts Camp?

_____

4 What should children wear to camp?

_____

5 What information do parents need to give about their child's doctor?

_____

Circle the number of the best answer for each question.

6 A family of an 11-year-old child is planning a vacation starting on August 1. They want to choose a camp that will be completed by that time. Which of the following camps could they choose for their child?
(1) Summer Day Camp
(2) Sports Camp I
(3) Sports Camp II
(4) Performing Arts Camp
(5) None of the camps will be completed by August 1.

7 What will happen if a child is not picked up by 3:30 P.M.?
(1) The camp director will call the parent.
(2) The child will be allowed to call one of the emergency contacts.
(3) The parent will be charged for Extended Care.
(4) The child will be released to go home with another family.
(5) The child will be driven home at 5 P.M. by the camp director.

8 If a child becomes ill, what will the camp do first?
(1) The camp will call the insurance company or medical group.
(2) The camp will call for emergency services.
(3) The camp will call the emergency contact listed on the form.
(4) The camp will call the child's doctor.
(5) The camp will try to contact the parent or guardian by telephone.

Read the directions and the diagram from a computer manual.

Setting Up Your New Computer

Before you begin setting up your new computer, make sure that you have chosen a location with sufficient room for the CPU, monitor, and other devices.

The CPU, or central processing unit, is the main box into which you will plug the other pieces of equipment, or peripherals. Each peripheral, including the monitor, printer, keyboard, and mouse, plugs into the CPU.

Each peripheral comes with its own connector. A connector is like a plug with a number of pins that stick out. The CPU has a number of ports, which are somewhat like electrical outlets, that accept the connectors. Make sure the connector lines up perfectly with the port. Then gently push the pins into the port.

Study the diagram below to plug in your keyboard, mouse, and monitor. Connect the speakers to the sound card and your phone line to the modem port. Attach power cords to the monitor and CPU. Finally, connect these cords to an electrical outlet through a high-quality surge protector. You are ready to turn on your computer.

Look closely at the shape of the connector on your mouse. If it is round, plug it into the PS/2 Port. Otherwise, use the Serial Port.

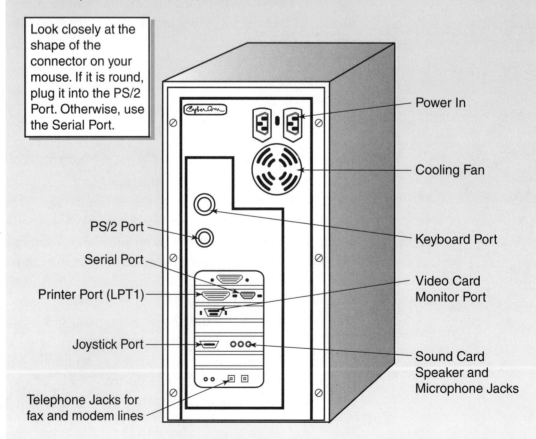

Look closely at the shape of the connector on your mouse. If it is round, plug it into the PS/2 Port. Otherwise, use the Serial Port.

Power In

Cooling Fan

PS/2 Port

Keyboard Port

Serial Port

Printer Port (LPT1)

Video Card Monitor Port

Joystick Port

Sound Card Speaker and Microphone Jacks

Telephone Jacks for fax and modem lines

Items 9–15 refer to the computer manual and diagram on page 210.

Complete each sentence by writing the correct term.

9   The monitor, printer, and keyboard are all _____ .

10   The letters *CPU* stand for _____ .

11   Each new piece of equipment will have a _____ that plugs into a port on the CPU.

12   The _____ card has a special jack that you can use to plug in a microphone.

Circle the number of the best answer for each question.

13   The connector on your mouse has a round shape. Where should you plug in the mouse connector?
(1)   the keyboard port
(2)   the serial port
(3)   the PS/2 port
(4)   the cooling fan
(5)   the sound card jacks

14   According to the diagram, which piece of equipment would you plug into the video card?
(1)   printer
(2)   monitor
(3)   keyboard
(4)   mouse
(5)   speakers

15   According to the manual, what is the last step in setting up the computer system?
(1)   Connect the speakers to the sound card.
(2)   Connect the mouse and keyboard to the CPU.
(3)   Connect the phone line to the modem.
(4)   Connect the monitor to the CPU.
(5)   Connect the power cords to an electrical outlet.

Read the following advertisement and graph.

There has never been a better time to fly Freedom Airlines.

Fly Freedom for $98 or Less

Are you planning a vacation this summer? You should, because now you can fly anywhere Freedom Airlines does for only $98 or less (each way with round trip purchase).

In a survey conducted by *Travel World* magazine, Freedom Airlines ranked #1 in customer satisfaction.

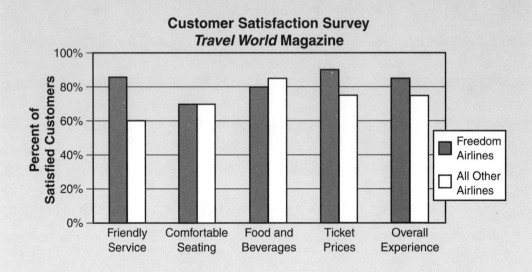

Customer Satisfaction Survey
***Travel World* Magazine**

Don't miss out on this great opportunity. Simply purchase your round trip ticket at least seven days in advance. You must pay for your ticket within 24 hours after making the reservation. Travel must be completed by August 31. Other restrictions are listed below.

Call your travel agent now. Remember, seats are limited. There may be no available seats on some flights during busy travel times and holiday periods.

Restrictions: Your travel plans must include a stayover of at least one night. If your travel plans change, your airline fare cannot be refunded, but the value of the ticket can be applied toward future travel on Freedom Airlines. Fares do not include airport and federal taxes.

Items 16–22 refer to the advertisement and graph on page 212.

Complete each sentence by writing the correct term.

⑯ This special deal has the following _____: your travel plans must include a stayover of at least one night.

⑰ The passenger made a _____ to travel to Chicago on May 24.

⑱ The cost of the ticket will not be _____ if you decide not to take the flight.

⑲ To get the special price, you must buy a _____ ticket.

Circle the number of the best answer for each question.

⑳ According to the graph, in which area did Freedom Airlines have the greatest percent of satisfied customers?
(1) Friendly Service
(2) Comfortable Seating
(3) Food and Beverages
(4) Ticket Prices
(5) Overall Experience

㉑ In what area in the survey did Freedom Airlines rank the same as the other airlines?
(1) Friendly Service
(2) Comfortable Seating
(3) Food and Beverages
(4) Ticket Prices
(5) Overall Experience

㉒ Based on the advertisement, which of these statements best explains what the airline wants the public to believe?
(1) Freedom Airlines is safer than other airlines.
(2) More customers fly on Freedom Airlines than on any other airlines.
(3) Freedom Airlines has more flights than other airlines.
(4) There are few restrictions on tickets purchased at Freedom Airlines.
(5) Freedom Airlines has the best ticket prices.

Prose and Visual Extension

Look through magazines for an advertisement that catches your attention. Write a brief description of the advertisement and explain why it appeals to you. Include the main idea of the advertisement as well as phrases that use emotional words to persuade you to buy the product or service. Which claims in the advertisement are facts? Which claims may not be true?

Reading Connection: Visual Information and American History

Our National Treasures

Art and the artists who create it are among our nation's greatest treasures. For many Americans, Ansel Adams and his photographs are examples of some of our nation's best artwork.

Much of Adams' art was based on natural landscapes and objects. His artistic eye, technical talents, and photography tools were used to manipulate the images. His technique heightened their visual impact, leaving the viewer with a powerful, memorable image. Although Adams used his camera to transform the way nature appeared, his art reflected the great respect he had for the American landscape.

Adams spent a significant part of his life taking photographs in another great U.S. treasure—the national park system. The photograph *Moon and Half Dome* taken in Yosemite National Park is an example of his work.

Photo of *Moon and Half Dome,* Ansel Adams, Yosemite National Park, California, 1960

History: The U.S. National Park System—Preserving the Lands for All to Enjoy

Yellowstone National Park, established in 1872, was America's first national park. Abraham Lincoln's approval of the Yosemite Grant in 1864 led the way. When Lincoln signed the legislation turning over the Yosemite territory to the state of California, the government began preserving and managing wilderness areas for use by all Americans.

By the time President Woodrow Wilson approved the National Park Service Organic Act in 1916, 40 national parks and monuments had already been set aside for the American public to enjoy. This new division within the Department of the Interior became responsible for protecting national parks like Yellowstone and Yosemite. It also established historic sites like Abraham Lincoln's birthplace in Kentucky.

Today, the U.S. National Park Service manages a diverse collection of wilderness, cultural, and historic areas. Its domain encompasses 80.7 million acres throughout the 50 states and the U.S. territories.

Use the material below and on the previous page to answer the questions.

The National Park Service Organic Act, 1916
"There is created in the Department of the Interior a service to be called the National Park Service, which shall be under the charge of a director....The service thus established shall promote and regulate the use of the Federal areas known as national parks, monuments, and reservations hereinafter specified ... as provided by law, by such means and measures as conform to the fundamental purpose to conserve the scenery and the natural and historic objects and the wild life therein and to provide for the enjoyment of the same in such manner and by such means as will leave them unimpaired for the enjoyment of future generations."

1 Ansel Adams is best known as a
   (1) president.
   (2) conservationist.
   (3) photographer.
   (4) national park director.
   (5) congressman.

2 All of the following statements are true except
   (1) Abraham Lincoln's birthplace is part of the national park system.
   (2) President Woodrow Wilson established the first national park.
   (3) the National Park Service is part of the Department of the Interior.
   (4) the National Park Service manages over 80 million acres.
   (5) the subjects of many Ansel Adams photographs can be found in nature.

3 The main purpose of The National Park Service Organic Act was to
   (1) give the Director of the Department of the Interior the power to build the national park system.
   (2) make certain that Abraham Lincoln's birthplace would not be destroyed by the American public.
   (3) ensure that wildlife would have a safe place to live in each state and U.S. territory.
   (4) set aside public areas to be protected and managed by the federal government.
   (5) prevent American citizens from destroying wildlife and historic and wilderness areas.

4 Look again at the photograph *Moon and Half Dome* on page 214. Describe what you see in the picture and the impression it makes on you.

_____

_____

Posttest

Read the following passage from the autobiography *The Story of My Life* by Helen Keller.

I remember the morning that I first asked the meaning of the word "love." This was before I knew many words. I had found a few early violets in the garden and brought them to my teacher. She tried to kiss me: but at that time I did not like to have any one kiss me except my mother. Miss Sullivan put her arm gently round me and spelled into my hand, "I love Helen."

"What is love?" I asked.

She drew me closer to her and said, "It is here," pointing to my heart, whose beats I was conscious of for the first time. Her words puzzled me very much because I did not then understand anything unless I touched it.

I smelt the violets in her hand and asked, half in words, half in signs, a question which meant, "Is love the sweetness of flowers?"

"No," said my teacher.

Again I thought. The warm sun was shining on us.

"Is this not love?" I asked, pointing in the direction from which the heat came. "Is this not love?"

It seemed to me that there could be nothing more beautiful than the sun, whose warmth makes all things grow. But Miss Sullivan shook her head, and I was greatly puzzled and disappointed. I thought it strange that my teacher could not show me love.

A day or two afterward I was stringing beads of different sizes in symmetrical groups—two large beads, three small ones, and so on. I had made many mistakes, and Miss Sullivan had pointed them out again and again with gentle patience. Finally I noticed a very obvious error in the sequence and for an instant I concentrated my attention on the lesson and tried to think how I should have arranged the beads. Miss Sullivan touched my forehead and spelled with decided emphasis, "Think."

In a flash I knew that the word was the name of the process that was going on in my head. This was my first conscious perception of an abstract idea.

For a long time I was still—I was not thinking of the beads in my lap, but trying to find a meaning for "love" in the light of this new idea. The sun had been under a cloud all day, and there had been brief showers; but suddenly the sun broke forth in all its southern splendor.

Again I asked my teacher, "Is this not love?"

"Love is something like the clouds that were in the sky before the sun came out," she replied.

Go on to the next page.

Items 1–6 refer to the passage on page 216.

Fill in each blank with a word that best completes the statement.

1 This passage is about how a visually and hearing impaired child learns

the meaning of _____ from her teacher.

2 The first conversation in the passage takes place in the

_____.

3 One clue to the fact that the child is visually impaired is that she does

not understand anything unless she _____ it.

Circle the number of the best answer for each question.

4 Which word or phrase is the best meaning for *abstract*?

    (1) not warm

    (2) not physical

    (3) important

    (4) hidden

    (5) confusing

5 What is the first mental process the child realized was going on in her head?

    (1) stringing beads

    (2) loving Miss Sullivan

    (3) thinking about the beads

    (4) smelling violets

    (5) being still

6 Miss Sullivan spells words into Helen's hand, and Helen talks partly in sign. These details support which inference?

    (1) Helen does not like to talk.

    (2) Helen is not very smart.

    (3) Miss Sullivan is a good teacher.

    (4) Miss Sullivan is not a very good teacher.

    (5) Helen is hearing impaired.

Read the poem "That Woman" by Wilma Elizabeth McDaniel.

Stuffed animals
mean a lot to Nina Dowley
much more than to some kids
on days
that I run into her house
on any day
to borrow baking soda
last Tuesday
it was pinking shears
and met number 60
she had found him
at the flea market
a dirty pink rabbit
with eyes that moved
by Wednesday
when I returned the shears
Nina had sprayed
and cleaned
and brushed the rabbit
until he looked like new
and placed him
in a wicker basket on glass eggs
that belonged to her mother
she is out of space in the room
bears are lined up
on the chesterfield
and only bears sit there
cats monopolize chairs
of comfort and over-size
and dogs are happy on the floor
guarding stuffed frogs
and crocheted turtles
there is friction
but all agree
they never had a home
like Nina's heart
and never heard a story
like the one
Nina tells them every night
It never changes.

Items 7–12 refer to the passage on page 218.

Write the answer to each question.

7 What does the number *60* refer to in this poem?

_____

8 What does Nina Dowley collect and love?

_____

9 Why is Nina "out of space in the room"?

_____

Circle the number of the best answer for each question.

10 What is the speaker's tone when she talks about Nina Dowley?

    (1) affectionate

    (2) amused

    (3) embarrassed

    (4) mocking

    (5) superior

11 Which conclusion is supported by the details that the speaker borrowed baking soda and pinking shears? The speaker is

    (1) the neighborhood gossip.

    (2) too poor to buy her own things.

    (3) a salesperson.

    (4) Nina's neighbor.

    (5) avoiding Nina.

12 What would Nina be most likely to do if she found a stuffed animal thrown out in the trash? She would

    (1) leave it there.

    (2) take it home and clean it.

    (3) throw it out again.

    (4) give it to someone as it is.

    (5) tear it up.

Read the following passage from the novel *Roots* by Alex Haley.

Every time he and his brother would be walking somewhere by themselves, Kunta would imagine that he was taking Lamin on some journey, as men sometimes did with their sons. Now, somehow, Kunta felt a special responsibility to act older, with Lamin looking up to him as a source of knowledge. Walking alongside, Lamin would ply Kunta with a steady stream of questions.

"What's the world like?"

"Well," said Kunta, "no man or canoes ever journeyed so far. And no one knows all there is to know about it."

"What do you learn from the arafang?"

Kunta recited the first verses of the Koran in Arabic and then said, "Now you try." But when Lamin tried, he got badly confused—as Kunta had known he would—and Kunta said paternally, "It takes time."

"Why does no one harm owls?"

"Because all our dead ancestors' spirits are in owls." Then he told Lamin something of their late Grandma Yaisa. "You were just a baby, and cannot remember her."

"What's that bird in the tree?"

"A hawk."

"What does he eat?"

"Mice and other birds and things."

"Oh."

Kunta had never realized how much he knew—but now and then Lamin asked something of which Kunta knew nothing at all.

"Is the sun on fire?" Or: "Why doesn't our father sleep with us?"

At such times, Kunta would usually grunt, then stop talking—as Omoro did when he tired of so many of Kunta's questions. Then Lamin would say no more, since Mandinka home training taught that one never talked to another who did not want to talk. Sometimes Kunta would act as if he had gone into deep private thought. Lamin would sit silently nearby, and when Kunta rose, so would he. And sometimes, when Kunta didn't know the answer to a question, he would quickly do something to change the subject.

Items 13–18 refer to the passage on page 220.

Fill in each blank with a word that best completes the statement.

13 The two boys in the passage are named _____

and _____.

14 The main idea of the passage is that the older brother wants to be able to

_____ his brother's questions.

15 The *arafang* the boys talk about is probably a _____.

Circle the number of the best answer for each question.

16 What causes Kunta's conflict with himself?

    (1) He wants to be back at home with the rest of his family.

    (2) He feels his father should have come along on the journey.

    (3) His brother refuses to learn about animals and the Koran.

    (4) He does not always know the answers to Lamin's questions.

    (5) He believes the spirits of his dead ancestors are in owls.

17 How does the older brother feel about the younger brother?

    (1) He resents the boy.

    (2) He dislikes the boy.

    (3) He cares about the boy.

    (4) He is not interested in his brother.

    (5) He does not want to be responsible for his brother.

18 What would Kunta probably do if Lamin suddenly became quiet?

    (1) He would probably grunt and ask him a question.

    (2) He would probably teach him about animals.

    (3) He would probably stop talking to him.

    (4) He would probably change the subject.

    (5) He would probably get angry with him.

Read the following passage from the play _Butterflies Are Free_ by Leonard Gershe.

DON: Right. And I don't meet a stranger and say, "Hi, Don Baker—blind as a bat."

JILL: I think you should've told me. I would've told you.

DON: Well . . . I wanted to see how long it would take for you to catch on. Now you know. Do you want to run screaming out into the night or just faint?

JILL: How can you make jokes?

DON: Listen, the one thing that drives me up the wall is pity. I don't want it and I don't need it. Please—don't feel sorry for me. I don't feel sorry for me, so why should you?

JILL: You're so . . . adjusted.

DON: No, I'm not. I never _had_ to adjust. I was born blind. It might be different if I'd been able to see and then went blind. For me, blindness is normal. I was six years old before I found out everyone else wasn't blind. By that time it didn't make much difference. So, let's relax about it. Okay? And if we can have a few laughs, so much the better.

JILL: A few laughs? About _blindness?_

DON: No, not about blindness. Can't you just forget that?

JILL: I don't know. You're the first blind person I've ever met.

DON: Congratulations. Too bad they don't give out prizes for that.

JILL: I've seen blind men on the street—you know, with dogs. Why don't you have a dog?

DON: They attract too much attention. I'd rather do it myself.

JILL: But isn't it rough getting around New York? It is for me!

DON: Not at all. I manage very well with my cane. I've got so I know exactly how many steps to take to the grocery . . . the laundry . . . the drugstore.

JILL: What about here in the apartment? Aren't you afraid of bumping into everything? You could hurt yourself.

DON: I've memorized the room. _(Moves around the room with grace and confidence, calling off each item as he touches it or points to it)_ Bed . . . bathroom . . . bookcase . . . guitar . . . my cane. _(He holds up the white aluminum walking stick, then puts it back on the shelf.)_

JILL: What are those books?

DON: Braille . . . Front door . . . tape recorder. _(Moving on)_ Dining table . . . bathtub. _(Walks quickly to the chest of drawers against the door to Jill's apartment)_ Chest of drawers. _(Touching the things on top)_ Wine . . . more wine . . . glasses. _(He opens the top drawer.)_ Linens. _(Closes the drawer; opens the front door and shuts it; moves on to the kitchen)_ Kitchen . . . _(He opens the cabinet over the sink.)_ Dishes . . . cups . . . glasses. _(He opens the next cabinet.)_ Coffee . . . sugar . . . salt and pepper . . . corn flakes . . . ketchup . . . et cetera. _(Returning to Jill)_ Now, if you'll put the ashtray back. _(She replaces the ashtray on the table, and Don stamps out his cigarette in it. He sits on the sofa and holds out his arms with bravura.)_ Voilà! If you don't move anything, I'm as good as anyone else.

Go on to the next page.

Items 19–24 refer to the passage on page 222.

Write the answer to each question.

19 What conclusion can you draw about Jill's attitude toward Don from their conversation?

_____

_____

20 Where does the story take place? What helped you figure this out?

_____

_____

21 When did Don realize that most other people are not blind?

_____

Circle the number of the best answer for each question.

22 What conclusion can you draw about Don's character?
  (1) He is bitter about being blind.
  (2) He is independent and funny.
  (3) He enjoys being taken care of.
  (4) He doesn't know how to laugh at himself.
  (5) He enjoys making people feel uncomfortable.

23 Why do you think Don objects to other people's attitudes about his blindness?
  (1) He hates the fact that he is blind and feels angry that others can see.
  (2) He would rather be accepted for who he is and for what he can do.
  (3) He would like other people to just leave him alone.
  (4) He worries about what other people might think about him.
  (5) He doesn't like to be reminded that he is blind.

24 Which statement from the passage best shows Don's attitude toward his blindness?
  (1) "I wanted to see how long it would take for you to catch on."
  (2) "Too bad they don't give out prizes for that."
  (3) "I never had to adjust."
  (4) "They attract too much attention."
  (5) "I don't feel sorry for me, so why should you?"

Read the following catalog advertisement and chart.

The Decorator's Den New Spring Collections!

The Cozy
Country Collection

The hand-hooked rugs in this new collection are made of 100% wool. Made with a thick and dense pile, these rugs are long lasting. The latex backing provides added durability.

The Cozy Country line features a solid color rug with a patterned border. The border pattern is a sprinkling of tiny and delicate flowers. These rugs will add a country flavor to any room or area. With the subtle pattern, you are not restricted in your choice of accessories. These versatile rugs will accent any room scheme. You can turn your home into a cozy country cottage!

A Azure: blue with white flowers
B Spring Meadow: green with white flowers
C Sandstone: beige with green flowers
D Rose Garden: dusty rose with blue flowers

Item Number	Dimensions	Price
12135	1'9" x 2'9"	$43
12136	2'6" x 4'2"	$89
12137	3'6" x 5'6"	$154
12138	5'3" x 8'3"	$349
12139	8' x 11'	$699
12140	4' round	$139
12141	6' round	$299
12142	8' round	$549
12143	5' x 7' oval	$579
12144	7'6" x 9'6" oval	$579

Go on to the next page.

Items 25–30 refer to the catalog advertisement and chart on page 224.

Write the answer to each question.

㉕ Suppose you order Item 12140, color B. Describe the color, size and price of the rug.

_____

㉖ Which is the most expensive rug in this collection? Give the item number, price, and size.

_____

㉗ Suppose that you want to cover an area that is about five feet by eight feet. Which is the least expensive rug you could get to do this? Give the item number, size, and price.

_____

Circle the number of the best answer for each question.

㉘ Which two features of the rug are emphasized in this advertisement?
   (1) inexpensive price and durability
   (2) texture and easy care
   (3) durability and versatility
   (4) versatility and inexpensive price
   (5) durability and easy care

㉙ Hand-hooked refers to
   (1) the texture of the rug.
   (2) the durability of the rug.
   (3) the color of the rug.
   (4) the way the rug is made.
   (5) the pattern on the rug.

㉚ What makes the rugs long lasting?
   (1) They are made of 100% wool.
   (2) They are a solid color.
   (3) They have a thick and dense pile.
   (4) They are available in a variety of dimensions.
   (5) They will accent any room.

Posttest Correlation Chart

The chart below will help you determine your strengths and weaknesses in reading and interpreting different forms of literature and other written material.

Directions

Circle the number of each item that you answered correctly on the Posttest. Count the number of items you answered correctly in each row. Write the number in the Total Correct space in each row. (For example, in the Fiction row, write the number correct in the blank before *out of 6*.) Complete this process for the remaining rows. Then add the four totals to get your Total Correct for the whole 30-item Posttest.

Content Areas	Items	Total Correct	Pages
Fiction (Pages 12–65)	13, 14, 15, 16, 17, 18	_____ out of 6	Pages 32–37 Pages 44–49
Nonfiction (Pages 66–131)	1, 2, 3, 4, 5, 6	_____ out of 6	Pages 80–85 Pages 86–91
Poetry and Drama (Pages 132–165)	7, 8, 9, 10, 11, 12, 19, 20, 21, 22, 23, 24	_____ out of 12	Pages 134–139 Pages 140–145 Pages 146–151 Pages 152–157
Prose and Visual Information (Pages 166–215)	25, 26, 27, 28, 29, 30	_____ out of 6	Pages 168–173 Pages 198–205

TOTAL CORRECT FOR POSTTEST _____ out of 30

If you answered fewer than 25 items correctly, determine which of the four content areas you need to study further. Go back and review the material in those areas. Page numbers to refer to for practice are given in the right-hand column above.

Answers and Explanations

INVENTORY

PAGE 2

1. hurts
2. free
3. smooth
4. **(1) All creatures suffer when they are trapped.** The bird is a symbol for any being that is not free. The poet understands its pain because people feel the same way when they are trapped. Option 2 is incorrect because it is too specific to be a general truth about life. The passage does not support option 3. Option 4 is a general truth about life, but not the one suggested by this poem. Option 5 is incorrect because singing is an expression of pain in the poem, not a way to solve the problem.
5. **(3) yearning** This option is correct because the bird wants what it cannot have. Options 1, 2, and 5 are the opposites of the emotion in the poem. The poem does not mention option 4.
6. **(4) a blues song** This option is correct because the blues express painful emotions and a search for something. Options 1, 2, 3, and 5 are incorrect because they are generally not songs that express pain.

PAGE 4

7. Joan Rivers, the main writer of the autobiography, is telling the story.
8. The author describes a "wave of hate" coming toward her. The audience was screaming, priests were yelling, and nuns were shaking their fists.
9. **(1) "The biggest scam ever pulled on me was that summer of 1960."** This option is correct because the passage is mainly the story of this scam. The other options are incorrect because they are details in the story.

10. **(5) embarrassed** This option is suggested because Joan Rivers says she felt terrible, and she told the audience she was "terribly sorry." Option 1 describes the feeling in the air before she went onstage. Option 2 describes the audience's feeling after they realize the truth. Option 3 is the opposite of what is suggested. The poem does not mention option 4.
11. **(1) amused** This option is supported by the author's humorous tone. The same tone indicates that options 2 and 4 are incorrect. Options 3 and 5 are feelings she might have had at the time but does not seem to have now.

PAGE 6

12. They have been married for eight years.
13. Nora will probably leave. The stage directions say that she has put on her cloak, hat, and shawl.
14. **(3) gap** The clue to the meaning is given by the words *opened between us* and *fill it up*. The other options are not logical substitutes for *abyss*.
15. **(2) He does not really understand what Nora wants.** Torvald keeps making the wrong suggestions in his effort to get Nora to stay. Option 1 is incorrect because this is what he offers to do, not what he has done. Options 3 and 5 are the opposite of what is suggested about his character. The passage does not mention option 4.
16. **(3) treated her like a pet or a toy** This option is correct because a skylark is a bird and a doll is a toy; this suggests how Torvald thought of Nora. Option 1 is incorrect because Torvald tells Nora that she thinks and talks like a child. The passage does not mention option 2. Option 4 is incorrect because it is a suggestion that Torvald makes but Nora rejects. Option 5 is incorrect because Nora does not like the way Torvald has treated her.

17. The old man and the girl have just come from the bus station.

18. Several answers are possible. Old Man Li wanted to eat everything, but he didn't want to spend money. He felt torn between these two impulses. He let his daughter order to avoid the discomfort of making a decision.

19. **(3) They decide to have breakfast.** This is stated in the passage. Option 1 describes what they decide not to do. Option 2 is incorrect because, although they are going to eat some New Year's dishes, there is no hint of a celebration. Option 4 is incorrect because they have already left the station. The passage does not mention option 5.

20. **(2) very strong** This is clear from the simile in the passage: *She was strong as a cow.* The passage does not mention the other options.

21. **(4) The restaurant was clean and impressive.** This is stated as the reason that Old Man Li changed his mind. Options 1, 2, and 3 refer to his original opinion. Option 5 did not affect his decision.

22. A person who does not live in Greensboro would pay $48.

23. Students don't need to own a tennis racquet to take a class. They can rent one from the pro shop.

24. A full class contains 12 students.

25. **(2) Advanced Beginner Tennis** Students who take this class must have taken at least one class or have some experience, know the rules, and understand how to score. Options 1, 3, and 4 are not reasonable for a player with the level of skill described. Option 5 is not true.

26. **(4) You would learn strategies for play.** The description of the Advanced Tennis class says that students will develop strategies for singles and doubles play. Options 1, 2, 3, and 5 are skills covered in other classes.

27. **(3) Tuesday from 7:00–8:00 P.M.** This is the day and time listed for Intermediate Tennis. Options 1 and 4 are the wrong day and wrong time. Option 2 is the wrong time. Option 5 is the wrong day.

UNIT 1: FICTION

SECTION 1

1. In the country; it's twilight.
2. Chee; a horse has been stolen.
3. Many answers are possible. In some cultures, death is greatly feared; in others it is welcomed and even celebrated.

b

1. He heard the sound of feet on earth and cloth scraping. He saw many things—for example, a black stocking cap, a pea coat, a boot, a leg.
2. a small girl, who is thin, Navajo, frightened, and speaks English

a

1. hogan
2. gusts
3. plausible
4. tentatively
5. forlorn
6. ponderosas
7. He heard coughing and sniffling; he thought no Navajo would go in a death hogan.
8. Chee was shaking, but the girl was not.
9. She says that she borrowed the horse because she plans to take it back.
10. The hogan belongs to Hosteen Ashie Begay, the girl's grandfather.
11. **(4) Other crimes besides the horse theft may have taken place here.** This option is correct because Chee says he was looking for Gorman last week, wonders where the grandfather is, and remembers a "missing St. Catherine's student." Options 1, 2, 3, and 5 are details rather than main ideas.
12. **(2) He had come to terms with the ghosts of his people.** This option is correct because it describes a spiritual challenge Chee has faced and dealt with successfully. Options 1, 3, 4, and 5 describe actions— what he does or sees—rather than character.

13. **(5) He looked along the ponderosa timber covering the slopes.** This option offers the best picture of the landscape. It tells the reader that the place is hilly, and the hills have pines. Options 1 and 2 describe things Chee feels and hears. Option 2 describes sound. Option 3 is not related to the land. Option 4 partly describes the land, but not as much as Option 5.

14. Many answers are possible. Find a place for the girl to stay; return the horse to its owner; look for Begay, to ask him questions about Albert Gorman.

15. Many answers are possible. Some students may describe a negative shock, such as surprising a burglar. Others may describe a positive event, such as a surprise birthday party.

SECTION 2

PAGE 20

1. Alfred Lanning, Dr. Susan Calvin, The Brain, and Robertson

2. Many answers are possible. Many people have had frustrating experiences with technology. Others are fascinated by computers, the Internet, even robots—and all other advancements produced during this age of technology.

PAGE 21

a

PAGE 22

b

PAGE 23

Possible clues are: they could see nothing but stars; no engines or controls are visible; the walls are very thick and might contain the engines.

PAGES 24–25

1. g
2. e
3. c
4. d
5. b
6. f
7. a
8. b
9. a
10. b

11. She doesn't want to upset The Brain and cause it to break communication.

12. The ship appears to be controlled by an outside source. Powell and Donovan do not know how to get control of the ship or bring it back.

13. **(1) The scientists have lost control of their own experiment.** This option is correct because it is the basis for all the events that take place in the story. Option 2 is incorrect because The Brain is quite happy; the people are angry and upset. The passage contains no evidence for option 3. Option 4 may be true in many cases, but certainly is not true here. Option 5 may be true of The Brain, but it is not the main idea of the story.

14. **(1) The Brain is worth a great deal of money.** This is probably true but has nothing to do with the main idea. Options 2, 3, 4, and 5 all give examples of The Brain's independent behavior.

15. **(4) He was out of his seat with sudden frenzied energy.** Jumping out of one's seat and "frenzied energy" best portray the idea of shock. Option 1 is too calm to portray shock. Option 2 is an unemotional statement of fact. Option 3 is a detail that describes tension rather than shock. Option 5 conveys irritation, but not shock.

16. Any of the three choices is reasonable. Dr. Calvin appears to have more power; she is the one in charge of The Brain. On the other hand, Dr. Calvin may be held responsible for losing control of the experiment. Dr. Lanning may be considered less at fault for the problems with The Brain. Other readers may choose to be a different character altogether—such as The Brain itself!

17. Many answers are possible. Some people believe that thinking robots are impossible. Other people believe that robots someday may be able to think much like humans do.

SECTION 3

PAGE 26

1. Mark
2. Words and phrases that have a scary feeling include: snapping of twigs, crept, but that didn't mean that they couldn't get people, eyes like the eyes of a toad, break a baby's arm and smile while he did it.
3. Many answers are possible. Some people like the thrill of being scared, especially when they know nothing bad is actually happening. Other people dislike feeling scared, even by fiction.

PAGE 27

a

PAGE 28

b

PAGE 29

a

PAGES 30–31

1. glimpse
2. methodical
3. pondering
4. hunkered
5. incline
6. cylindrical
7. momentarily
8. synchronized
9. Answers should include two of the following: he got his father's target pistol; he took a piece of ash from the wood pile; he whacked one end into a rough point.
10. He didn't want to be seen or heard; the twigs on the ground would break and make noise if he stepped on them carelessly.
11. She's sneaking around Straker's house; she's carrying a stake.
12. **(2) She turned around and looked at him.** This is the only sentence that tells what Sue is seeing; all the other options tell what Mark saw or felt.
13. **(1) Yellow ash would burn longer and cleaner in the living room fireplace.** Option 1 tells something that Mark's father has taught him but does not reveal anything about the place where Mark and Sue are hiding. Option 2 indicates that some trees are big enough to hide behind. Option 3

states that this place is hilly and has many trees—enough to have a break in them. Option 4 mentions the twigs on the ground, again emphasizing the many trees in the area. Option 5 again mentions the hilliness (incline); the "carpet" probably refers to the grass, leaves, and twigs that cover the ground.

14. **(5) Mark had seen Straker go out to the driveway, look down the road, and then go back in the house.** Option 5 suggests that Straker is looking for something. Options 1–4 simply describe him or tell where he is.
15. Many answers are possible: Sue is relieved to have a partner in this adventure; she's mad because she wanted to handle this herself; she doesn't like Mark because he thinks he knows everything.
16. Many answers are possible. Some people like the camaraderie of working with other people. Other people prefer the independence or control they have when working alone.

SECTION 4

PAGE 32

1. Many answers are possible, but the mood is fun-filled and lively.
2. a teenaged boy, Mattie, Etta Johnson
3. Many answers are possible. Often both happy and sad feelings are involved when such a reunion occurs.

PAGE 34

a and c

PAGE 35

a

PAGES 36–37

1. e
2. f
3. a
4. b
5. c
6. d
7. Ciel has been in San Francisco.
8. Miss Eva was Ciel's grandmother, and she was a good cook who made great angel food cake.

9. She's worried that they won't approve.

10. They approve of him because he is both good to her and good for her. They don't care that he isn't black. These ideas are supported by the way the women volunteer to take part in Ciel's wedding.

11. Many answers are possible. They argue with each other, but they've known each other for years, and they're like family to each other.

12. **(3) at an outdoor neighborhood party** The passage mentions dancing in the street, the outdoor grill and other food, and the number of people present. Etta also refers to the event as a party. Options 1 and 2 are wrong because the passage does not mention reunions or birthdays. Option 4 is wrong because they are in Brewster Place—not San Francisco. The only mention of a wedding refers to the future, so option 5 is wrong.

13. **(1) She had some kind of personal trouble.** This is suggested by Ciel's references to her "scars, " and to getting over all that happened. She got to the ocean because she "just kept going," not because she intended to go there, so option 3 is wrong. The passage does not support options 2, 4, and 5.

14. **(5) Etta likes to go out and party, while Mattie is a motherly at-home type.** The passage clearly portrays Etta as loving to dance and have a good time. Mattie is the one who holds Ciel, dries her tears, and calls her "child." The passage does not support options 1, 2, or 3. Option 4 is the opposite of what the passage suggests.

15. Many answers are possible. Some people see themselves as outgoing and social, like Etta. Other people think of themselves as more quiet and less social, like Mattie.

16. Many answers are possible. Reasons for wanting to stay in the same neighborhood might include the security of being in a familiar place and near people that are known. Reasons for wanting to move might include the joy of experiencing new places and meeting new people.

SECTION 5
PAGE 38
1. Two characters; they are fishing.
2. Many answers are possible. Some families face war or political upheaval; others struggle over money. For others, personality differences lead to conflicts.

PAGE 39
b

PAGE 40
b

PAGE 41
a

PAGES 42–43
1. furrow
2. churned
3. listlessly
4. abode
5. subsided
6. relented
7. He believes that fishing for carp is bad luck, though he doesn't know why.
8. He is excited and interested but also a little nervous. He's never heard a story like this before.
9. One of the gods loved the people very much and argued that they should be saved.
10. **(3) muddied water carried many secrets** This option is correct because a human quality—the ability to carry secrets—is given to water. Option 1 uses figurative language but does not attribute human qualities to something non-human. Option 2 describes the actual behavior of the carp in the water. Options 4 and 5 simply tell what happened to the people in the story.
11. **(1) that the boy thought of his mother while Samuel was talking** This option is correct because the boy did not speak of his mother; he only thought of her. If the story were told from Samuel's point of view, Samuel would not know what the boy was thinking. The other options are all part of the story Samuel tells, so the reader would still know about them.

12. **(2) after the people had been turned into carp** This option is correct because the god chose to be turned into a carp so he could take care of the people. The other options are not supported by the story.

13. Many answers are possible. Some people learn about their culture from family stories; some learn about their culture through reading. Others learn through classes, visiting museums, educational opportunities, or by other methods.

14. Many answers are possible. Some people are more motivated to follow a rule if they know the reason for it. For others, knowing that something is not allowed is enough to motivate them to follow the rule.

SECTION 6
PAGE 44
1. He is very nervous.
2. his hearing
3. Many answers are possible. Most people find such experiences upsetting, but some may be fascinated by all the things they can hear.

PAGE 45
a

PAGE 46
b

PAGE 47
a

PAGES 48–49
1. g
2. j
3. c
4. b
5. d
6. i
7. h
8. a
9. e
10. f
11. the old man's strange-looking eye
12. On the first seven nights, the man's eyes were closed. When the narrator couldn't see the eye, he didn't feel the need to kill the old man.
13. He sensed that the black shadow of death stalked him.

14. **(2) entered my brain** This option is correct because the word *conceived* comes in the phrase right after it, restating the meaning of having the idea in his brain. The passage does not support options 1, 4, or 5. Option 3 describes how he felt after conceiving of the idea.

15. **(5) For a whole hour, I did not move a muscle.** This sentence adds to the scary feeling of the passage because it emphasizes how sneaky the narrator is and how slowly the time is passing. Options 1 and 2 add little to the mood of fear the author is trying to establish. Option 3 states a fact, and option 4 tells something about the old man, who is not the main subject of the passage.

16. **(1) The sound of the old man's heartbeat haunts the narrator after he kills the old man.** This prediction fits best with the haunted, nervous personality of the narrator, his acute hearing, and the title of the story. Options 2 and 4 are extremely unlikely considering the personality of the narrator. Option 3 cannot be correct because, as he is telling the story, he keeps insisting that he isn't mad. Option 5 is possible, but less likely than option 1, considering the title of the story.

17. Many answers are possible. The narrator is crazy. His reason for killing the old man is not the thinking of a sane man.

18. Many answers are possible. People who like suspense will enjoy many of Poe's stories; people who like more cheerful fiction probably will choose to read other authors.

SECTION 7
PAGE 50
1. a mother and a daughter named Waverly
2. Chinese and American
3. Many answers are possible. Some children and parents believe they differ from each other in significant ways such as their ages, family circumstances, education, personalities, or the time period in which each has grown up. Other children and parents believe that the family culture is so strong that they do not differ from each other in significant ways. Feelings such as pride, joy, puzzlement, resentment, and many others may be involved.

a

b

b

1. pursuing
2. opportunities
3. blend
4. fabulous
5. advantage
6. circumstances
7. American circumstances and Chinese character
8. Many answers are possible. She feels her mother might make a mistake without her daughter's guidance, or she wants to make sure her mother looks just right for the wedding.
9. Mr. Rory says that Mrs. Jong and Waverly look very much alike. Waverly probably doesn't like this comment because she thinks of her mother as old-fashioned and not stylish. This is not the image Waverly has of herself.
10. **(1) The Chinese are more careful and quiet and observant than Americans.** This is the best option because it's the idea that underlies everything Mrs. Jong says. Options 2, 4, and 5 are not supported by the passage. Option 3 may be true, but it is not the focus of the passage.
11. **(2) They look directly at each other.** The mother's criticism implies that Americans do the opposite of the Chinese. Option 1 is what she says about Americans. The story does not support options 3, 4, and 5.
12. **(3)". . . her famous Mr. Rory . . ."** This option suggests that the mother doesn't think much of the hairdresser. She is making fun of how well known he is. Options 1 and 4 reveal how the mother thinks Waverly feels. Option 2 is a comment by Waverly. Option 5 is a judgment unrelated to the daughter's ideas.
13. Many answers are possible. Mrs. Jong's "American" face is like a mask that hides her true feelings; her "Chinese" face shows her true feelings.
14. Many answers are possible. Some people see Americans as superficial in their relationships with one another and therefore not "really looking at one another." Others may consider Americans to be very open, honest, and direct in their relationships.

READING AT WORK

1. You should have checked: To suggest new books for customers to read; To keep the most popular books in stock.
2. Let Me Hear It Again
3. Answers may vary. A sample is below:
   I enjoy reading horror stories the most. I love they way they grab and play with my emotions. Some parts of the book make me shiver and shake. A really good horror story can make me so scared that I leave on the lights when I go to bed.

UNIT 1 REVIEW

1. c
2. a
3. b
4. **(1) proud** This option is supported by Marsha's comments about how beautiful her baby is. Options 2 and 3 reveal the way Victor feels. The story does not support options 4 and 5.
5. **(3) The baby is not normal.** This option is supported by the fact that the baby clearly focuses on Victor's eyes. Option 1 is wrong because the passage states that the baby is a newborn. The passage does not support options 2, 4, and 5.
6. **(5) shock and fear** These words are used to describe Victor's feelings as he looks into the infant's eyes. Option 1 is wrong because the words refer to reactions of the resident and the mother. Option 2 is wrong because the baby's eyes are blue. Option 3 is wrong because the words refer to Marsha's and Victor's observations. Option 4 is wrong because eye color does not affect how Victor feels.

PAGE 61

7. work
8. hunger, anger
9. cannery
10. **(1) slowly to grow dangerously angry** This option is suggested by the fact that the people's hunger was slowly turning into anger. Option 2 has nothing to do with the passage. The story does not support options 3 and 4. Option 5 is the opposite of what is meant.
11. **(4) uneasy** The migrants are restless, and the author suggests that the situation will soon change for the worse. Options 1 and 2 are too positive for the situation described. The passage does not support options 3 and 5.
12. **(4) desperate** The two words suggest the extremes of hunger and violence. Options 1 and 3 are the opposite of what is suggested. The passage does not support options 2 and 5.

PAGE 63

13. perceived
14. lariat
15. yelping
16. trotting
17. **(3) a horse** This is stated directly in the passage. Option 1, a pony, and Option 2, a dog, are both mentioned in the passage, but they are not Baba. Baba is an animal, and not a human as in Options 4 and 5.
18. **(5) she had been separated from him** You can infer this when Ramona says that they will never be parted. Option 1 is wrong because Alessandro brought her the surprise. Options 2, 3, and 4 are mentioned in the discussion but are not the cause of her happiness.
19. **(2) Ramona is rich and Alessandro is not.** It is possible to infer that Ramona is rich because Alessandro refers to her in a respectful manner and because she owns a horse. Alessandro's manner implies an employer/employee relationship. There is no basis in the selection to choose Options 1, 3, 4, and 5.

READING CONNECTION

PAGE 65

1. **(3) the weather** All the examples used in the passage are weather conditions.
2. **(3) They could read their father's moods.** The selection says that the children were "adroit [skillful] weathermen who charted the clouds, winds, and high pressure areas of his fiercely wavering moods...."
3. **(1) a meteorologist** The other choices are conditions which can create weather.
4. d, c, a, b
5. Answers may vary. Some people feel depressed on gray, overcast days. Some think storms are scary, while others find them exciting. Still other people believe the weather doesn't affect their moods at all.

UNIT 2: NONFICTION

SECTION 8

PAGE 68

1. The story is about Langston Hughes. It takes place in Harlem.
2. The character is excited about being in Harlem.
3. Many answers are possible. Some people get excited by being in a new place; other people find the experience intimidating or frightening.

PAGE 69

b

PAGE 70

a and c

PAGE 71

c

PAGES 72–73

1. marquee
2. dazzled
3. anchorage
4. fraternity
5. flurry
6. Hughes spent his time learning everything he could about Harlem. His activities included visiting the Harlem Branch Library and the Lincoln Theatre.
7. Hughes dreamed of being Harlem's poet.
8. His final grades included three Bs and a C.

9. He had few skills and he was an African-American.
10. They did not get along.
11. **(3) Hughes spent hardly any time on campus and all the time he could in Harlem or downtown.** If Hughes liked the university, he would want to spend more time there. Options 1 and 5 have nothing to do with Columbia University. Option 2 describes Hughes' feelings about Harlem, not about the university. Option 4 tells Hughes' grades, but it doesn't show how he feels about Columbia University.
12. **(3) a publication that included poetry.** The facts that he meets editors at *The Crisis* while in New York City and that his poem appeared there support the idea that *The Crisis* is some kind of publication that includes poetry. The passage does not support the remaining options.
13. **(5) try to make a living writing poetry.** The passage describes how much Hughes likes to write poetry and that he dreamed of being Harlem's poet. Option 1 is wrong because Hughes' father never answered the letter. Option 2 is wrong because Hughes didn't like Columbia University. The material does not support options 3 and 4.
14. Hughes' father probably was angry because his son quit school. Not replying would be a way to express that anger.
15. Many answers are possible. Responses should reflect feelings, dreams, hopes, or disappointments about a particular place.

SECTION 9

PAGE 74
1. The biography is about Luis W. Alvarez.
2. He was a scientist who worked to develop radar systems.
3. Many answers are possible. Responses might discuss inventions in communication, transportation, war technology, information storage, or others.

PAGE 75
b and c

PAGE 76
b

PAGE 77
b and c

PAGES 78–79
1. radiation
2. fossil
3. radar
4. nuclear
5. geologist
6. inspire
7. Alvarez may be best known for his idea that about 65 million years ago a body from space hit Earth, causing a giant explosion. He suggested that dust from the explosion covered Earth, blocked the sun, and killed most plants and animals.
8. Many answers are possible. He built the hydrogen bubble chamber, developed a radar system, and worked on the atom bomb that ended World War II.
9. Alvarez helped to develop the bomb. He also witnessed the bombing and worked with the team that measured the energy released by the blast.
10. Alvarez received the Nobel Prize in 1968. In 1988, a newly discovered asteroid was named in his honor.
11. **(2) Future wars would be avoided.** Alvarez referred to this possible cause-and-effect relationship in a letter to his son. The passage does not support the other options.
12. **(2) A clay layer formed on Earth at the same time that the dinosaurs disappeared.** This option is correct because there is no evidence of fossils in the layer. Option 1 is a hypothesis, not a fact. Option 4 is true but does not support the conclusion. Option 3 does not discuss the differences between the layers and why they are important. Option 5 does not explain the animals' death.
13. **(3) They proved that the large amount of iridium could not have come from erupting volcanoes.** Proving that the iridium came from space rather than from volcanoes would have required extensive scientific tests. Options 1 and 2 are hypotheses. Options 4 and 5 are true but don't include evidence of careful testing practices.

14. Many answers are possible. Some people might be more afraid of war because of the terrible destructive capabilities of nuclear weapons. Others might feel safer because the destructive power of the weapons would deter governments from starting wars.

15. Many answers are possible. Accomplishments or inventions might relate to medical care, food production, transportation, communication technology, science, interpersonal relationships, or others.

SECTION 10

PAGE 80

1. Willie Mays
2. He is in the Army.
3. Many answers are possible. Answers should describe feelings about returning to a job or other activity after leaving it for a time. Did returning feel like a homecoming, or was it a negative experience? How did writers adjust to changes that had taken place during the absence? How did they apply newly acquired experience and knowledge to this familiar setting?

PAGE 81

a

PAGE 82

1. a
2. so

PAGE 83

b

PAGES 84–85

1. morale
2. authority
3. technicality
4. suspicious
5. ordeal
6. Mays wanted to leave the Army to take care of his brothers and sisters.
7. Mays and Leo had a close relationship. Leo cared about Mays, and Mays wanted Leo's respect and affection.
8. The team has a good chance of winning the pennant (the league championship) with Mays playing.

9. Mays is open-minded and willing to learn from others. He respects authority and is motivated mainly by his love for baseball, rather than money.

10. **(3) were dressed in odd-looking clothes** Forbes' overcoat was too big for Mays; Forbes used newspapers to stuff his jacket. Option 1 is wrong because the tip to the FBI was not made by Forbes or Mays. The story does not support options 2 and 5. Option 4 is wrong because it was the way they looked, not the way they acted, that was suspicious.

11. **(3) He took too long getting his snack in New Orleans.** Because he took too long, the train left without him, making him late for spring training. Option 1 is wrong because he started the trip on time in Washington. The passage does not support options 2 and 5. Option 4 is wrong because Leo was only a little annoyed at the delay.

12. **(2) To illustrate how ball players treat each other** To understand Mays' life as baseball player, readers need to know as much as possible how players communicate their feelings. The story does not support options 1 and 5. Option 3 is wrong because it has nothing to do with the silent treatment. Option 4 is true but not the best answer because Eddie Logan is not the only person who gave Mays the silent treatment. Mays is trying to describe how ball players interact with each other.

13. Many answers are possible. Some people would be happy because Mays was a great baseball player and the Giants were having a bad season before he returned. Others might feel nervous or worried about how this change would affect their positions.

14. Many answers are possible. Responses may describe something done as a hobby, as a volunteer, as part of a job, or for or with a family member.

SECTION 11

PAGE 86

1. the start of a journey
2. unhappy

3. Many answers are possible. Some people get quite homesick when traveling; others find it interesting or exciting to be away from home.

PAGE 87

b

PAGE 88

b

PAGE 89

c

PAGES 90–91

1. d
2. c
3. e
4. a
5. f
6. b
7. b
8. a
9. Black Elk left home to perform with Buffalo Bill's Wild West Show. He wanted to learn about the white man's ways so he could help his people live in peace with the new settlers.
10. Black Elk thought that New York City was too big and crowded. He didn't like the way the people treated one another.
11. The weather was rough and stormy.
12. **(4) the end of the Native American way of life** This option is supported by Black Elk saying that throwing away the animals was like throwing away part of the power of his people. The material does not support options 1, 2, 3, and 5.
13. **(5) He felt like he had lost his spirit.** For a holy man, being without a vision is like having no spiritual support. Option 1 uses the wrong meaning of the word vision. Options 2 and 3 have no support in the passages. Option 4 is wrong because Black Elk faces death bravely.
14. **(3) Black Elk performed for six months with the Wild West Show in London.** The last statement of the story says that they stayed in London for 6 moons (6 months). Options 1, 2, 4, and 5 happened before Black Elk got to London.
15. The Wasichus had a different way of life than the Sioux. Black Elk was unhappy living this way, because it seemed like a strange, cruel, spiritless way to live.

16. Many answers are possible. Some people try to adjust to situations in which they feel out of place; other people try to change the situation or escape from it.

SECTION 12

PAGE 92

1. The topic is street directions. The author will likely make the point that giving and getting street directions is a difficult task.
2. The topic is money or value of the dollar. The author will likely make the point that the value of a dollar has decreased over the years.
3. Many answers are possible. Most people will note that the dollar has lost at least some value during their lives. Answers should include a specific (and probably negative) way this change has affected the writers' lives.

PAGE 93

b

PAGE 94

a and c

PAGE 95

humorous

PAGES 96–97

1. obligations
2. abruptly
3. retain
4. realign
5. prior
6. hierarchy
7. People who are not familiar with the streets in many cities may have difficulty finding their way around.
8. The government in Washington no longer understands the value of a dollar.
9. Arkin is critical of the government. She uses a sarcastic tone in her writing.
10. **(5) "If America want to save gas, it ought to . . . give everyone directions on how to give directions."** This option is humorous because it offers a highly unlikely solution to a problem. Options 1–4 are examples of factual statements.

11. **(3) Government workers should be paid minimum wage for vacation time.** This option is an exaggerated solution to the money problem with the government. Options 1, 2, and 4 are all true statements. Option 5 is a serious and valid opinion that is not exaggerated.

12. **(2) Both essays could be considered complaints.** This option states a similarity between the two essays; therefore, it is a comparison. Option 1 describes a cause-effect relationship between making money and spending it. Options 3, 4, and 5 don't mention similarities among two or more items.

13. Many answers are possible. Topics might range from the personal to the political. Answers should include a suggestion for solving the problem.

SECTION 13

PAGE 98

1. An air fight between the English and the Germans is taking place.
2. Women can use their minds to fight for freedom.
3. Many answers are possible. Some people believe that we can work toward world peace; others believe that human nature makes peace an impossible goal.

PAGE 99

a and c

PAGE 100

b and c

PAGE 101

b

PAGES 102–103

1. subdued
2. disarmament
3. sterile
4. imperative
5. compensate
6. She describes the feeling as "dull dread."
7. Without creative outlets, men will return to fighting as an instinctive response.
8. When the fear has gone, the mind instinctively tries to create. Fond memories return.

9. **(5) "The young airman in the sky is driven by voices in himself."** This option is a judgment, or opinion, and cannot be proved true. Options 1, 3, and 4 are wrong because they are facts about what is happening. Option 2 is wrong because it is a quotation from someone other than the author.

10. **(3) to compare women's responsibilities with men's** To explain how difficult it would be for men to give up fighting, the passage compares something women might be asked to do to achieve peace. Option 1 is wrong because the passage does not suggest that women are better than men. The essay does not support options 2, 4, and 5.

11. **(2) "We must free him from the machine."** In this statement the author uses the strong word *must* to motivate the reader to act. Options 1 and 3 are facts. Options 4 and 5 are quotations and are not the author's ideas.

12. Many answers are possible. Most writers would think about their personal safety and fear the possibility of being killed.

13. Many answers are possible. Issues might be related to politics, health, charitable contributions, and others. Answers should include the outcome of the persuasive effort.

SECTION 14

PAGE 104

1. Smith and Carlos
2. The event is a race and involves some kind of action or statement that occurred in a past Olympic Games.
3. Many answers are possible. Some people are in favor of public protest against racial injustice; others suggest different ways to deal with this serious problem.

PAGE 105

1. b
2. b

PAGE 106

a and c

PAGE 107

a

PAGES 108–109

1. deprived
2. irrevocable
3. reprimanded

4. vindication
5. calculated
6. gesture
7. The Olympic audience included people from many countries. Some would not understand a protest spoken in English.
8. Norman wore an Olympic Project for Human Rights button.
9. Smith wasn't expected to win the final race because Carlos had achieved the best time in the semifinals and because Smith had injured a leg muscle in the second semifinal.
10. They felt angry about racial injustice in the United States. As African-American men, they believed they weren't treated fairly by the International Olympic Committee.
11. **(2) He slowed down.** "I pulled back on the reins" is a figurative way of saying that Carlos intentionally slowed down. The material does not support options 1, 3, and 5. Option 4 is the opposite of the facts stated in the passage.
12. **(4) Carlos would have won the race and set a world record.** This is supported by the statement "America deprived our society of seeing what the world record would have been." The passages do not support options 1, 3, and 5. Option 2 is not true because Smith hurt himself before the final race began.
13. **(3) They were suspended from the rest of the Olympic Games.** This option is supported by the fact that Norman was severely reprimanded, so it is likely that Carlos and Smith were too. The information in the article does not support options 1, 4, and 5. Option 2 is wrong because Brundage, the president of the International Olympic Committee, was not a strong supporter of civil rights issues.
14. A gesture can be understood by everyone, no matter what language they speak. Also, gestures can sometimes be more powerful than words.
15. Many answers are possible. Responses may focus on racism, sexism, religious or cultural discrimination, or other issues involving injustice or unfair treatment. Writers should include a method of protest they think would effectively make their point.

SECTION 15

PAGE 110
1. *NYPD Blue*
2. Jimmy Smits
3. Many answers are possible. People often change jobs for better pay, better working conditions, or better opportunities in the future. Major changes in one's job or other circumstances can alter life for the better or be an unfortunate disappointment.

PAGE 111
b

PAGE 112
1. b
2. a

PAGE 113
1. a
2. a, c, e, and f

PAGES 114–115
1. subtler
2. meticulous
3. turbulent
4. passive
5. improvise
6. reinvigorated
7. Jimmy Smits is an excellent performer who is dedicated to his work.
8. They like Smits and think he is a great actor.
9. The review states that Milch is "pumped" and finds it easy to write scenes for Franz and Schroder. *NYPD Blue* probably will continue to be a success after Schroder's character replaces Smits'.
10. Detective Andy Sipowicz, Detective Diane Russell
11. **(4) Smits enjoys changes and he felt that it was time to move on.** This is one reason why he decided to leave. Option 1 is true, but Smits fulfilled his contractual agreement before leaving the show. Options 2, 3, and 5 are not reasons for Smits' leaving *NYPD Blue*.
12. **(3) A man feels like he has done the best job possible but decides that it's time to look for a different job.** This implies that the man, like Smits, is looking for a change and possibly a challenge. Options 1, 2, 4, and 5 describe reasons for leaving that are different from Smits' reasons.

13. **(1) Jimmy Smits was an important member of the *NYPD Blue* team for four years. He thrives on challenges and felt it was time to move on.** This statement summarizes the different reasons he has for leaving. The review does not support Options 2 and 4. Option 3 refers to Milch's work process, which may have influenced Smits to leave, but it's untrue that he broke his contract. Option 5 does not explain why Smits is leaving.

14. Many answers are possible. Some people might choose to stay at a job that is familiar and successful; others might leave for another job and a different challenge.

15. Many answers are possible. Some people like change; other people fear it; still others have mixed feelings about it. Some people believe that change is inevitable and unavoidable, regardless of their feelings.

SECTION 16

PAGE 116

1. *Get Shorty*
2. a humorous crime story
3. Many answers are possible. Some people consider financial or sales industries to be dishonest; others disagree with this opinion. Answers should include objective examples of the business' dishonesty.

PAGE 117

1. a
2. b
3. a

PAGE 118

1. b
2. Many answers are possible. The book review includes the following slang words and phrases: *gonna, messed up, loan shark, skips off, has-been, Angeleno,* and *Jack-of-all-crimes.* Answers should include an alternate and more formal definition of the slang term selected.

PAGE 119

1. a and b
2. a

PAGES 120–121

1. zinger
2. moral

3. cynic
4. protagonist
5. acidic
6. villains
7. The detail *It wouldn't be a Leonard novel without colorful villains* shows that the reviewer has read many of Elmore Leonard's books.
8. Chili looks like a nice guy when compared with Ray Bones and Bo Catlett.
9. Many answers are possible. The reviewer calls the book a splendidly entertaining crime tale. He also says the novel contains nice twists and snappy action scenes.
10. **(3) humorous** This option is supported by the word choices and use of exaggeration throughout the review. Examples include: *Ronnie is a jack-of-all-crimes; he knows enough—which isn't all that much—to get into the filmmaking business; I've been a fan of yours ever since* Slime Creatures. The passage does not support options 1, 2, 4, and 5.
11. **(5) the movie industry** This option is suggested in the first sentence and is supported in the last sentence of the review. Option 1 is wrong because the "hero" of the novel is a crook. The review does not support options 2, 3, and 4.
12. **(4) The reviewer states that the story has nice twists.** This statement implies that the reviewer is biased in favor of the story. Option 1 is a description of a character. Options 2 and 5 are statements about the plot. Option 3 is an example of one way the reviewer achieves a humorous tone.
13. Many answers are possible. Other reviewers might describe the main character as gutsy, funny, or smart.
14. Many answers are possible. Some people might enjoy reading the book because it sounds humorous; others might not like mysteries or might think the book is silly.

READING AT WORK

PAGE 123

1. **(4) Spring Meadows will help Carverton build its community center.** Option 4 states the main idea, as demonstrated in the headline chosen for the article. The other options are details that support the main idea of the passage.

2. **(4) Spring Meadows residents will receive a discounted membership.** Option 4 is correct because discounted memberships at the community center may be a powerful selling point for the development. The article does not support option 1. Option 2 is untrue because the Spring Meadows Development Company is building the center. Options 3 and 5 are true but not as important as the discount in membership fees.

3. Answers may vary.
   a. A new community center is being built in Carverton.
   b. The community center will house two pools, a fitness center, an indoor track, a gymnasium, meeting rooms, and locker areas.
   c. Spring Meadows residents receive a discounted membership rate.

UNIT 2 REVIEW

PAGE 125

1. The narrator is Tammy Wynette.
2. She thinks Billy felt sorry for her.
3. Many answers are possible. Most responses will include the message that those who set big goals must be persistent.
4. **(1) The woman enters the office and sees the man.** This option is correct because it is the first action. Options 2, 3, 4, and 5 occur later.
5. **(2) nervous** This option is supported by Wynette's own statement in paragraph 2. Options 1, 3, and 4 are wrong because they do not describe how she felt. Option 5 describes how Billy acted, not Wynette.
6. **(4) the casual way Billy offered to record her** This option is supported by Wynette's statement. The passage does not support options 1, 2, 3, and 5.

PAGE 127

7. h
8. e
9. d
10. b
11. c
12. a
13. f
14. g

15. The word jam means a performance or recording session in which musicians play improvised, unrehearsed material.
16. In the reviewer's opinion, the collection is complete and well documented.
17. "If Brown was, as advertised, 'the hardest working man in show business,' the guys who worked in his backing band were tied for second."
18. **(1) To give an example of how unusual James Brown is** This option is supported by the first sentence in the paragraph about the sax player: "Brown was always a character." The passage does not support options 2, 4, and 5. Option 3 is the opposite of what is suggested.

PAGE 129

19. mountains, hills
20. "A beautiful symphony of brotherhood" means a society in which people of all races live in harmony.
21. **(1) hope** This option is correct because the author is talking about a positive idea that he has. He also says that he has hope and faith. Option 2 is wrong because his dream is the opposite of despair. Option 3 does not contain the vitality of a dream. Options 4 and 5 may or may not be included in achieving a dream.
22. **(5) By working together, all people can become free.** This is the general message suggested by Martin Luther King's examples. Options 1 and 2 are too negative to be the theme of this uplifting speech. Options 3 and 4 may be true, but they are not suggested in this passage.
23. **(1) ". . . we will be able to work together . . .," (2) "I have a dream today.", (3) "This is the faith that I go to the South with."** Option 1 shows that King wants to work with other people; option 2 shows his strong desire for change, and option 3 shows that he is taking action to achieve his dream. Option 4 repeats the words from a song and is not about what King is doing. Option 5 is wrong because it is just a description of the mountains.

READING CONNECTION

PAGE 131

1. **(2) Make your life something to be proud of.** Option 2 offers the best summary of the main idea. Option 1 is included in the letter but isn't the main idea. Options 3 and 4 only partially or indirectly capture ideas stated in the letter. The letter does not contain the idea expressed in option 5.

2. **(1) wants his son to know how much he loves and respects him** Option 1 best captures the father's motivation for writing. The letter indicated that options 2 and 5 are already true, and option 4 is unnecessary. Option 3 is true but not the main motive for the correspondence.

3. **(4) serious and loving** Option 4 best describes the tone of a wise and caring father who knows he is at the end of his life. Options 1 and 2 are true but don't convey the depth of feeling expressed in the letter. Options 3 and 5 are untrue.

4. Answers may vary.

December 18, 1999

Dear Mr. Chou:

Since you are the principal of Lincoln Elementary School, I would like to make you aware of the unsafe behavior I see on my children's school bus. I have already spoken to the bus driver many times. Unfortunately, my talks with him do not seem to make the ride any safer.

I have seen children standing on the bus while it is moving. Many of the children are talking too loudly. Some are even screaming. Not only are these behaviors distracting to the driver, but they are also dangerous to the other children.

It is my hope that you will speak personally with the driver of bus #23. I also hope that you will speak to the children who ride this bus. They too are responsible for making the bus a safe place for all.

Thank you for helping to correct this problem.

Sincerely,

Rosa Hernandez

UNIT 3: POETRY AND DRAMA

SECTION 17

PAGE 134

1. Meg, Babe, and Lenny

2. Meg and Babe are getting a birthday cake ready to surprise Lenny.

3. Many answers are possible. Some people may have attended or given a surprise party; others may have had a party given for them. Some people feel special to have a party given for them; others may feel embarrassed.

PAGE 135

a

PAGE 136

b

PAGE 137

a and c

PAGES 138–139

1. ravenously

2. glimmer

3. improvising

4. superstition

5. spontaneous

6. Lenny wishes to have a moment with her sisters, just being together and laughing.

7. Babe means that Meg should watch to see if Lenny is coming. She wants to be sure the surprise isn't spoiled.

8. If you tell someone what you wish for when you blow out the candles, the wish won't come true.

9. Students may mention that the celebration was a day late, and that they celebrated at breakfast, an unusual time for a birthday party.

10. **(3) She says that Lenny's wish will come true if she makes it deep enough.** This is a "fact" that Babe makes up to convince Lenny to tell her wish. Options 1 and 4 are facts about Babe that are stated in the story. Options 2 and 5 are opinions that Babe has.

11. **(2) ". . . we've just got to learn how to get through these real bad days here."** The phrase *real bad days* indicates that the sisters have some problems. The remaining options are lines spoken by the characters, but the words contain no sign of conflict.

12. **(5) All the sisters were having problems.**
The first line in the play supports this
option. Option 1 is the opposite of what is
stated. The passages do not support options
2 and 4. Option 3 is wrong because Lenny
loves making birthday wishes.

13. Yes. Lenny wants her sisters to laugh with
her. In the last minutes of the play they do.
They have gotten to that magical moment.

14. Many answers are possible. Answers should
include a wish that was truly meaningful, and
specific actions taken to help it come true.

15. Many answers are possible. Some students
may discuss feeling nervous when speaking
in public; others may mention feeling
nervous when discussing a conflict or an
embarrassing subject. Answers should
describe the situation and the outcome.

SECTION 18
PAGE 140

1. Beneatha, Walter, Ruth, and a white man
named Karl Lindner

2. Walter, Beneatha, and Ruth are members of
the same family. Walter and Beneatha are
brother and sister. Walter and Ruth are
husband and wife.

3. Many answers are possible. Conflicts about
noise, animals, property maintenance, or
racial differences are possibilities. Answers
should include a reasonable solution to the
conflict described.

PAGE 141
a

PAGE 142
1. a and b
2. b

PAGE 143
b

PAGES 144–145
1. affirmation
2. quizzical
3. consulting
4. deplore
5. labored
6. expectantly

7. Beneatha is suspicious. The stage directions
say that Beneatha watches the man
carefully, and answers dryly, and is the only
one who gets Lindner's two meanings.

8. The Youngers treat Lindner politely, offering
him a drink and a comfortable chair.

9. He is probably referring to racial conflicts.

10. Many answers are possible. Lindner is
planning to talk about something difficult,
and this makes him feel uncomfortable.
Lindner feels uncomfortable because he is
talking to people he perceives as different.

11. **(3) suggest in a nice way that they sell the
house** This option is supported by
Lindner's awkward way of getting to the
idea that there is a problem. He is gentle
and hesitant and thinks he is being
reasonable. Options 1 and 5 do not fit with
Lindner's personality so far. Options 2 and
4 would mean that the association had no
problem with African-American families.

12. **(4) Lindner suggests that people should
sit down and talk to each other.** This
answer is reasonable because people can't
understand another's point of view if they
don't discuss it. Options 1 and 2 don't
relate to the stated theme. Options 3 and 5
are not ideas mentioned in the story.

13. **(2) Mrs. Younger bought property in the
neighborhood.** This is the only option that
has nothing to do with the association.
Options 1, 3, 4, and 5 all explain the
association's responsibilities.

14. Many answers are possible. Some people
would agree that we need to talk about
differences and would set up neighborhood
meetings to discuss issues. Others would get
insulted and possibly choose to evict
Lindner instead of talking.

15. Many answers are possible. Some people
may have experienced prejudice because of
race, age, sex, or disability. Answers should
describe the prejudice, including how it was
shown and what was done about it.

SECTION 19
PAGE 146
1. a woman who is 38 years old
2. as a plain, ordinary woman

3. Many answers are possible. Some people feel disappointed by their accomplishments; others feel proud of their hard work.

PAGE 147
b

PAGE 148
b

PAGE 149
a and b

PAGES 150–151
1. embrace
2. mantel
3. precious
4. extend
5. awkward
6. countenance
7. smaller, more beautiful, wiser in African ways (the poet uses the spelling *Afrikan*), more confident
8. Both characters have lost their mothers.
9. The boy is looking for a mother's love. The meeting with the woman in the store does not truly comfort him because the woman can fill his need for only a few moments.
10. As a mother herself, the woman understands how much the boy misses a mother's love. She hugs the boy in an attempt to comfort him.
11. **(3) She has tried to be like her mother.** The speaker has dreamed dreams for her mother and has made her mother alive again, both of which suggest she wants to be like her mother. Option 1 is wrong because the speaker admires her mother. Options 2 and 4 are not mentioned in the poem. Although option 5 is probably true, it's not the meaning of the given statement.
12. **(3) The mother's picture was placed next to the vase.** This fact is not needed to understand the poem. The remaining options explain how the boy feels and why. These are the important details about the poem.
13. **(5) " . . . out of my mother's life into my own"** This phrase shows that the speaker wants to stop imitating her mother and start developing her own identity. Options 1, 3, and 4 describe her present life. Option 2 describes the way the speaker has tried to be like her mother.

14. Many answers are possible. Some responses may mention how much the mother loved her son and explain that she is always with him in his heart.
15. Many answers are possible. Answers may include the feelings such as anger, fear, disbelief, grief, or even numbness.

SECTION 20
PAGE 152
1. The speaker is trying to choose which one of two roads to take.
2. It seems to be a difficult choice.
3. Many answers are possible. Some people may mention making a choice about a job, marriage, or having children. Others may discuss choices related to addictive substances or gang membership. Responses should include the factors used in making the decision and the writers' current feelings about their choices.

PAGE 153
a and c

PAGE 154
1. b
2. b

PAGE 155
b

PAGES 156–157
1. minuet
2. trodden
3. diverged
4. arrayed
5. fluttered
6. claim
7. He stood and looked down the two roads.
8. The granddaughter found it hard to imagine an old woman who naps every day as a young, pretty girl.
9. The suicide was a surprise because Cory seemed to have everything, with no hint of problems.
10. **(2) just as attractive** This option is supported by the phrases *really about the same, grassy,* and *both that morning equally lay.* The poem does not support options 1, 3, and 5. Option 4 is incorrect because the poem is about one path being less traveled than the other is.

11. **(3) You can't judge a book by its cover.**
This option is correct because the saying
means that decisions should not be based
on appearances. The poem does not
support options 1, 2, and 4. Option 5 is
wrong because the poem does not suggest
that Richard Cory was evil or that money
had anything to do with his death.

12. **(5) Sometimes you can get more out of
life if you do something different and
don't just follow the crowd.** The
speaker states that the route he took "made
all the difference" in his life. Option 2 says
the opposite of the stated main idea.
Option 3 is incorrect because the speaker is
not talking about physical travel. Options 1
and 4 are not mentioned in the poem.

13. Many answers are possible. Some people
may like the choice because taking a road
less traveled is probably unusual and
interesting. Others may think this choice is
frightening because travelers may find
themselves alone, without help from others
readily available.

14. Many answers are possible. Some people
may mention that family, love, or honesty
are more important than money. Some
reasons for Cory's suicide might be that he
was disappointed in love, or that he'd done
something very wrong and couldn't live
with himself.

READING AT WORK
PAGE 159

1. **(4) expose the children to a wide variety
of stories, poems, and songs** This option
is stated in the final sentence of the first
paragraph.

2. **(3) the center wants children to develop a
love of reading and literature** This option
is stated in the first sentence of the passage.

3. **(5) "The Wild Hog," a poem about a
mean hog who kills many men** This
option is supported by the second bullet
item on the list.

4. Sample answer:
I always liked "Row, Row, Row Your Boat."
Even though it is a silly song, I like how it
sounds when people sing it in rounds, with
singers starting the song at different times.

UNIT 3 REVIEW
PAGES 161–163

1. They have been trying to pick up radio
signals from deep outer space.

2. Friday

3. If they know the future they would be able
to make money by betting on football
games or other events. Knowing the scores
ahead of time, they can never lose.

4. They are husband and wife; they work
together.

5. **(3) were expecting to receive radio signals
from outer space** This answer is provided
by the narrator's introduction, which
describes Adela's and Marcos' work. The
passage does not support options 1, 2, and
5. Option 4 is the opposite of what is stated.

6. **(4) do something good** This option is
correct because Adela and Marcos might
prevent a death if they share the news
bulletin. Option 1 is wrong because the
information about football scores, not the
bridge, could make money. Option 2 is
inconsistent with the goal of scientific work,
which is to discover evidence or proof, not to
fool people. Option 3 is wrong because only
one unsubstantiated broadcast is insufficient
as proof. Option 5 is wrong because the
broadcast is anything but ordinary.

7. **(4) go to the authorities and try to
convince them that the bridge will
collapse** Option 1 is incorrect because the
discovery is too important to ignore.
Option 2 is incorrect because they could
make more money if they kept the radio.
The passage does not support option 3.
Option 5 may be true in the future, but it is
not the first thing they would do.

8. The couple divorced.

9. The speaker talks about how bad the nights
were.

10. The speaker has torn them up.

11. **(1) arguing bitterly** This option is correct
because it suggests that the two tried to hurt
each other's feelings with words in the same
way they might hurt each other physically
by throwing the furniture. Option 2 is
wrong because the couple did not really
throw furniture. The poem does not support
options 3, 4, and 5.

12. **(3) They lived in different parts of the country.** This option is correct because the poem implies that the two are separated by distance, and states that they now communicate by a yearly letter. The poem does not support options 1, 2, 4, and 5.

13. **(5) "held on tight, and let go"** This option is correct because it states that, although reluctant to do so, the couple eventually parts voluntarily. The other options are wrong because they refer to how the couple acted before the end of the marriage.

POETRY AND DRAMA EXTENSION

Pick a play or poem that is interesting to you. Your summary should include a description of the main characters, the main idea, and details that illustrate the main idea.

READING CONNECTION

PAGE 165

1. **(3) kettle-steam is hard to hold on to, like her dream** This is the only option that captures the elusive nature of dreams.

2. **(1) remembered she had a dream, but did not remember the specifics** This is the only accurate option.

3. **(2) Dreams experienced during stages 3 and 4 are the most memorable.** All other options are accurate. Option 2 is the only statement that is not true.

4. **(5) the REM state** Although some dreams occur in Stages 3 and 4 of NREM sleep, most occur during REM sleep, and they are the most easily remembered.

5. Sample answer:

   Oddly, I keep having the same dream over and over. I seem to have this dream when I am nervous or anxious about something I must do.

   The dream takes place in high school. I arrive at school to take a test that day. I get very nervous in the dream because I haven't studied for the test. I get even more nervous as the dream goes on, because I can never find the room where the test is being given.

   I always wake up from this dream with my heart racing. I often get confused that this dream is, in fact, reality.

UNIT 4: PROSE AND VISUAL INFORMATION

SECTION 21

PAGE 168

1. Yes. The words "Too Much" in the title of the brochure and negative impact of television named in the three main headings suggest that the author believes that watching a lot of television can harm a child's ability to learn.

2. Yes, the product will probably be expensive. The heading "Don't You Deserve the Best Technology Money Can Buy?" tries to persuade the customer that this product is worth a high price.

3. Many answers are possible. Brochures and advertisements can help people find out about new medicines and treatments. They can also be used to teach people how to make good health-care decisions.

PAGE 169

a

PAGE 170

1. b
2. b

PAGE 171

1. a and b
2. b

PAGES 172–173

1. allergic
2. enhanced
3. symptoms
4. clarity
5. hypnotized
6. antibiotics
7. There are three reasons given in the brochure. Television can shorten a child's attention span, it can weaken a child's language skills, and it can weaken a child's reading skills.
8. When sound effects and music are ignored, it becomes apparent that the characters speak in short phrases and incomplete sentences.
9. Antibiotics fight to kill bacteria that can cause some sore throats and earaches.

10. Many answers are possible. Answers should list two of the claims that were made about the CD player. The sound from the CD player's small speakers is unlike anything expected from a CD player, is high quality, with clarity never before possible from a small CD player and can fill a concert hall, and you will never want to listen to music on any other CD player once you hear this one.

11. **(2) Watching television may weaken a child's language skills** The heading for paragraph 3 states the main idea of that paragraph. Only option 2 restates that idea. While options 1 and 3 may be true, these ideas are not the focus of the brochure. Options 4 and 5 are false according to the information in the brochure.

12. **(5) For antibiotics to work well, you need to take them on a schedule.** The second tip says to take the medicine at the same time every day. This is the only option mentioned in the list of tips. Options 1, 2, 3, and 4 are all false statements according to the facts in the brochure.

13. **(4) The CD player will delight you.** Option 4 is the only option that is a claim that might not be true. Options 1, 2, 3, and 5 are facts about the CD player that are true.

14. Many answers are possible. Answers should include the name of the product bought, the information that inspired the purchase of the product, and whether the advertising claims were true.

15. Many answers are possible. Answers should express an opinion and include reasons for the opinion. Some might state that watching a lot of television is bad for adults because it takes time away from more worthwhile activities and because the quick cuts and flashing lights may shorten an adult's attention span in the same way that it can shorten a child's. Others might not think watching a lot of television is bad for adults.

SECTION 22
PAGE 174
1. Many answers are possible. The shipping and receiving schedule shows the times shipments will arrive and leave the loading dock, the origin or destination of each shipment, and what route each truck will take.
2. The work schedule gives the days and times each employee is scheduled to work during the week of July 6.
3. Many answers are possible. Answers should describe the type of calendar used, the information it contained, and an opinion about how helpful the calendar was.

PAGE 175
1. a
2. c

PAGE 176
1. b
2. a
3. c

PAGE 177
1. c
2. c

PAGES 178–179
1. international
2. punctuality
3. intermediate
4. destination
5. personnel
6. b
7. b
8. a
9. **(3) Advanced Gymnastics and Mad Scientist Club** Find the column for Wednesday and check the times for each class listed. Three classes begin after 3 P.M., but only Advanced Gymnastics and Mad Scientist Club are for five-year-olds.

10. **(1) Two shipments will be unloaded after the lunch break.** According to the schedule, the lunch break ends at noon. Only two shipments will be unloaded after that time— the shipment from Jensen Office Supplies and the shipment from A&S Computer Warehouse. Options 2, 3, and 4 are false because the times given in the statements do not agree with the times on the schedule. Option 5 cannot be true because Truck 9 will have already been loaded and sent to Freemont before the shipment from Jensen Office Supplies arrives.

11. **(3) 3:30 P.M.** Max is scheduled to work from 8:30 A.M. to 5 P.M. and Lamar is scheduled to work from 1 P.M. to 9:30 P.M. Lamar will not be at work during the times given in options 1 and 2. Max will not be at work during the times given in options 4 and 5. Of the choices given, only option 3 is a time at which both Max and Lamar are at work.

12. Many answers are possible. Answers should explain a method for keeping track of things that need to be done and include ideas for how to make the method more effective. Some might make a list and then number the items from most important to least important. The system might work better by writing down a time to do each item on the list.

13. Many answers are possible. Answers should describe a system and explain why it works. One such system might be to hang a large chalkboard on the kitchen wall and make a schedule with each person's name on it and use different colors of chalk to list different types of activities, such as chores, jobs, and social events. As each task or activity is completed, it would be crossed out, so it is clear what tasks have been completed and what must still be done.

SECTION 23

PAGE 180

1. The employer uses this section to gather information about the jobs an applicant has held before.

2. This form is probably used by an insurance company to pay dental claims.

3. Many answers are possible. Responses should name a legal agreement, such as renting an apartment, arranging to make payments on a large purchase, or opening a checking account. Some responses may state that there are so many forms to sign that it is difficult to read them all or that the language is difficult to read. Answers should include ways to get help in understanding what is being signed, such as asking the person presenting the form to explain it.

PAGE 181

1. a
2. c

PAGE 182

1. b
2. b Every patient should sign lines 13 and 15. Only patients who want their benefits paid directly to the dentist sign Line 14.

PAGE 183

1. a
2. a

PAGES 184–185

1. constitute
2. references
3. specify
4. introductory
5. authorize
6. certify
7. This question must be answered by applicants who are under 18 years old.
8. The purpose of Box 2 is to find out how the patient is related to the employee who has the dental insurance.
9. Box 13 requires a signature so that information about the treatment and dental history can be released to the insurance company.
10. The interest rate will increase to 19.9% if the cardholder is late paying his or her bills twice during a six-month period.
11. **(2) The position you are applying for** The headings in Section 2 call for all the information listed in options 1, 3, 4, and 5. Option 2 is information asked for in Section 1, not Section 2.

12. **(3) The employee should sign and date Line 14.** Line 4 of the instructions tells the employee to sign and date Line 14 in order to have the payment sent directly to the dentist. Options 1, 2, and 5 cannot be correct because every employee filing a claim must fill out boxes 1 through 4, sign Line 15, and attach any dental bills to the form. Only employees who have other dental insurance should check box 11 so Option 4 is incorrect.

13. **(5) "if you use your card to borrow cash"** These words introduce the information about cash advances in Section E. They make it clear that the credit card can be used to get cash, not only to make purchases. Options 1 and 2 are found in the section on cash advances but refer to the fee, not the term *cash advance.* Option 3 applies to the introductory rate in Section A. Option 4 appears in Section C, not Section E.

14. Many answers are possible. Answers may include any of these ideas: Always read the instructions on a form carefully and provide all the information the form requires. Print neatly and make sure all answers are true and complete.

15. Many answers are possible. Answers should express an opinion about how legal documents should be written and include reasons or personal experiences to support the opinion.

SECTION 24
PAGE 186
1. Many answers are possible. Responses might include a question such as What is a probationary period? When do employee health benefits start? How much sick (or vacation or other type) leave does an employee get each month?
2. If You Need Service
3. Many answers are possible. Answers should include a description of an actual or an imaginary emergency experience, how a real emergency was handled, or how to know or find out how to handle an imaginary emergency.

PAGE 187
1. a

2. b
PAGE 188
1. b
2. a
PAGE 189
1. b
2. b
PAGES 190–191
1. precautions
2. probationary
3. technicians
4. contaminated
5. eligible
6. reinstated
7. The supervisor will give the employee a written evaluation.
8. An employee can use sick leave for any illness, for pregnancy, for doctor or dentist visits, or for illness in the employee's immediate family.
9. Hot food enclosed in bags and closed containers can produce steam which can cause burns.
10. **(4) Family Leave** If your friend is going to need to take more than a few days off, she will need some type of leave. Family Leave allows an employee to take off up to four months. Options 1 and 2 are not about taking a leave of absence. Neither Maternity Leave (option 3) or Vacation Leave (option 5) apply to this situation.
11. **(1) to allow you to cook food for a certain amount of time** The section titled "Using the MicroTime Feature" explains that the MicroTime button allows you to enter the amount of time that you want to cook the food. Only option 1 includes this information. Options 2 and 3 are about other types of settings. Neither option 4 nor option 5 is about how to cook the food.
12. **(5) Dispose of the paper towels in a red trash bag.** Step 2 of the safety procedure on page 189 has two parts. The first gives the instruction to wipe up the fluids with paper towels. The second part tells the worker to dispose of the paper towels in a red trash bag—option 5. Option 2 is unnecessary in this situation. Options 1, 3, and 4 come later in the procedure.

13. Many answers are possible. Answers should include reasons to support the *yes* or *no* response. Some might say it is important to read the entire employee handbook as soon as possible after starting a new job because the handbook may contain information that your supervisor has forgotten to tell you. In addition, once an employee is given a handbook, it becomes his or her responsibility to know what is in it.

14. Many answers are possible. Answers should include a description of the features of the perfect instruction manual and an explanation of how these would make the manual easy to understand.

SECTION 25
PAGE 192
1. Many answers are possible. Responses might indicate that the drawing could show where to load the paper or where to find the button to turn on the printer.
2. The chart shows how an employee in a store should handle the return of merchandise.
3. Many answers are possible. Answers should state whether drawings helped make written instructions clearer, and how the drawings helped. Responses might also include a description of when drawings might help, such as to make a complicated process less confusing.

PAGE 193
a

PAGE 194
1. a
2. b

PAGE 195
1. b
2. a

PAGES 196–197
1. implement
2. irregular
3. inventory
4. anchor
5. connection
6. ascend

7. The on/off switch is on the front of the printer directly below the control panel.

8. Begin stretching the bandage in Step 2 when bringing it across the back of the hand, after wrapping the bandage loosely around the wrist once in order to anchor the end of the bandage.

9. Using a clip, fasten the bandage to the layer beneath.

10. A check of the inventory price list (computer code 94) would give the last known price of an item.

11. **(3) It connects to the computer.** The printer cable connects the printer to the computer (option 3). Option 1 refers to the paper jam access door. Option 2 refers to the power cord connection. Options 4 and 5 do not directly refer to any feature shown in the drawing.

12. **(5) The bandage should end part of the way up the lower arm.** In the final step, you are told to wrap the bandage gradually up the wrist to the lower arm. The bandage will end on the lower arm. Only Option 5 describes the correct location. Options 1, 2, 3, and 4 refer to locations on the hand.

13. **(4) Ask the customer for the sales receipt.** Follow the flowchart. No matter what the situation is, the salesperson's first task is to ask the customer for the sales receipt (option 4). Options 1, 2, 3, and 5 all refer to later steps in the flowchart. Eventually, the salesperson may perform some of these steps, but the first task is to ask for the receipt.

14. Many answers are possible. Answers should explain when flowcharts are helpful such as describing the kind of job—like for learning a new job, repairing or building something, or serving customers—or a situation—when a job involves many decisions, to figure out what to do next, to avoid missing any important steps, or to solve problems.

15. Many answers are possible. Answers should tell about an experience learning how to use an unfamiliar piece of equipment, describing whether and how diagrams or drawings made the task easier.

SECTION 26

PAGE 198

1. The chart compares different kinds of checking accounts offered by a bank to help make the decision about which account is right.
2. The graph could be used to see the trends in the number of injuries from skiing and snowboarding and to predict how many injuries might occur in the coming year from these activities.
3. Many answers are possible. Answers should describe an experience using information in a chart or graph and the type of information or the kind of information that would be helpful to have in a chart or graph.

PAGE 199

1. b
2. a

PAGE 200

1. b
2. b

PAGE 201

1. b
2. b
3. b

PAGE 202

1. a
2. a
3. b

PAGE 203

1. a
2. b

PAGES 204–205

1. bimonthly
2. overdraft
3. projections
4. allocated
5. priorities
6. There is no monthly service charge for the Silver Checking plan.
7. The Linens department is expected to have the lowest sales. Its projected sales are about $8,000.
8. There were about 123 skiing injuries in 1995. Answers between 120 and 125 are correct.
9. The School Council plans to spend the least amount—about 5% of the budget—on Art Supplies.
10. (3) Standard Checking Look at the columns labeled "Minimum Balance Required" and "Monthly Service Charge." Only the Standard Checking plan has an amount in each column. All other checking plans have the word "None" in one or both of the columns.
11. (1) March–April Comparing the bars for each two month period shows that for all periods except March–April the bars are nearly the same length. For the March-April period, the bar for this year is much shorter than the bar for last year.
12. (3) There will be more snowboarding injuries than skiing injuries. The line for snowboarding injuries is moving up at a steep slope. The line for skiing injuries is coming down. Imagine that you add one more space for 1999 at the bottom of the graph. If the two lines extend to 1999, the snowboarding line will cross and go above the skiing. None of the other options could happen unless the direction of one or both lines changes.
13. Many answers are possible. Responses might suggest that snowboarders may take greater risks than skiers or that since snowboarding is a new sport, there may be less safety equipment available for it. Another reason might be that as a new sport, many more people are trying snowboarding each year and as more people engage in a sport, more are likely to be injured. There is no way to tell from the graph whether skiing is safer than snowboarding because the graph does not indicate how many people engaged in the sports safely.
14. Many answers are possible. Answers should state whether a budget is used and how a circle graph might help understand spending. Responses might indicate that a circle graph makes it easy to understand which expenses are expected to require the most money and may help the household make better decisions about how to spend its money.

READING AT WORK

1. **(2) capitalized and bold type** Option 2 agrees with Rule 1. Options 1, 3, 4, and 5 describe how other types of text are treated.

2. **(4) every, own** Option 4 contains the two words that are underlined in Rule 5 for emphasis.

3. **(4) Capitalize the first letter of the first word after a bullet.** Option 4 reflects the fact that the second bullet in Rule 5 states that the first letter of the first word after a bullet should be capitalized; however, this rule is not followed. The rules in options 1, 2, 3, and 5 are followed in the directions.

4. **(1) font** According to Rule 3, specialized vocabulary words should be in bold type as in option 1. The rules do not support the other options.

UNIT 4 REVIEW

1. Parents must read and agree to the policies and procedures on page 14 of the Summer Camp Guide.

2. A parent can authorize a friend to pick up a child by listing the friend as an emergency contact.

3. Children must be between 8 and 14 years of age to attend Performing Arts Camp.

4. Children should wear camp T-shirts to camp.

5. Parents need to give the doctor's name and phone number.

6. **(4) Performing Arts Camp** Sports Camp I and Performing Arts Camp (Options 2 and 4) are over by August 1. However, Performing Arts Camp can be attended by an 11-year-old child. Options 1 and 3 do not meet the date requirement. Option 5 is not true.

7. **(3) The parent will be charged for Extended Care.** Only option 3 is stated on the form. The other options are not stated as policies of the camp.

8. **(5) The camp will try to contact the parent or guardian by telephone.** If a child becomes ill, the camp will try to call the parent first (option 5). Afterwards, if the situation is serious, the camp will call for emergency services (option 2). The form does not explain if or when the camp would call the insurance company (option 1), the emergency contacts (option 3), or the child's doctor (option 4).

9. peripherals
10. central processing unit
11. connector
12. sound
13. **(3) the PS/2 port** According to the diagram, a mouse can plug into either the PS/2 port or the serial port. Only the PS/2 has a round port, making option 3 the only correct choice.
14. **(2) monitor** Find the label for the video card on the diagram. The label shows that the video card has a monitor port. The other pieces of equipment in options 1, 3, 4, and 5 plug into different cards or ports.
15. **(5) Connect the power cords to an electrical outlet.** Options 1, 2, 3, and 4 are all described in the manual as happening before option 5. The word *finally* in the instructions is a clue that this step happens last.

16. restriction
17. reservation
18. refunded
19. round trip
20. **(4) Ticket Prices** Look only at the bars for Freedom Airlines. Compare the heights of those bars. The bar representing Ticket Prices is highest.
21. **(2) Comfortable Seating** For each category shown at the bottom of the graph, compare the two bars. The bars are exactly the same height in the area of comfortable seating (option 2). The bars are different lengths in all the other categories.
22. **(5) Freedom Airlines has the best ticket prices.** This advertisement offers a special low ticket price—$98 or less. The survey shows that a high percent of Freedom Airline's customers are satisfied with its ticket prices. Option 5 is the main idea of the advertisement. The advertisement does not tell us anything about Freedom Airline's safety record (option 1), how many people actually fly on Freedom Airlines (option 2),

or whether it is has more flights than the other airlines (option 3). Option 4 is not the correct choice because the advertisement actually contains many restrictions.

PROSE AND VISUAL EXTENSION

Your description should summarize the main idea of the advertisement. It should also include examples of facts that give you important information, phrases that try to appeal to your emotions, and claims that may not be true. The main idea of the advertisement was that I would feel beautiful with a new hair color. The phrase "Show the world who you really are" appealed to my emotions; it painted a picture in my mind of a glamorous, daring person. The claims that the hair color does not contain peroxide and that it does contain some natural ingredients, are useful facts. The claim that coloring my hair will make me feel vibrant, alive, and young is probably not true.

READING CONNECTION

PAGE 215

1. **(3) photographer.** Only option 3 is correct about Ansel Adams.
2. **(2) President Woodrow Wilson established the first national park.** Options 1, 3, 4, and 5 are stated in the information. Only option 2 is untrue.
3. **(4) set aside public areas to be protected and managed by the federal government.** Only option 4 is correct. The information does not mention the other options.
4. Many answers are possible. The photograph shows a moon over a cliff at Yosemite National Park. Some might think the light, shadows, and large cliffs with the small moon over them look haunting and spooky. Others might think it looks romantic, peaceful, or exciting.

POSTTEST

PAGE 217

1. love
2. garden
3. touches

4. **(2) not physical** The clues that this option is correct are in the sentences that tell how Helen Keller came to understand what thinking is. Thinking is not physical; it cannot be touched. The poem does not mention option 1. Options 3, 4, and 5 may be true in part, but they are more characteristics of abstract ideas than they are definitions.
5. **(3) thinking about the beads** In the tenth paragraph, the author clearly states that thinking was Helen Keller's "first conscious perception of an abstract idea." Options 1, 4, and 5 are physical, not mental, processes. Option 2 is incorrect because Helen reports that Miss Sullivan loved her, but Helen does not say that she returned that love.
6. **(5) Helen is hearing impaired.** The fact that other people must communicate tactually with Helen to be understood suggests that she is hearing impaired. The passage does not mention options 1, 2, and 4. Option 3 is true but cannot be inferred solely from her knowledge of finger spelling and sign language.

PAGE 219

7. The number 60 refers to the number of stuffed animals in Nina Dowley's house.
8. Nina Dowley collects and loves stuffed animals.
9. Stuffed animals take up all the space in the room.
10. **(1) affectionate** This tone is present throughout the entire poem. The passage does not mention options 3, 4, and 5. Amusement (option 2) may be mildly perceived by some readers, but it is not the primary tone of the poem.
11. **(4) Nina's neighbor** Neighbors often borrow things from each other. The passage does not mention options 1, 2, and 3. Option 5 is obviously not true.
12. **(2) take it home and clean it** This option is correct because Nina did the same thing with the rabbit. The other options are inconsistent with Nina's character.

PAGE 221

13. Kunta, Lamin
14. answer
15. school, book, or teacher

16. **(4) He does not always know the answers to Lamin's questions.** This option is suggested in the last sentence. Options 1 and 2 are not mentioned in the passage. Option 3 is untrue. Option 5 is stated in the passage, but it does not cause conflict in Kunta.

17. **(3) He cares about the boy.** This option is clear from Kunta's willingness to take on the responsibility of teaching his brother and from the pleasure he seems to feel being with the boy. The other options are inconsistent with Kunta's actions and thoughts.

18. **(3) He would probably stop talking to him.** The last paragraph states that Mandinka home training taught that one never talked to someone who did not want to talk. Although the other options are things that Kunta might do in other situations, they are not the Mandinka way of responding to silence.

PAGE 223

19. Jill is confused by Don and a little uncomfortable. She does not know much about people who are blind, and she does not understand how he can joke about being blind.

20. The story takes place in Don's apartment. This is first clear from Jill's remark about his apartment and is supported by the stage directions and by Don's pointing out the parts and furnishings.

21. He realized that most people aren't blind when he was six years old.

22. **(2) He is independent and funny.** Don refers to how well he can get around, and he also makes a number of jokes. Jill's statement that Don is well adjusted indicates that option 1 is wrong. Options 3 and 4 are the opposite of the correct answer. Don's words . . . *let's relax about it* indicate that option 5 is wrong.

23. **(2) He would rather be accepted for who he is and for what he can do.** Everything Don says and does supports this option. He doesn't tell anyone that he is blind, and he wants no help or pity. Everything in the passage contradicts the other options.

24. **(5) "I don't feel sorry for me, so why should you?"** Don's lack of self pity summarizes his feelings about being blind. He has accepted his blindness, and he wants others to do the same. Options 1–4 relate loosely to the fact that Don is blind, but they don't clearly show his attitude toward blindness.

PAGE 225

25. The color is green with white flowers. The size is 4 feet round. The price is $139.

26. Item number 12139 is the most expensive rug. It is 8 feet by 11 feet. The price is $699.

27. The least expensive rug to cover this area is item number 12138. The dimensions are 5 feet 3 inches by 8 feet 3 inches. The price is $349.

28. **(3) durability and versatility** The advertisement mentions that the rug is long lasting, can be matched with any accessories, and will accent any room. The other options include features that are not mentioned in the advertisement: inexpensive price and easy care.

29. **(4) the way the rug is made** The word hand indicates that the rugs are handmade. The other options describe features of the rug (what), not manufacturing processes (how).

30. **(3) They have a thick and dense pile.** The advertisement clearly states that the rugs are long lasting because they have a thick and dense pile. Option 1 may be correct, but the ad does not state that the wool adds to durability. Options 2, 4, and 5 refer to the appearance of the rugs, not to durability.

Annotated Bibliography

Most of the passages you have read in this book are parts of longer works such as novels, magazine articles, essays, biographies, and plays. If you liked a particular passage, you might want to read the entire work it was taken from. On the following pages is more information about the longer works for most of the passages in this book. Look for these works in your local library.

Anaya, Rudolfo A. *Bless Me, Ultima*. Berkeley: Tonatiuh-Quinto Sol International, 1972, reprinted 1988. An award-winning Hispanic novelist tells the story of a boy growing up in a traditional culture.

Arkins, Diane C. "Back When a Dollar Was a Dollar." *USA Today*, November 2, 1989, p. 10A. A newspaper columnist uses a humorous tone to write about modern economic problems.

Asimov, Isaac. "Escape," in *I, Robot*. Garden City, New York: Doubleday and Co., Inc., 1950. A short story about the role of computers in the future as told by a respected scientist and science-fiction author.

Clifton, Lucille. "The Thirty Eighth Year," in *Women in Literature: Life Stages Through Stories, Poems, and Plays*. Englewood Cliffs, New Jersey: Prentice Hall, Inc., 1988. An African-American woman expresses her feelings about getting older.

Codye, Corinn. *Luis W. Alvarez*. Austin, Texas: Steck-Vaughn Co., 1991. The discoveries of an Hispanic scientist who won the Nobel Prize for physics in 1968 are described in this biography.

Cook, Robin. *Mutation*. New York: G.P. Putnam's Sons, 1989. This novel is a medical thriller about genetic engineering.

Dodge, Mary Mapes. "The Minuet," in *One Hundred and One Famous Poems*, ed. Roy J. Cook. Chicago: The Cable Company, 1928. A poet recalls her grandmother's tales of what it was like to be a young woman in America in the nineteenth century.

Dunbar, Paul. "Sympathy," in *Black Writers of America*. New York: Macmillan and Co., 1972. Dunbar, the son of a slave, reflects on the idea of freedom in a moving poem.

Frost, Robert. "The Road Not Taken," in *An Introduction to Robert Frost*. New York: Holt Rinehart Winston, 1971. A poet considers making an important decision at a crossroads in life.

Gershe, Leonard. *Butterflies Are Free*. New York: Random House, 1969. This play tells the story of a visually impaired young man living independently in New York City.

Haley, Alex. *Roots: The Saga of an American Family*. New York: Dell Publishing Co., 1976. This novel tells the story of Kunta Kinte. Kinte is the ancestor of the African-American author who has traced his ancestry back to Africa.

Hansberry, Lorraine. *A Raisin in the Sun*. New York: Random House, 1958. The experiences of an African-American family living in a predominantly white neighborhood in the 1950s are dramatized in this play.

Henley, Beth. *Crimes of the Heart.* New York: Viking Press, 1982. This play is a comedy in which three sisters work out some of their differences and re-establish their family ties.

Hillerman, Tony. *The Ghostway.* New York: Avon Books, 1984. In one of a series of mystery novels, a well-known fiction author relates the investigations of a Navajo detective.

Hughes, Langston. "Theme for English B," in *Literature: An Introduction to Reading and Writing*, eds. Edgar V. Roberts and Henry E. Jacobs. Englewood Cliffs, New Jersey: Prentice Hall, 1986. A prominent member of the Harlem Renaissance literary movement writes about one of his early educational experiences.

Ibsen, Henrik. *A Doll's House*, in *Four Great Plays*, translated by R. Farquharson Sharp. New York: Bantam Books, 1959, reprinted 1962. This play, written in the mid-nineteenth century, is a social drama. It tells about the tensions in a marriage and is an early example of a drama dealing with women's rights.

Jackson, Helen Hunt. *Ramona.* Boston: Little, Brown and Company, 1884, reprinted 1939. This novel tells the story of a romance between an Hispanic woman and a Native American man during the time when the West was being settled. It was one of the earliest literary works to examine the mistreatment of Native Americans.

Keller, Helen. *The Story of My Life.* Garden City, New York: Doubleday and Company, Inc., 1954. This autobiography is the inspiring story of a woman who achieved international fame and success in spite of the physical disabilities of being blind and deaf.

King, Martin Luther, Jr. "I Have a Dream," in *The Writer's Craft*, eds. Sheena Gillespie, Robert Singleton, and Robert Becker. Glenview, Illinois: Scott, Foresman and Company, 1986. A leading civil-rights activist made this famous speech during a protest march on Washington, D.C., in 1963.

King, Stephen. *Salem's Lot.* New York: A Signet Book, New American Library, 1975. This novel tells the story of a small town terrorized by vampires. Stephen King is one of the United States' most popular thriller writers.

Lee, C. Y. *The Flower Drum Song.* New York: Grosset and Dunlap, 1957. The conflicts between cultures and generations are played out in this novel about a Chinese-American family.

Mathis, Cleopatra. "Getting Out," in *Sound and Sense*, ed. Laurence Perrine, 7th edition. New York: Harcourt Brace Jovanovich, 1987. The breakup of a marriage is described from a woman's point of view.

Mays, Willie, with Lou Sahadi. *Say Hey.* New York: Simon and Schuster, 1988. A legendary baseball player tells the story of his life and his experiences in major-league baseball.

McDaniel, Wilma. "That Woman," in *The Red Coffee Can.* Fresno, California: Valley Publishers, 1974. This poem describes how a lonely woman finds a way to spend her time and the love she has to offer.

Meltzer, Milton. *Langston Hughes: A Biography.* New York: Thomas Y. Crowell Company, 1968. The life story and struggles of the African-American poet Langston Hughes are described in this biography. See also Hughes, Langston.

Moore, Kenny. "A Courageous Stand," in *Sports Illustrated*. Vol. 75:6, August 5, 1991, pp. 62–73. This magazine article recounts a protest against racial discrimination made by two American athletes at the 1968 Olympics.

Naylor, Gloria. *The Women of Brewster Place*. New York: Penguin Books, 1982. This novel follows the lives and complex relationships of several women in an inner-city neighborhood.

Neihardt, John G. *Black Elk Speaks*. Lincoln, Nebraska: The University of Nebraska Press, 1961. A holy man of the Oglala Sioux tells the dramatic true story of his travels in the United States and Europe.

Poe, Edgar Allan. "The Tell-Tale Heart," in *Complete Tales and Poems*. New York: The Modern Library, 1938. One of the earliest mystery and thriller writers sends chills up the reader's spine with this story of murder and obsession.

Reeves, Robyn. *The Tomorrow Radio*, in *On Stage, A Readers' Theater Collection*. Austin, Texas: Steck-Vaughn Co., 1992. In this modern science-fiction drama, two scientists accidently discover a way to know what will happen in the future. The play also shows the difficulty they face convincing other people to believe in their discovery.

Rivers, Joan, with Richard Meryman. *Enter Talking*. New York: Delacorte Press, 1986. The autobiography of Joan Rivers shows that the life of a comedienne is not all laughs. Rivers recounts the struggles of her early career as she tries to break into show business.

Robinson, Edwin A. "Richard Cory," in *Sound and Sense*, ed. Laurence Perrine, 7th edition. New York: Harcourt Brace Jovanovich, 1987. This poem was written by the first winner of the Pulitzer Prize for poetry. The poem suggests that people are not always what they seem to be.

Rooney, Andy. "Street Directions," in *And More by Andy Rooney*. New York: Atheneum, 1982. A TV commentator takes a humorous look at giving, receiving, and trying to follow directions.

Steinbeck, John. *The Grapes of Wrath*. New York: Penguin, 1939, reprinted 1987. The terrible effects of the Great Depression of the 1930s are described in this novel. It is about an Oklahoma farming family who was forced to leave their farm and move to California.

Tan, Amy. "Double Face," in *The Joy Luck Club*. New York: Ivy Books/Ballantine Books, 1989. This collection of connected short stories describes how the conflicts between people of different generations can be complicated by changes in cultural values.

Walker, James. "A Picture on the Mantel," in *Contemporary Poets of America*. Bryn Mawr, Pennsylvania: Dorrance and Company, Inc., 1985. A modern poet tells about the emotions of a little boy whose mother has died.

Woolf, Virginia. "Thoughts on Peace in an Air Raid," in *The Death of a Moth and Other Essays*. New York and London: Harcourt Brace Jovanovich, 1942. An English novelist expresses her opinions on war and peace.

Wynette, Tammy. *Stand by Your Man*. New York: Simon and Schuster, 1979. This autobiography describes the life and career of a country-and-western singer.

Acknowledgments

Pages 258–260 constitute an extension of the copyright page.

Grateful acknowledgment is made to the following authors, agents, and publishers for permission to use copyrighted materials. Every effort has been made to trace ownership of all copyrighted material and to secure the necessary permissions to reprint. We express regret in advance for any error or omission. Any oversight will be acknowledged in future printings.

p. 3
From *Enter Talking* by Joan Rivers. Copyright © 1986 by Joan Rivers. Used by permission of Dell Publishing, a division of Random House, Inc.

p. 5
Excerpt from Act III of "A Doll's House" by Henrik Ibsen, translated by R. Farquharson Sharp and E. Marks-Aveling from *The Complete Major Prose Plays of Henrik Ibsen*. Reprinted with permission of David Campbell Publishers Ltd.

p. 7
Reprinted by permission of C.Y. Lee, c/o Ann Elmo Agency, Inc. From the book *Flower Drum Song*. Copyright © C.Y. Lee.

pp. 15–17
Excerpt from *The Ghostway* by Tony Hillerman. Copyright © 1984 by Tony Hillerman. Reprinted by permission of HarperCollins Publishers, Inc.

pp. 21–23
From *I, Robot* by Isaac Asimov. Copyright 1950 by Isaac Asimov. Used by permission of Doubleday, a division of Random House, Inc.

pp. 27–29
From *Salem's Lot* by Stephen King. Copyright © 1975 by Stephen King. Used by permission of Doubleday, a division of Random House, Inc.

pp. 33–35
From *The Women of Brewster Place* by Gloria Naylor. Copyright © 1980, 1982 by Gloria Naylor. Used by permission of Viking Penguin, a division of Penguin Putnam Inc.

pp. 39–41
From *Bless Me, Ultima*. Copyright © Rudolfo Anaya 1974. Published in hardcover and mass market paperback by Warner Books Inc. 1994; originally published by TQS Publications. Reprinted by permission of Susan Bergholz Literary Services, New York. All rights reserved.

pp. 51–53
"Double Face" from *The Joy Luck Club* by Amy Tan. Copyright © 1989 by Amy Tan. Used by permission of Putnam Berkley, a division of Penguin Putnam Inc.

p. 58
From *Mutation* by Robin Cook. Copyright © 1989 by Robin Cook. Used by permission of G.P. Putnam's Sons, a division of Penguin Putnam Inc.

p. 60
From *The Grapes of Wrath* by John Steinbeck. Copyright 1939, renewed © 1967 by John Steinbeck. Used by permission of Viking Penguin, a division of Penguin Putnam Inc.

pp. 69–71 From *Langston Hughes, A Biography* by Milton Meltzer. Reprinted by permission of Harold Ober Associates Incorporated. Copyright as in 1992 edition.

pp. 75–77 From *Luiz W. Alvarez* by Corinn Codye. Copyright © 1991, Steck-Vaughn Company.

pp. 81–83 Reprinted with permission of Simon & Schuster, Inc. from *Say Hey: The Autobiography of Willie Mays* by Willie Mays with Lou Sahadi. Copyright © 1988 by Willie Mays.

pp. 87–89 Reprinted from *Black Elk Speaks* by John G. Neihardt by permission of the University of Nebraska Press. Copyright 1932, 1959, 1972 by John G. Neihardt. Copyright © 1961 by the John G. Neihardt Trust.

pp. 93–94 "Street Directions" reprinted with the permission of Scribner, a Division of Simon & Schuster from *And More by Andy Rooney* by Andrew A. Rooney. Copyright © 1982 Essay Productions, Inc.

p. 95 "Back When a Dollar Was a Dollar" by Diane C. Arkins. Reprinted by permission of the author.

pp. 99–101 Excerpts from "Thoughts on Peace in an Air Raid" in *The Death of the Moth and Other Essays* by Virginia Woolf, copyright 1942 by Harcourt Brace & Company and renewed 1970 by Marjorie T. Parsons, Executrix, reprinted by permission of the publisher.

pp. 105–107 Reprinted courtesy of *Sports Illustrated* August 5, 1991. Copyright © 1991, Time Inc. "A Courageous Stand" by Kenny Moore. All rights reserved.

pp. 111–113 "Keeping a watch on TV. Jimmy, we hardly knew ye—the real story behind Smits' departure from NYPD" by Bruce Fretts from *Entertainment Weekly*, 10/23/98. Copyright © 1998 Entertainment Weekly Inc., reprinted by permission.

pp. 117–119 "Review of Get Shorty" by Ralph Novak, *People Weekly*, 10/30/95. Copyright © 1995 Time Inc. Reprinted by permission.

p. 124 Reprinted with the permission of Simon & Schuster, Inc., from *Stand by Your Man* by Tammy Wynette with Joan Dew. Copyright © by Tammy Wynette.

p. 126 "Review of Star Time: James Brown" by David Hiltbrand, *People Magazine*, 6/10/91. Copyright © 1991, Time Inc. Reprinted by permission.

p. 128 Excerpt from "I Have a Dream" by Martin Luther King, Jr. Reprinted by arrangement with The Heirs to the Estate of Martin Luther King, Jr., c/o Writers House, Inc. as agent for the proprietor. Copyright 1963 by Martin Luther King, Jr., copyright renewed 1991 by Coretta Scott King.

pp. 135–137 From *Crimes of the Heart* by Beth Henley. Copyright © 1981, 1982 by Beth Henley. Used by permission of Dutton Signet, a division of Penguin Putnam Inc.

pp. 141–143 From Act II, Scene 3, *A Raisin in the Sun* by Lorraine Hansberry. Copyright © 1958 by Robert Nemiroff, as an unpublished work. Copyright © 1959, 1966, 1984 by Robert Nemiroff. Reprinted by permission of Random House, Inc.

pp. 147–148 Lucille Clifton: "the thirty eighth year" copyright © 1987 by Lucille Clifton. Reprinted from *Good Woman: Poems and a Memoir 1969-1980* with the permission of BOA Editions, Ltd., 260 East Ave., Rochester, NY 14604.

p. 160 "The Tomorrow Radio" in *On Stage, A Reader's Theater Collection* by Robyn Reeves. Copyright © 1992 by Steck-Vaughn Company.

p. 162 "Getting Out" by Cleopatra Mathis. Reprinted by permission of the author.

p. 164 "Waking Up" by Eleanor Farjeon from *Siver-Sand and Snow*, 1951. Reprinted by permission of David Higham Associates.

p. 218 "That Woman" by Wilma Elizabeth McDaniel. Reprinted by permission of the author.

p. 220 From *Roots* by Alex Haley. Copyright © 1976 by Alex Haley. Used by permission of Doubleday, a division of Random House, Inc.

p. 222 From *Butterflies Are Free* by Leonard Gershe. Copyright © as an unpublished work, 1969 by Leonard Gershe. Copyright © 1970 by Leonard Gershe. Reprinted by permission of Random House Inc.

Glossary

advertisement a public notice designed to attract attention or customers

autobiography the true story of a real person's life written by that person

bar graph a graph that uses vertical or horizontal bars to represent numerical data

bias a strong preference for a particular point of view

biographer the writer of a biography

biography the true story of a real person's life written by another person

brochure a booklet or pamphlet containing descriptive or advertising material

calendar a list of events giving dates and details

cause a person, thing, or event that brings about a result

cause-and-effect relationship a situation in which one event happens as a result of something else

character a person in a story or a play

chart a map, graph, or table that gives information in a form that is easy to read

circle graph a graph in the shape of a circle that shows how a total amount has been divided into parts

classic literature literature that has set a high standard of excellence, remains meaningful, and continues to be read after many years

column a vertical arrangement of items typed or printed on a page

comedy a play that is meant to be funny

compare to find the ways things are alike

conclusion a judgment or opinion based on facts and details

conflict a struggle or problem between characters or forces

context the words and sentences surrounding a word or phrase. The context of a word helps show what that word means.

contrast to find the ways things are different

detail a fact about a person, place, thing, event, or time. Details answer the questions *who, what, when, where, why,* and *how.*

diagram a drawing designed to clarify the relationships among parts or show how something works

document an official paper used as the basis, proof, or support of something

double-bar graph a graph that uses two bars to compare information

drama a story written in dialogue and meant to be acted on stage

effect the result of a cause

essay a short piece of nonfiction writing that gives the author's opinion about something

fact a statement that can be proved true

fiction writing that is about people, places, and events invented by the author

figurative language words used in a special way to make a point. Personification is an example.

flow chart a chart or diagram showing the sequence or progress of a specific project

folk novel an elaborate work of fiction that people tell over and over for generations. Folk novels explain how people believe things began and include many events, people, and experiences.

folktale a story that people tell over and over for many generations. Folktales often explain how people believe things began.

form a printed document with blank spaces to be filled in with specific information

format a general form or organization of a publication; the way information is arranged on a page

graph a diagram used to show numerical information

handbook a concise reference book covering a particular subject

head a headline; an important main caption or title

implied main idea a main idea that is not directly stated but is suggested by the author

inference an idea that the reader figures out based on clues an author presents and what the reader already knows

key something that gives an explanation, such as the meaning of symbols on a map or graph

line graph a graph that uses lines to show changes over a period of time

main idea the most important point in a paragraph or passage

manual a reference book used to give instructions on how to do something or operate something

metaphor a comparison that says on thing is another thing. Example: She is a ray of sunshine.

mood the atmosphere the author creates in a written work

mystery novel a story about solving a puzzle. The main character of a mystery is usually a detective who has to figure out who committed a crime.

narrator the character telling the story

nonfiction writing that is about real people, places, and events

novel a long work of fiction that can include many events, people, and experiences

opinion a judgment or belief

personification a type of figurative language that gives human qualities to something that is not human. Example: The leaves danced in the wind.

persuasive essay an essay that is meant to get the reader to think or act a certain way

persuasive writing writing that is meant to convince the reader to think or do something

play a story that is written in dialogue and is meant to be acted on a stage

plot the series of events that create the action of a story

poet a writer of poetry

poetry literature that uses words in special ways to show feelings and create images. Poetry is usually arranged in short lines.

point of view the way the action is seen by the narrator or author of a story

popular drama recently written plays

popular fiction recently written works including short stories, novels, and plays. Fiction comes from the author's imagination.

popular novel a recently written book about people and events that are not real

popular poetry recently written poetry

popular short story a recently written work of fiction that is shorter than a novel but has a full plot and a single theme

predict to tell what you think will happen in the future

prose ordinary written or spoken language; not poetry

purpose the reason something is done

review a short piece of writing that tells what a writer or critic thinks of a book, movie, TV program, musical performance, or work of art

row objects, words, or numbers arranged in a horizontal line

scan to look at quickly; to browse for information

schedule a plan or timetable of events

science fiction fictional stories based on the possibilities found in science. Science fiction shows what life and people might be like in another time or place, usually in the future.

sequence the order in which events occur; time order

setting the time and place in which the events of a story take place

short story a work of fiction that is shorter than a novel but has a full plot and a single theme

skim to read something quickly, looking for main ideas and main characters

social drama a play that deals with a major social issue

stated main idea a statement that tells clearly the most important point of a paragraph or story. To restate a main idea means to put it in different words.

subhead a heading of a part (as in an outline); a caption, title, or heading of less importance than the main heading

summarize to state briefly the most important ideas of a longer piece of writing

summary a short statement of the main idea and most important supporting details of a passage

synonyms words that have the same or nearly the same meaning. Examples: *paste* and *glue*

theme a general truth about life or human nature that is suggested in a work of literature

thriller novel a work of fiction that is meant to scare the reader; also called a horror novel

tone the author's attitude or feeling about a subject

tragedy a serious play with a sad ending

trend a line of general direction or movement reflecting change

visualize to form a picture in your mind

Index